The
SOUL
of
SEX

THOMAS MOORE

The
SOUL
of
SEX

Cultivating Life as an Act of Love

HarperPerennial

A Division of HarperCollinsPublishers

A hardcover edition of this book was published in 1998 by Harper-Collins Publishers.

THE SOUL OF SEX. Copyright © 1998 by Thomas Moore. All rights reserved. Printed in the United States of America. No part of this book may be used or reproduced in any manner whatsoever without written permission except in the case of brief quotations embodied in critical articles and reviews. For information address HarperCollins Publishers, Inc., 10 East 53rd Street, New York, NY 10022.

HarperCollins books may be purchased for educational, business, or sales promotional use. For information please write: Special Markets Department, HarperCollins Publishers, Inc., 10 East 53rd Street, New York, NY 10022.

"We Drink Your Health" and "Bridesmaids," by Sappho from *Sappho: A New Translation,* trans. Mary Barnard, Copyright © 1958 by The Regents of the University of California. "Man of Tyre," "Glimpse," "What Does She Want?" by D. H. Lawrence from *The Complete Poems,* ed. V. de Sola Pinto and F. W. Roberts, Copyright © 1964, 1971 by Angelo Ravagli and C. M. Weekley, Executors of the Estate of Frieda Lawrence Ravagli; used by permission of Viking Penguin, a division of Penguin Books USA, Inc. and Laurence Pollinger Limited, U.K. *(continued on page 308)*

To Hari Kirin

Quella che 'mparadisa la mia mente

DANTE, *Paradiso*, xxviii

CONTENTS

Writing about sex somehow participates in the topic, whether the form is a love letter, an essay, or pornography, which could be translated "courtesan writing," the ancient spirit of which I have tried not to exclude from the book. I have attempted to write a book about sex that enriches our appreciation of it while demonstrating one of its main themes: everything we do and make can be sexual. Those who love books with passion know that a book can be sensual.

I feel indebted to the many authors and artists devoted to eros over the centuries who had the courage to speak for it and the grace to speak of it beautifully: Sappho, Plato, Epicurus, Plotinus, Ficino, Wilde, Dickinson, Sade, Jung, Hillman, and others, some of whom appear in the end notes.

I would like to thank friends and coworkers who helped in

many different ways to keep this project on eros erotic. With valuable humor, criticism, and charm, Jerriann Boggis helped at every step. Ken Tate, a remarkable architect of the sensuous, gave me important directions and hints. Pat Toomay, as always, kept me safe from the cool traps of the reasonable. Gurucharan Singh Khalsa gave me some good leads, perhaps without knowing it. Dr. Lee Doyle, therapist of desire, long ago taught me unforgettable lessons in erotic life. Hugh Van Dusen is widely recognized as an editor with heart, passion, and civility, and he found inspired ways to get my preoccupations to the public. Jisho Warner and Carol Williams helped me reconstruct a rough first draft and then do the polishing. Rose Carrano brings unexpected warmth, and therefore eros, to the important work of marketing. In recent postcards and in many long-past conversations James Hillman supplied me with a direction and a few remarkable sources. Merle Worth, a genius in film, always keeps me mindful that the soul is made of images, not ideas about images. Michael Katz has become an intimate coworker. He was unusually forceful in helping to shape and present this book, and if there is any Zen fragrance on its pages, it is a gift from him. Finally, Joan Hanley's painting and companionship breathes life into all my writing, as in the tale where Aphrodite gently drops a butterfly on the sculptor's marble creation to bring it to life and give it soul.

This is a book about human sexuality, but it contains no information on biology, anatomy, or health, and it has little to say about techniques and relationship. It begins with the assumption that a human being is a whole world of meanings, emotions, dreams, wishes, fears, a past, a cultural milieu, and an interior life of thought and fantasy—in short, a soul. The soul comes into its fullness at the place where it encounters God, the infinite, or whatever we want to call the object of religious concern. Although I would prefer a less obvious phrase, this book is truly about the soul of sex.

All my life I have had a special attraction to eros. I remember my early childhood years as filled with interest in the body. I see now in my young children their relatively innocent fascination for words, body parts, and sensual delights that are thoroughly erotic in their own way.

Although I was brought up in a thoroughly Catholic environment, which is well known to be prudish and reticent about sexual matters, I deeply appreciate the erotic life. I'm not fascinated by erotica, but I do enjoy a good painting or photograph of the naked human body, or an intelligent erotic film. It's clear to me that sex is one of the most important aspects of human life, second perhaps only to religion, and these are often inseparable.

I write about the spirits and ghosts that engage the soul in sex. Sex is infinitely more mysterious than we usually imagine it to be and it is only superficially considered when we talk about it in terms of hormones and the mechanics of lovemaking. I approach sex here as a lover of mysteries.

I have written about eros in all my books, but here I focus in on sexuality itself. I take a long look at the body, especially as it is presented in art and religion, for signs of the mysteries involved in bodies and lovemaking. When I tease out those hidden meanings, I apply them to life and culture on a larger scale with the idea that we might be less depressed and less confused if we were to make our surroundings more sexual and allow pleasure to be a valid goal in life.

As a psychotherapist, I discovered that the soul often manifests itself in the sexual areas of life. Many of the men and women who consulted with me over the years came with sexual concerns, which eventually were revealed as containers of the central mysteries of the person's life. In some ways sex is the facade of the soul, and when we deal with it thoughtfully, the whole interior cosmos comes into the foreground.

Why should modern life become more sensuous and sexual? We are already deluged with sexual images in all the media. We are obviously a sex-obsessed society. Why make it worse?

In response, I call upon Freud. He enunciated a principle I find useful: we display outrageously and obsessively that which we do not fully possess or have deeply at our disposal. If we are displaying sex with unseemly exaggeration and pre-occupation, then we have not found the heart of sex and made it a fully integrated part of individual and social life.

Given our obsession with sex, we need to get more of it, not in quantity but in quality. It's like a person addicted to junk food. He eats as much as he can because there is nothing there. If he were to eat real food—unprocessed, close to its earth origins, wonderfully prepared—he might leave the addiction behind.

We need more sex, not less, but we need sex with soul. What that means is, of course, the burden of the book.

When lovers lie on a bed, and embrace each other
so closely that the arms and thighs of the one are
encircled by the arms and thighs of the other, and
are, as it were, rubbing up against them, this is
known as Tila-Tandulaka, an embrace like the
mixture of sesamum seed with rice.

Kama Sutra

What does she want, volcanic Venus,
as she goes fuming round?
What does she want?
She says she wants a lover,
but don't you believe her.
She's seething like a volcano,
and volcanos don't want lovers.

D. H. LAWRENCE

Some say a squadron of horse, some, infantry,
some, ships, are the loveliest thing
on the black earth. But I say
it's what you desire.

SAPPHO

The Soul of Sex

CHAPTER I

The Nymph of Sex

Divine Eros and Human Sexuality

We have a habit of talking about sex as merely physical, and yet nothing has more soul. Sex takes us into a world of intense passions, sensual touch, exciting fantasies, many levels of meaning, and subtle emotions. It makes the imagination come alive with fantasy, reverie, and memory. Even if the sex is loveless, empty, or manipulative, still it has strong repercussions in the soul, and even bad sexual experiences leave lasting, haunting impressions.

In general, we treat the body as though it were a skeleton wrapped in muscles and stuffed with organs. When illness comes along, we go to a doctor and expect X rays, pills, or surgery. We don't talk about the way we're living, strong feelings that may be related to the illness, or whether life has meaning. We separate the body, mind, and emotions as though they were properly contained in individual and unrelated compartments.

The philosophy characteristic of our culture, in which the body is treated as unrelated to our emotions, our sense of meaning, and our experiences, has deep implications for sexuality. Not only do we deal with sexual problems mechanically, we may well approach our lovers mechanically—without the deep engagement of the soul and spirit that would give sex its depth and humanity.

Against this point of view, the eighteenth-century poet William Blake, who used his power of words to fight against the rationalistic and mechanistic thinking of his own time, made a statement that could fittingly be printed at the bottom of every page of this book:

> Man has no Body distinct from his Soul for that calld
> Body is a portion of Soul discernd by the five Senses, the
> chief inlets of Soul in this age.

Unless we have lost imagination completely, when we look at the body we are seeing the soul, and when we have sex, we experience the body as a way to the most penetrating mysteries of the soul.

It may be tempting at times to imagine sex as purely physical. Then we might not have to deal with feelings, personalities, and repercussions. We may try to avoid the complexities that always appear in relationships and look for liberated sex in "free love." How pleasant it would be, we may think, to have sex without strings attached, without all the painful emotions and partings and reunions. But the soul has its own life and its own will. It won't submit to our manipulations. The attempt to have sex without implications may backfire, and through a meaningless sexual fling we may find ourselves in the biggest emotional mess of our lives.

This human body that we have been conditioned to see as a system of chemicals, pulleys, pumps, and plumbing is an expressive entity of great subtlety and nuance. This subtle body is alive, diaphanous, full of meanings, poetic, expressive in every organ and part, intimately connected to emotion and feeling, and, by no means least, beautiful. This is the body that engages in sex, a body with so much soul that any attempt to deny its layers of meaning will likely come back to haunt us.

Obviously, the body can be appropriately studied, measured, and treated at a merely chemical and physiological level. But at the same time the body is infinitely more, and to grasp its sexuality we have to go far beyond the scientific imagination. We can appeal to artists, poets, and mystical writers, and to the rites and images of religion to get a fuller picture of its sexuality and to glimpse the myriad of ways the body can be sexually expressive.

The key to going any further in this book is to set aside our habit of looking at the body and its sexuality materialistically and to realize, as fundamentally as we can, that there is no such thing as a human body without emotion and imagination. The larger part of human sexuality is inaccessible to the materialist's viewpoint. Beyond it lies a whole world of sexual meaning. By looking at the sexual myths we live out, and at our spiritual attitudes, however developed and conscious they may be, we will find the roots of our desires and the sources of our satisfactions. Here lie secrets critical to our problems and unfulfilled hopes, here a way to educate the young in their sexuality, and here the means of reconciliation between sex and morality and between the body and the spirit.

Evoking Venus

The *Homeric Hymn to Aphrodite,* an ancient story about sex,
describes what I believe is the key to keeping the "human" in
human sexuality. Zeus, to the Greeks the divine governor of
life, wants to make certain that immortals and humans inter-
penetrate. This great mystery, related in Christianity to the
incarnation, addresses the human condition, in which spirituality and ordinary life go together to complete our humanity. We are made up of spirit and body, with an animating
soul in between, and any embodiment of spirit is an incarnation. The story begins with Zeus instilling in Aphrodite, goddess of sex, a desire for a mortal man.

As the story opens, Aphrodite goes to her temple at Cy-
prus, takes a bath, oils her body, and clothes herself in beautiful garments and golden jewelry. Then she finds Anchises, a
young shepherd, and disguises herself as a youthful virgin.
Taken aback by her beauty, Anchises suspects that she may
be a goddess, but she says no, she is the daughter of the ruler
of Phrygia. Hermes snatched her from her home, she says,
to be the wife of Anchises and the mother of their children.

Convinced that she is mortal, Anchises makes love with
her, but then she wakes him from his sleep and reveals herself
in all her divine glory. "When I first saw you, I knew you were
divine," says Anchises, worried about the consequences of
sleeping with a goddess, including loss of potency. She assures him that everything is fine and in accord with the divine will. Their son will be raised by the big-breasted mountain nymphs, the same, she says, who live long lives and eat
divine food and make love with Hermes in the corners of
their charming caves. Then she gives Anchises a warning:

When anyone asks who the mother of his child is, tell them she is a flowerlike nymph who lives in the mountain woods.[1]

This lovely erotic hymn to the goddess of sex offers many fascinating insights, but the theme that has kept me ruminating on it for years is the idea that sex is part temporal and part eternal. The son whom Aphrodite and Anchises conceived at their remarkable rendezvous, Aeneas, would go on to found Rome. His powerful creativity is an indication that lovemaking between a human and a deity, the union of spirit and body, can be extraordinarily fruitful.

Aphrodite's last comment also hints that one's partner in sex is more than human—he or she is a nymph. A man or woman can inspire such deep fantasy and emotion that through the loving embrace of our partner's body we may break through the limits of the human condition to touch upon another level of reality. The sex spirits come to us as from another world and can't be reduced to pieces of human personality. Sex with soul is always a form of communion with another level of existence, and that quality alone may be a major reason for its compelling attraction.

I find this nymph pictured in many places: in the lovely ancient Cycladic figures of the Mediterranean where she is shown almost without a face, her body erect and breasts small, and the pubic area a luminous triangle; in Lucas Cranach's nudes; in African wood-carved statues of woman; in Edward Weston's photographs; and in almost every picture of

Cycladic Figure

Marilyn Monroe. In these images the nymph is given form, but I also sense her, invisible, in certain groves, gardens, and bedrooms. I smell her in some perfumes, and I feel her in a scarf. I enter her bower whenever I visit certain exceptional stores and salons where she is present in all her beauty and where the sensitive shopkeepers are sacristans of the goddess of sensuality.

When Aphrodite says she is a flower nymph, she is also revealing something of great importance about herself and about sexuality. The divine pleasure granted to Anchises has come from the simple beauty of a flower. Aphrodite's Roman counterpart, Venus, was honored as the goddess of gardens. Nature's beauty, not just her functioning organs, is the essence of sexuality. In a sense, this book is inspired all the way through by this simple revelation of the goddess: if you want to know what sex is, think long and hard about a flower, especially its beauty and its appeal to the senses. Then think about all of nature and your own place in it. Whatever makes a flower glow with enchantment is the essence of your own sexuality.

Something deep in the human makeup needs and longs for a taste of eternity—at least a momentary release from the relentless pace of time. We don't usually place eternity in our list of needs, but the soul is only half satisfied with the things of this world. Traditional literature states over and over that the soul needs to break free from time and place. It needs regular excursions out of busy life, demanding relationships, and incessant productivity. For the monk, contemplation is one kind of deliverance from clock time and busyness, while for the average person sex can serve the same purpose.

The soul wants union not only with other persons but also with another dimension altogether, one we can call eternal, immortal, mythic, or a host of other names. As we'll see at the end of our journey through the many realms of sex, the soul craves the mystery lover, who inhabits and transcends the known partner. We'll also see how this world, including our flesh-and-blood lover, is not necessarily an obstacle but offers a positive route to the eternal and spiritual realm.

The brief sex-play of Anchises and Aphrodite gave birth to an entire civilization, and when our sex has soul it too can create worlds—families, communities, friendships, and personal vitality. Without the mystery dimension sex is not fully human, and it may feel incomplete or even empty. Sex is not something apart from life but is implicated in every aspect. The goddess is a mere flower nymph, but the ancients also called her the soul of the world.

In the *Homeric Hymn,* Aphrodite presents herself as both goddess and mortal. I used to think of the story she tells Anchises as a manipulating fiction, an aspect of her skill at seduction and persuasion, but now I suspect that more is going on. The whole tale is one of incarnation, an immortal taking on human flesh. The story she tells Anchises gives her a human family and place, a context that lasts admittedly for only the brief time of their lovemaking, but that gives their sex both humanity and divinity.

The nymph of sex is essential in lovemaking, but so too, obviously, is a human partner. We need to find the man or woman who can evoke this spirit for us. Sexual attraction is not at all a purely physical event. The soul is always in search of whatever will complete its desire, and our physical eyes are never separate from the eyes of the soul.

It also helps to have a place for love that is suitable for the nymph, because these nature spirits show themselves only in particular places and at special times. Marsilio Ficino, a fifteenth-century Florentine philosopher and magus—someone skilled in lore and magic—taught that by living with a degree of artfulness we can attract the various kinds of spirit, including the sexual spirit, that we need to live a full human life. The whole pleasant work of sex is to incarnate, to call down the spirit that will quicken our physical world and give home to eros.

Most people know that you can go through the motions of sex, even have an orgasm, and still not be fully present. Sometimes the sexual response may feel incomplete. A person may be impotent, emotionally cool, or in some other way unable to be involved in the lovemaking fully, despite an intention to be fully present. In the realm of sex intention isn't as important as it is in ordinary life. Usually we explain sexual problems in personal terms, as though the ego were somehow at fault, but the hymn teaches us that sex is more mysterious and not so dependent on the ego as we might expect.

Lovemaking is a ritual that invites the goddess of sex to be present. The love and affection we may feel toward our partner, the preparations we make for lovemaking, and all the activities that go into foreplay are intended to invoke the nymph of sex, so that what goes on between people is inspired and infused with this spirit. Without the presence of the nymph, sex becomes mechanical. It lacks soul because the soul requires that we attend to both the temporal and the eternal aspects. If we leave out the vertical dimension, our deep feelings and our high aspirations, in any activity, including sex, we disengage the soul and are left with a functional experience that may feel hollow.

When the spirit or genius of sex enters lovemaking through evocative words, touches, and actions, the soul of sex comes into play, and the lovers sense an inexplicable depth in their union. The sexual experience may feel effort-less and even glorious. We may think of sex as something we should do well, with skill and healthy motives. But health and technique, valuable as they may be, are not enough to evoke the depths of sex, which calls for imagination, rever-ence, and full presence.

Lovemaking is a ritual that, like all religious rites of the world, tries to make present the spirit that will make the human activity magically effective. Like all ritual, too, sex re-quires art, attention to details, and a devoted imagination. It calls for the kind of humility proper to religious ritual, in which the devotee doesn't force but requests the presence of the god or spirit. We may go to dinner, dress attractively, have an intimate conversation, listen to music—all with the thought of invoking the spirits of sexuality. In the midst of lovemaking we may be guided by deep intuition and imagi-nation to do those particular things that not only please our-selves and our partner but take us away from the cool world of the ego and place us in the warm, dreamlike cloud of sex-ual trance and charm. In this cloud of Aphroditic enchant-ment—scholars have translated the name Aphrodite as "shin-ing cloud"—the mystery that is sex takes place effectively and powerfully, as though it were a sacrament in the religion of this goddess whose task it is to deepen human sexuality, giv-ing it a more than human level of meaning.

Eros and the Soul

In modern times the word eros has been corrupted to refer to plain physical sexual acts, and even to the lowest kinds of sex. The word is actually abhorrent to some people, a surpris-ing development since in classical literature it was a highly spiritual, cosmic, and lofty kind of love. In Greek literature eros is nothing less than the magnetism that holds the entire universe together, and human love in its many forms is simply a participation in that greater eros.

The ancient poet Hesiod, writing around 800 B.C. about the origins of things, places Eros among the first beings, but he also warns of the terrible power of the erotic, and perhaps it is this tendency to overwhelm us that makes people wary of eros. Hesiod writes:

> Eros, who is love, handsomest among all
>   the immortals
> who breaks the limbs' strength
>   who in all gods, in all human beings
> overpowers the intelligence in the breast,
>   and all their shrewd planning.[2]

Later, the Greek philosopher Empedocles taught that the entire universe runs on the two principles of love and strife. He identified love with both Eros and Aphrodite, linking the binding attraction that keeps all things connected and working in harmony with the allures and desires that ordinarily we call sexual. The tie between this greater notion of eros and ordinary sexuality is a key idea in our search for the soul of sex. We don't want to leave sex behind and focus on some ethereal and generic idea of the erotic life, nor do we wish to reduce sex to physical behavior. Somewhere in between is a valuable way of seeing the erotic within sex, expanding our idea of sexuality without losing its immediacy and intimacy.

Many writers who have described the erotic life help create a picture of eros that might be useful in deepening our notion of sexuality. Plato, for instance, says of lovers that "the deepest insights spring from their love." Eros is a guide to knowledge, and for that reason Socrates, Plato's archetypal wise person, refers to himself as a lover.[3]

In some cultures it is said that to have sex with someone is to know the person in a deep way, and to have sex for the first time is to know life in a way that is entirely new and transforming. Sex is a kind of gnosis or holy knowing. In sex we get to know a person in a way that is more than special. Sex reveals much that is unconscious to both people, and so the unveiling that goes on at the physical level is mirrored as the soul itself sheds its protective covering.

In sex we also discover the power and direction of our deepest desires. The pleasures we may find in sex—sweet sex, aggressive sex, inventive and explorative sex, sadomasochistic games, dressing and undressing, body parts and kinds of kissing, places and settings—all of these preferences, tied so closely to passion show us who we are, where our soul wants to lead us, and what our complexes, obstacles, and inhibitions look like. In sex we see the private parts of the soul with all its particulars.

In his dream seminars, C. G. Jung once made the comment that "people think that eros is sex, but not at all, Eros is relatedness."[4] Eros is not the physical expression in sex alone, but is rather the physical and the emotional combined. More accurately, it is the meaningful connection established by sex, felt and understood by the people making love. This eros we feel in sex and romance is also the broader magnetism that holds the universe together, the go-between spirit said to keep the planets in orbit and the seasons on track. What we seek in sex is not only bodily satisfaction, but a response to the soul's need for all that eros offers, for a world that holds together and a whole life that is creative and motivated by love.

In her elegant book *Eros the Bittersweet,* Anne Carson notes that the Greeks played with the word eros by adding "pt" to it, making it *pteros,* wing. When the penis is pictured having wings, or when bird-women like the Sirens tempt and seduce, this idea of a flying, lofty eros finds direct expression. When the Greeks and Romans personified Eros in their art and literature, they sometimes pictured him as a young man with large and lovely wings. Eros seems to move through the air, and he has this quality of taking us, as Anne Carson says, "from over here to over there."[5] When we long for someone or something, we are being invited to make a move, to soar in spirit out of the status quo and into a new world. Maybe this is yet another reason why we're afraid of the erotic and the sexual—it disturbs our current equilibrium. On the other hand, it is also the very source of vitality and animation.

Georges Bataille, a French writer who devoted his life to the study of eros, says that eros always involves a transgression of some kind. "Unless we see that transgression is taking place, we no longer have the feeling of freedom that the full accomplishment of the sexual act demands,"[6] he writes. Now this is a strong statement that could easily be misread, fitting nicely into the fear many people have that eroticism is evil and sinful by nature. But the transgression in sex may be more a psychological one than a literally moral one.

As eros entices us into new worlds, it may entail breaking through current modes and even codes of behavior, and so it can feel like a transgression. The first sexual experience overreaches inhibitions that may have been in place for a long time. The first intimacy with a particular lover breaks the reserve that has kept the couple within certain limits in their contact with each other. The first experiment with a new style of lovemaking may involve the feeling of breaking rules or habits. The very point of sexual experimentation may be to sense together, in mutual generosity and complicity, the joy of transcending rules and expectations. In this spirit communities have often celebrated important religious festivals with orgies and other kinds of sexual license, breaking into the realm of spirit by means of sexual overstepping.

Throughout his writing Plato discusses the role of eros in life, but especially in the *Symposium,* where Socrates is taught the nature of love. "Eros," Plato writes, "is a coming to life in beauty in relation to both body and soul." This is an aspect of eros that can easily be overlooked or taken too lightly. In our erotic desires we may be in search of beauty, pure and simple. However close to or far from cultural ideals of beauty, a lover introduces us to beauty's soul and the soul's own beauty.

We live in a world that gives scant attention to beauty. We're willing to build cities that function but have little beauty and to make homes that are convenient and affordable but not necessarily beautiful. We believe that beauty is expendable. But to the soul beauty is more important than almost anything, and so it plays an important role in our desires and cravings. It lies at the heart of sexuality and is responsible for a good portion of the pleasure we find there.

In Plato we also find that Eros is the child of Want and Plenty. Our erotic lives may feel full for a while, then empty, or maybe even full and empty at the same time. If we knew that both emptiness and fullness were natural to the erotic life, we might live out this natural rhythm sympathetically rather than demanding that eros always be full and feeling abnormal or incomplete if it isn't.

A man in his mid-fifties once told me that he was puzzled to see his sexual dreams, cravings, and fantasies diminish at the mid-point of his life. He thought the change might be due to his age, and yet at the same time he had finally found a partner he could live with and love. Sometimes we expect eros to feel empty, but instead we discover a surprising fullness. At other times we may assume that life will be erotically full, when in fact we still feel some of its emptiness.

At the end of the twentieth century we seek hungrily for sexual satisfaction, but we don't give much attention to eros in the whole of life. Our craving never seems satisfied, or if it is, it may be temporary and not connected with the rest of life. Some work all day drudgingly at a computer and come home to watch a sexy movie on cable television. In their lives eros and work belong to separate categories. Thinking literally and negatively about the erotic life, we don't give eros a place of honor among our values, and yet at the same time we are overwhelmed by our desires and by our basic but misunderstood appetites.

Sex and eros are related, as the Greeks said, like mother and son. If we could recover a sense of the holiness of eros and its creative, divine place in the nature of things, we might see how absurdly small our view of sex has been, and we might reinstate it without moralism at the center of life, where it can offer vitality and intimacy of unrivaled power. Before we can give depth and richness to our sexuality, we have to discover the value of deep pleasure and desire and at the same time relax our anxious attention to the control of the emotions, the justification of our lives by work and restraint, and our belief in the value of repression and suffering.

In our society sex is wounded by a deep-seated masochism, which finds distorted satisfaction in the suppression of desire. This masochism is a symptomatic and destructive form of surrender. Instead of giving in to our passions, allowing emotion to course through our bodies and psyches, and generously offering ourselves to intimacy, we surrender our joy in life to any authority we can find, and we find many authorities willing to condemn us for our longings and pleasures.

At the very heart of sex lies a profound affirmation of life, giving us a reason for living, optimism, and energy. At every step, this process can be wounded and weakened by a fear of vitality and a failure to trust in life, in others and in oneself. Everywhere we are told to set limits on eros, to be careful that we are not lost in its passion. But if we listen to these worried cautions, we may end up with only a modicum of self-possession purchased at the cost of life's passion. Eros may go underground as seething, dark desire, and the surface of life may turn mechanical and controlled, cheerless and humorless.

When anyone asks who is your lover, Aphrodite says to the shepherd, tell them your lover is a flower nymph who can be found in the woods. Sexual desire always offers an invitation to the world's soul through the nymph responsible for the beauty and vitality of our woods and their plants and flowers. Sex keeps us connected to our deepest natures and links us to our roots. In that way it expands the source from which we live our lives.

The *Orphic Hymn to Eros* calls him "great, pure, lovely, and sweet" and prays to him to banish evil inclinations from our hearts. What change of heart would be required of us to call on the spirit of desire and pleasure to rid us of evil? Yet sex has the capacity to pacify our raging and distressed hearts, if only we would grant it its soul.

CHAPTER 2

The Erotic Body

Beauty, Face, Hair

I F W E T A K E seriously William Blake's reminder that the body is the soul manifested by the senses, then we have to look at the body in a new way. This view of the body, quite unlike anything we find in modern culture, offers two challenges: how to see the soul when we look at the body, and how to use our senses as the primary means of knowing the soul. Usually we think of the body in purely physical terms and consider the soul abstractly. People often ask for definitions of the soul, as though it could be grasped intellectually. They want to know if it is immortal and how it functions. Blake invites us to think about the soul in a different way, as something to be discovered through touch, smell, hearing, taste, and sight.

We make a mistake when we think of sensation as a purely physical experience. Like everything human, sensation cannot be separated from imagination. We are always living in a story, always surrounded by images, and always perceiving with imagination. Sensation is a particular way of imagining, fully grounded in physical perception, but nevertheless determined by fantasy. Ralph Waldo Emerson said as much when he observed that only the poet can really see the stars. At a mundane level, a person eating pasta that his mother has cooked all his life will have a sensory experience heavily influenced by past memories and by affection for his mother. Sensation is never separated from fantasy, which gives it meaning.

Everyone is aware that sex is a physical experience. What we sometimes forget is that even in the midst of ecstatic sensation, we are still deep in the imagination as well. We can't appreciate the deeper dimensions of sex unless we consider the poetics of this body that speaks to us through sensation.

The Landscape of the Body

The body is an erotic landscape with regions of special interest, some common to all people, some proper to certain cultures and individuals. It's always difficult to read the symbolism or imagery of the body, but in general the body and its various parts echo certain themes in a person's psychology. It doesn't take much effort, for instance, to see a child's attachment to mother in a man's attraction to big-breasted women. But what is the meaning of an interest in feet or shoes? What is going on in the attraction to a man's pectoral muscles or to a woman's calves or thighs? What does it mean when we're fascinated by a man's or woman's "buns"? I've never been able to accept the common idea among scholars that the thigh is a euphemism for the genitals. Thighs have their own eros. And what exactly is the lure of underclothes, and what is it about the eyes that can be erotically hypnotic?

The body is a mythology, entire and complete in itself. Just as we can turn to any culture's traditional stories and rituals and find gods of war, nymphs of groves and streams, and spirits of place, so we can look at the body and find nurturing breasts, protective muscles, luxuriant hair, adventurous feet, and boyish buttocks. Each part of the body, differing slightly from person to person, is a window onto a world of meaning and allure. This stirring of fantasy and desire shows that the body expresses the soul, or even, in Blake's language, *is* the soul.

The Freudian body is a mythological terrain of nurturing breasts, retentive anus, and sexual phallus. But it would be a mistake to limit the meaning of any body part to a Freudian interpretation, no matter how imaginatively nuanced. In the writings of the Marquis de Sade, for instance, the anus is mysteriously an object of adoration, and in statues of Artemis the breasts seem to have nothing to do with nurturing.

The body is always available for poetic reading, and there is no need to become rigid about a particular way of interpreting it. Each person, each culture, each historical period, and each theory has the right to its own storytelling based on images that lie piled on each other in every inch of human tissue. The skin is thick with stories, told and untold, already explored and yet to be discovered.

Some ancient sculptures show trim, muscled men running races, throwing spears, and fighting in battle. Some depict a mother nursing her child. Aphrodite appears preparing for a bath, loosening a sandal, placing her hands over her breasts and pubic area, glancing back over her shoulder to see her buttocks, or tending to her bracelets and other adornments. She seems to enjoy looking at herself and being looked at, and she is often preoccupied with things we might consider peripheral and nonessential. She seems generally happy in her apparently unproductive, insignificant preoccupations.

These delightful images of the goddess of sex may help correct our biases. To the soul it may be fruitful to look at our bodies, to take time at the bath, to consider our jewelry and body ornaments. The soul may be restored by a long soaking or an hour stolen from a busy life for a fragrant sauna. The soul may need attention to nails and skin and hair.

In Aphrodite, the entire body is alive with significance and pleasure—her smile, the placing of her hands, the crook of a leg, the shape of a breast. We have to remember that statues of Aphrodite are icons, a holy presencing of the goddess and not just portraits of her, and so each subtle element has profound implications for sexuality at the personal level and for life in its largest sense. The curve of her hip may be attractive, and it may also say something about curves in all of nature and all of culture. Her seductive smile may remind us of a friend, and it may also offer some deep insight into the allure of nature and of things. Her gestures are so precise that they appear to be mudras, sacred signals representing holy truths. We will look closely at these mudras in the next chapter.

Aphrodite's body is the archetype of the human body and also of the body of the world. The human body is a miniature world, each of its parts mirroring nature, culture, and ordinary human life. If we could give up some of our modern biases, we could look at the body and see signs of life's deepest mysteries. Every body is a mystical body, each part a poem. If it's possible to see the whole world in a grain of sand, we can glimpse the meaning of life in an eyebrow, a nipple, a penis, and, in the holy spirit of Aphrodite, a rounded backside.

The Erotic Body

The only way I can understand the enormous curiosity and fascination attached to the human body is to recall William Blake's instruction that the body is the soul perceived by the senses. The body subtly expresses the mystery of the person and of the human race. How fascinating it is to watch bodies go by in a crowded public space. We never tire of contemplating the subtle differences and presentations of bodies in advertising and in serious photography. Artists never cease painting the body in myriad styles and tonalities, and we gaze intensely at our own bodies in the mirror and in family photographs.

It is as if the body holds the secret to who we are and what we are to become. One wonders if the many religions and philosophies that have been repressive and dismissive of the body, seeing it as an obstacle and weight, are merely defending themselves against the vitality promised by the body's eroticism. Spiritual worry about the body seems to come from an undervaluation of physical life that parallels an overvaluation of eternity.

Women tormented by anorexia and bulimia have told me how they wish from the depths of their hearts to be relieved of their bodies. Some are embarrassed to have breasts and curves, some develop an overpowering need to cut off their hair, and some just want to waste away until they have no body at all. I've witnessed profound liberation in such women when they begin to accept their desires and the unique direction of their attractions.

Often spirituality is motivated by an anti-Venus retreat into an ethereal and bodiless realm where we can escape our humanity. We may see in individual cases of anorexia a battle, enacted in the culture at large, to live virtuously in the undeniable presence of the body. The obvious materialism of our age covers over an extreme spiritualism, in which we deny the necessities of Venus and live as though we could ignore the body. Often men and women are so focused on future success in work and business that they first take note of their bodies in serious illness and in sexual attractions that disturb them.

Men can be extremely self-conscious of their bodies. Some can't urinate in public rest rooms because of their deep embarrassment. Many men obsessively devote themselves to weight lifting and fitness, suffering their bodily existence rather than enjoying it. Obviously not comfortable with themselves, men may strut and brawl as though they need to display their physical power and presence.

One of the first achievements to be made in the reconciliation of body and spirit, which is a prerequisite for a deepened, soul-filled sexuality, is a rediscovery of the virtue and value of the body's eroticism. We may have to realize in the starkest terms that the historical and psychological splitting of body and spirit, of transcendence and sensuousness, and of virtue and desire is a neurosis, a disturbance of the soul. It is not a philosophical choice, not a cultural emphasis, and not a spiritual necessity. It takes many forms both within religion and outside of it, both in explicit spiritual devotion of all kinds and in less obvious forms of dedication, as in business and politics.

These divisions lie at the base of modern Western culture, and as such they lie in the individual hearts of us all, contaminating our marriages and our lovemaking. They are false divisions, unnecessary oppositions that affect every aspect of modern life, from our personal emotional stability to the building of bridges. To find the soul of sex we have to wrench it out of the materialistic and mechanistic body that we have created by means of our modern philosophies and reunite it with the subtle, fantasy-filled, mythologized body of the imagination.

Body and spirit marry in the chapel of the soul. They marry every minute of every day, in all activities and in all inactivity, in all thoughts and in all actions, or they marry not at all. If they don't marry, we do not know sexuality with soul, and therefore our sexuality remains incomplete and insufficiently human. We do not find the soul of sex by spiritualizing the body but by coming to appreciate its mysteries and by daring to enter into its sensuousness.

The Beautiful Face

One curious epithet for the goddess Aphrodite is *philommeides*. A tradition going back to ancient literature understands *philommeides* to mean both "lover of smiles" and "lover of the genitals." Aphrodite is often shown with a slight smile on her face, the kind we find both mysterious and intriguing in Leonardo da Vinci's Mona Lisa. The smile cannot be reduced to any single meaning, but in relation to other qualities associated with the goddess we can see in it her delight in ordinary physical pleasures, the joy she brings to life, and, not unrelated, her unashamed appreciation for the sexual body.

Aphrodite's mystery is expressed in a smile because she

knows that the face can be used with extreme subtlety to invoke the atmosphere of sex, to attract a partner, and to lure a lover to her sensual rituals. This goddess of the alluring smile is the patroness of seduction. Look closely at statues of Venus and you will find much to read in her smile and in the tilt of her head.

Some people are attractive simply for their facial beauty and handsomeness. With little effort they can work sexual magic, a talent that can be a great gift or a terrible burden. A person with a beautiful face is born into the world of Aphrodite and has to learn how to live in it. As with any immortal gift of birth, such a gifted person has to discover over time how to enjoy it without narcissism and without making it a slave of the ego.

Most of the truly beautiful people I have known confess both their gratitude and their sense of luck for having been born handsome or beautiful, and at the same time they admit that beauty can get them into trouble and can be a weight to carry. They also express their fear of losing their beauty to age, wondering how they are going to get along without it. Their physical beauty becomes part of their makeup and plays a central role in the unfolding of their soul. But the same is true for all of us. Archetypal human beauty shines through in every body and every face, especially to a lover or a parent, and that beauty, with its seductiveness, is part of the life of the soul.

In Marilyn Monroe people encountered the nymph of sex, and she often complained that people looked at her without really seeing *her*: "People had a habit of looking at me as if I were some kind of mirror instead of a person," she said. People didn't exactly see themselves in her, because this mirror performed a special magic. In her they saw their idealization of the body and of sex, and beyond that they perceived the sex spirit herself, our nymph, the goddess, who so possessed the actress that the person was hardly to be noticed.

Marilyn Monroe also observed, "The real lover is the man who can thrill you by touching your head or smiling into your eyes or by just staring into space."[1] This simple line captures the sensation of stumbling into Aphrodite's world simply by means of a smile or a stare. All it takes are deep dark eyes, an arch in the eyebrows, flawless skin, a chin of authority, or a delicate throat to do her magic.

The nymph takes residence in men as well as women, and when she is there people react to her presence, sometimes with extraordinary clumsiness, and call it beauty. Cary Grant began his life as Archie Leach, an English actor who worked hard at creating the persona of the suave screen lover—the look, the walk, the accent. His biographer Graham McCann refers to Grant's persona as "a cluster of idealized qualities" and quotes the film critic Pauline Kael describing Cary Grant as "the most publicly seduced male the world has known." He notes that the outrageous Mae West once looked him up and down and said, "You can be had."[2]

We can all take on the Aphroditic task of making the most of the raw beauty we've been given. The face allows us to eroticize our very persons creatively. Lips, teeth, noses, eyebrows, and skin, along with all the care and medical attention we may bring to them, serve the spirit for whom the body and its sexuality are at the center of life, even though we may judge them superficial.

Cosmetic dental repairs and plastic surgery can be written off as the work of vanity, but they can also be soul-saving resources through which our deep, life-giving sexuality is sustained and cared for. Our sexual nymph may not keep the heart beating and the brain at work, but she makes life worth living and her work is essential for the survival of the soul.

Erotic Hair

Eyes, dimples, foreheads, cheeks, shoulders—any of these can launch a thousand ships in a person's imagination, becoming a loving obsession as we remember, sketch, photograph, and discuss some small feature of a person we love. One element that has drawn particular attention in literature and painting is the hair. Brushed, dyed, shaved, and shaped according to dictates of meaning, pleasure, and allure, hair has drawn particular attention in life as in art. In the realm of sex hair works a special magic.

Hair is of great importance in religion and in communities dedicated to celibacy, where not giving much attention to hair is a matter of serious concern. When I lived in a Catholic religious order, I was instructed to wear my hair short, preferably about three-quarters of an inch long. The rules forbade the use of shampoo and the growing of beards and mustaches. For centuries, of course, monks were recognized by their tonsure, the small shaved bald spot that was a sign of their initiation into religious life. Eastern monks still shave their heads entirely, while yogis never cut a single hair.

Having short, plain hair may help the monk keep his vow, while the evangelist might benefit from the sexual display of his luxurious coiffure—religion is full of concealed erotic signals. As is often the case, religion shows us in the extreme certain patterns that are common in our daily lives. Deep shifts may be taking place in the soul in those ordinary but crucial moments when we decide to change our hairdo or shave off a beard or, certainly, change hair color.

The many rituals and stories surrounding hair also provide some hints about the life fantasies that mingle with our
sexuality. When I was growing up in a Catholic school and
family, it was the strict custom for women to have their hair
covered whenever they were in church. I never thought much
about the meaning of covering the head and always assumed
that it was a tradition signifying reverence, parallel to the in-
junction that men not wear hats in church.

C. G. Jung offers an interesting reason for the practice, one
I never heard from the nuns or priests. He says that according
to tradition the problem was not that men in the congregation might be tempted by the sight of uncovered feminine
hair, but that angels might be thrown into rapture in its presence.[3] He explains that in some traditions angels are not as
pure as we might think. Sometimes they display an eagerness
for sex that matches any human desire, and apparently they
can't resist the allure of hair.

We are often told, in one form or another, to resist the
temptations of the world, the flesh, and the devil. But to live
a vibrant spiritual life the angels and spirits have to be enticed
into our daily lives. This legend about angels being attracted
by beautiful human hair says something profound about
both the spiritual life and the power of sexy hair. Lovely, attractive earthly life is epitomized in beautiful hair, and the
cultivation of this life, including the sexual potency of hair,
plays an important role in our full participation in our humanity.

Renaissance philosophy sees physical beauty as part of a
chain from body to spirit. In his book on love Ficino says that
we can ascend from body to soul to angel to God by means
of beauty.[4] I take these levels of reality in very ordinary ways.
I can be enraptured by my daughter's hair, but that beauty

only leads me immediately to feelings of love for her, and through her to a love of life, and through that love of life to an appreciation of absolute and infinite beauty. I am easily persuaded of the existence of God through the old argument of beauty, and the chain begins with a child's lovely red hair.

As part for the whole, hair can represent earthly human life in all its sensuousness. In 1922 British sculptor and calligrapher Eric Gill published a wood engraving entitled *Nuptials of God*, showing a woman standing with outstretched arms against the body of Jesus as it hangs on the cross. Except for her arms and two small patches of leg, all you see is her body-length hair covering the entire torso of Jesus. For Gill, this coming together of the suffering Christ and human hair represents the deepest mystery of the spiritual life, the erotic union of Christ and his church.

Eric Gill, *Nuptials of God*

The engraving was objectionable to some, of course, not only because of the woman's body pressed against the crucified Christ's, but also because almost all you see of her is her long flowing hair. She echoes the traditional image of Mary Magdalen, of course, a woman in legend recognizable for her hair and her sexuality. She is also the sensuous soul finding completion in loving embrace of the exalted spirit. All my life I have been drawn to the bold, sensuous theology of Eric Gill and to his beautiful images that blend, with extraordinary originality, passionate spiritual practice with passionate sensuality. With rare intuition his erotic, spiritual engravings and sculptures heal the wound that occurs whenever body is torn from spirit and the two try to survive apart from each other.

The monk shaves his or her head in the name of transcendent spirituality, while the person dedicated to a different, more earth-rooted spirituality, no less important or virtuous, braids her locks or enhances his appearance with styling gel. The man or woman standing in front of a mirror brushing straggling hairs into place is engaged in a ritual, a true rite in the religion of Aphrodite. Combing your hair is way of caring for your soul. Of course it can be empty and narcissistic, but any human activity can be either genuine in its unselfconsciousness or neurotic in its egotism. Aphrodite is a face of the soul, and her world of alluring beauty and body care is a valid and effective way to the soul.

The Soul's Own Beauty

Beauty, a quality of body and character, lies deep within the province of Aphrodite, but for all our attention to physical beauty we often ignore beauty in the soul and in the world.

The myths associated with Aphrodite encourage us to see beauty not only as a physical quality but as the evocation of a spirit. The gorgeous yet almost surreal Venus figures of Botticelli and those of Lucas Cranach conjure this spirit of beauty in a variety of ways that are alluring and arresting.

Sandro Botticelli, *The Birth of Venus*

Such Venus bodies of art, dressed in mere hints of clothing, are not literal depictions of the human body. Rather, they show that a spirit body lies visible just beneath the clothes and adornments of a human person. Cranach's many representations of Adam, too, evoke a primordial beauty in his perfect proportions, handsome face, and vulnerable postures. These and countless other erotic images from art demonstrate the many ways in which the sex nymph can be called forth in our ordinary lives and through our ordinary bodies.

Life-enhancing beauty does not require that a person be pretty or handsome; it may consist in quite inconspicuous signs of the nymph's presence. I once knew a man whose face was rather deformed, but his voice was angelic. Hearing him

speak, you would immediately be charmed and would see
the music of his speech give a beatific cast to his face. A person may not be a typical beauty and yet you can be sent reel-
ing in pleasure by the erotic shape of a cheek or the turn of a
lip. Because it is more than the product of cosmetics and aesthetics, beauty casts a spell. It is the work of magic and serves
sexuality because it offers pleasure and gives rise to the desire
for union.

James Joyce's analysis of beauty, based on the writing of
Thomas Aquinas, considers the radiance of a thing to be a
primary source of its beauty, a radiance that can be appre-
hended "luminously" by the human mind, causing an "enchantment of the heart."[5] It's interesting in this regard that
the Greeks described Aphrodite as one who shines like the
dawn. In a poem about a new bride, Sappho conjures up this
same idea of beauty:

> charming to look at,
> with eyes as soft as honey,
> and a face that Love has lighted
> with his own beauty.

In Sappho it is love that inspires the radiance we perceive
as beauty. Especially as part of sex, beauty is the result of attraction, desire, and enjoyment rather than a fixed physical
quality. It is the radiance of the soul showing itself in a facial
expression, an innate facial figuration, or the face as it has
been shaped into a certain glowing visage through years of
experience. We perceive these rays shining invisibly through
a charming face, even though that face may fail to move others and may by all current standards be plain. We may be cap-
tivated, unable to think of anything else, and want desper-

ately never to have this presence taken from us, so powerful and meaningful is its beauty.

Growing old diminishes a kind of beauty that is undeniably potent, but it doesn't destroy the beauty that is the soul's radiance, because the body as soul exists partly outside of time and therefore is differently affected by the passing of years. It may take a person of unusual perspicacity to perceive this beauty, or it may require only a person of experience. In Marcel Proust's *Remembrance of Things Past,* when Marcel sees the ageless Odette after a lapse of many years, he says: "I failed at first to recognize her, not because she had but because she had not changed."[6] Soul beauty is perceived through the senses, yet it is timeless.

Whatever its source, the radiance of the face plays a central role in sex, so much so that in the moment of passion a person may look at his or her partner and catch a glimpse of Aphrodite herself, no longer disguised as the person who slipped into the bed. Perhaps the central goal in sex is to achieve this apotheosis in which the human lover calls forth a momentary perception of divine beauty, thereby turning the lovemaking into true ritual. What we call "good sex" may be nothing less than a timeless rite carried out so effectively that we are deeply affected by the Aphroditic spirit that has been so effectively summoned.

D. H. Lawrence, who was acutely aware of this mystery of divine sexuality, wrote:

> What's the good of a man
> unless there's the glimpse of a god in him?
> And what's the good of a woman
> unless she's a glimpse of a goddess of some sort?

In this definition anyone and everyone can be beautiful. Perhaps only a lover can see the soul's beauty reflected in the face or body of the beloved, but even so that beauty is real, and it plays an important part in sex. It's a sign that Venus has been called and that she has responded. And, as the ancients said, she is the sine qua non of sex. She gives new meaning to the word nymphomania, which we can define along the lines of Plato and many of his followers as erotic madness or frenzy. Nympho-mania becomes an altered state of consciousness in which we succeed in beholding the nymph in a male or female body, the nymph whose task it is to grace human life with sensual and sexual wonders.

Near the end of his extraordinarily complex novel *Lolita*, Vladimir Nabokov places a lovely sentence that captures the essence of his unusual story about a man on the edge of sanity, fiercely in love with a young girl: "the very attraction immaturity has for me lies not so much in the limpidity of pure young forbidden fairy child beauty as in the security of a situation where infinite perfections fill the gap between the little given and the great promised—the great rosegray never-to-be-had." Humbert Humbert would be called a nymphomaniac, but Nabokov reminds us that sexual desire can be life desire, the craving for immortal perfections expressed in earthly attractions.

The theme is even stronger in the ancient tale of Eros and Psyche, where in a crucial moment Psyche, the soul, breaks her vow not to look at her lover and gazes at Eros, who is Love himself, "a handsome god lying in a handsome posture." She looks long on his beautiful face, his luxuriant hair, his "hairless and rosy body."[7]

These and other ancient stories tell of the soul's attraction to the human body and especially the face. Beyond its mystical and profound psychological implications, we might simply acknowledge the importance of our own beauty and allure, however great it is, however slight and relative. Renaissance philosophers said that beauty is one of the graces of human life, a gift and a power that should not be underestimated.

Eros and Psyche

CHAPTER 3

Phallic and
Vaginal Mysteries
Meaning and the Sex Organs

T HE SIMPLE presence of the body inspires worlds of meaning. The human body is crammed with significance in all
its parts. Even the prohibitions against sex—how much cleav-
age can be shown in an approved movie, whether frontal
male nudity is more objectionable than frontal female nudity, whether the nudity is brief or extended—betray a studied interest in the erotic significance of the most finely measured displays of the body. So powerful and fascinating are its
details that we measure sex in centimeters.

The ante is raised when we focus on the sex organs per se,
the penis and the vagina. The sex organs give rise to such
primitive and fundamental thoughts and feelings that they
elicit both extreme interest and extreme measures of control.

As we continue to track down the soul of sex in the body,

we can see the sexual body as a constellation of images rather than a collection of mechanical organs, and we can find the soul in unexpected places. The sexual organs not only have a huge role in our imagination of sex, they have given rise to religious ritual, meaning, and art. In fact religion demonstrates that the sex organs and the body's capacity for sexual expressiveness are not only meaningful, they convey the grandest and deepest truths about human life.

The Penis and the Phallus

I keep in mind a lesson I learned from a friend, Professor Rafael Lopez-Pedraza, that the soul sometimes manifests itself most directly in the freakishness of human life. I want to begin our search for the soul in the sex organs with the odd interest shown in their weight and size.

Japanese erotic drawings show the penis being weighed and measured, and I recently came across an image of a woman holding her breast on a scale. Men's magazines discuss penis length and girth, sometimes in fun and sometimes to reassure men who are anxious about the relative size of their penis. A well-hung man or a well-endowed woman is something of an ideal that people aspire to, and they often have corresponding feelings of inferiority when their organs don't match up. I've counseled women who are deeply disturbed by the large or small size of their breasts, and men who have become preoccupied with the proportions of their penis.

This anxiety doesn't make much sense at the purely biological level, and usually magazine writers assure men that physically they can have satisfying sex regardless of the size of their penis. What the writers fail to see is that the worry may have more to do with the symbolic resonance of the phallus than with the physical penis. This is a source of confusion in sex: taking organs, desires, fetishes, images, and ways of making love too literally, and failing to bring a sufficiently rich imagination to everyday sexual concerns.

The simplest psychological analysis sees a parallel between penis and ego—the bigger the penis, the more confident the ego. But what is it about the penis that inflates the ego? And why would breast size have such deep emotional importance for both men and women?

The penis is an unusually fertile source of mythology. Just as the rosy light of early morning inspired the Greeks to imagine the mythological figure of Eos, Dawn, who was then identified with the "brilliant" Aphrodite, so the penis, a natural phenomenon in the geography of the body, can stir the imagination. The phallus is the penis mythologized and fantasized, and mythical fantasy extends, of course, to every aspect of the male and female pubic area.

Penis size has long been part of this mythology. Men seem to be proud of whatever it is that a large and long penis gives them, and it's too simple to describe that gift as ego or personal power. In some cultures the phallus is an image of divine potency. Perhaps some men, without consciously being aware of it, find real magic in a large penis, the ample size being sufficient to transform the penis into the phallus. The bigger the penis, the greater the myth. As the story usually goes, a man so endowed can give superhuman pleasure to a woman, and the man takes pride in the intensity of her response. Women may express their concerns about the penis size of their partner, and there, too, may lie a fantasy about the greater meaning of the penis.

Because of our secular ways of thinking, we see personality issues where other cultures might see myth and religion.

When we study images in which the penis or breast is being measured and weighed, we tend to see the anxious ego, wondering if it measures up. From a less secular point of view we might realize that the penis represents life's potency in the largest sense, something we all need and crave. There is nothing neurotic or egotistical about desiring the fertility and potency that are epitomized and compacted into the image of the penis.

A man wants to give his partner pleasure, and he feels powerful and fulfilled through her or his responsiveness and enjoyment. Eros is a vast source of power and satisfaction. If the world loves you, you are not going to feel weak and insignificant. A man's wish for a bigger penis might more deeply be a search for the phallus, the source of erotic vitality. The advice columnists are correct—penis size is not essential. Nevertheless, the story about wanting a big penis *is* important, because everyone, man and woman, encounters a particular aspect of life's possibility in the penis. The larger the penis, the more we may sense the myth and the more we may imagine the erotic power stored in that image.

The women of ancient Greece waved huge wooden phalluses during religious processions. They weren't advertising for bigger penises; they were celebrating the phallic potency in life, the divine power that grants a more-than-human passion for life. It is the phallus we want in marriage, in love and sex, not necessarily a big penis. In that spirit the Japanese drawings of the weighing of the penis tell the story of the weight eros has in life—nothing is as simple or as literal as it appears to be, especially in the area of sex.

Literature on the phallus that explores its importance in male experience is often rich and full of insight, but if we consider the phallus solely as the penis, just as an aspect of male physiology and psychology, we are in danger of literalizing and limiting its meaning. Unlike the penis, experienced subjectively by males, the phallus is available to both men and women, whether they are waving it in procession, pleasuring it in sex, or strapping on a rubber one. In imagination the phallus is not limited to literal gender.

The small penis has its own allure in the imagination. The nonthreatening, normal, ordinary, flaccid penis is also, in my view, part of the myth of the phallus. The male knows the ups and downs of desire partly through his penis, and the ordinary state of being limp is as important as arousal. To be always tumescent is an undesirable condition, whether in the actual penis or in the emotions of desire and excitement.

An ancient note on Aristophanes' play *The Acharnians* refers to the people who carried large images of penises in processions as *phallophoroi*, phallus-bearers, and it says that once, when the citizens of Athens refused to honor Dionysus, "a grievous disease attacked their men in their private parts," a malady called satyriasis, compulsive sexuality.[1] Could our social satyriasis be due to a neglect of the religious aspects of sex? Today we still use the word priapism, after the phallic god Priapus, for the condition in which a man cannot get rid of an erection—a physical analog of compulsive sexuality. Honoring the penis only in its erect state may be a psychological variant of *priapism*, the inability to find relief from our preoccupation with sexual excitement.

Fascination with the phallus is not merely about power. It is a numinous source of mystery as well. On one hand the penis is common, ordinary, and insignificant, and on the other it is the focus of curiosity and interest out of all proportion to its size and function. The organ is relatively small, but the myth is big, and it is the myth that means so much to the imagination and to the soul's quest for meaning. Interestingly, the word "fascination" is a phallus term, used by the ancient Romans to refer to an amulet in the shape of a penis worn around the neck to ward off the evil eye.[2]

Many explanations have been offered as to why the ancient Greeks placed at their doors a herm, a stone pillar topped with a bust of Hermes, often with a phallic image attached. Among other things it must have been an emblem of protection. They also placed phallic images at gravesites, presumably because Hermes, an especially phallic god, guided souls to the underworld. An image of divine power that provides reassurance in the face of death must also have healing properties, if for no other reason than that it serves the life principle.

Why not extend this idea into everyday life and imagine that sex can be healing? The display of each other's bodies and especially the private parts, the organs usually veiled, may help heal a marriage or keep each person lively and vibrant and, as the Greeks would say, in touch with immortality. Naturally, an anxious person may use this power of the phallus for personal gain, but the abuse of phallic power neither defines nor negates its healing potentiality.

Technologically primitive societies use sexual power to sustain community and to remain in sympathy with nature, while we reduce sex in our collective imagination to physical and emotional dimensions and then try to live a vibrant life cut off from the wellspring of sexuality. The phallus represents life itself—procreative, pleasurable, rising and falling, penetrating, healing, enduring. Our powerful attraction to images like the phallus and the breast, even the buttocks and crotch, may serve simply to spur us on to living a lively and abundant life. In the ancient world the sexual organs were associated with the cornucopia, the horn of plenty, an image of life's copious gifts.

Perhaps the ultimate healing is to find a way to break through the wall of habit and culture and let nature's raw vitality penetrate our small ideas and fearful repressions. Orgasm in the broadest sense is an important gift of sex—a collapse of control accompanied by a healing infusion of vitality.

In a time of neurotic male dominance and jealous defensiveness, it's difficult to recommend honoring the phallus, but we have to get beyond personal matters and gender battles if we want to tap into the deep soul of sex. We should be able to distinguish between neurotic abuse of phallic power and genuine honoring of sexuality. Ancient myths and rituals give us a taste of the vast meaning of the phallus that far transcends our current biological and psychological attitudes toward the penis. This new appreciation for sex and its imagery encourages us to leave behind our nervous and life-suppressing prudishness. Our anxiety about sexual imagery is not as righteous and high-minded as it appears to be; it may contain more than a little fear of life's basic fruitfulness and vitality.

The phallus is not an image of the male ego; it is a representation of earth's potency and life's capacity for creativity and pleasure. Ancient and primitive celebrations of the phallus were carried out with joy, laughter, comedy, and celebration. This phallus is not exactly *symbolized* by the ancient images of trees, bulls, and lightning that are associated with it. Rather it represents the power of life we encounter in these overwhelming revelations of nature. The phallus is in fact that power coursing through us, men and women, and in that spring of vitality we can find the creativity and energy we need to get along, survive, and thrive. Ancient humans knew that the ego is insufficient for making a truly creative life. They knew through their ideas of magic, in which the phallus is profoundly implicated, that we need nature's power in us, and that there is no better example of nature dwelling in us effectively than our sexuality, with its autonomous responses and its ineffable capacity to generate new human life.

The penis we see in pornography is not the true phallus; it is rather a poor attempt to restore the phallic dimension to the penis. Pornographic penises are symptomatic of our need to rediscover the phallus and with it a religious appreciation for life's mysterious potency. Like the ancients carrying huge penises in their processions, we fantasize penises of unusual dimension and photograph them in ways that make them seem huge and detached from individual personality. But we don't yet have a religious appreciation for the penis as the presentation of life's almighty power. Religious institutions remain close to pornography, sometimes in their art and sometimes in their ingenious means of repression, because ultimately both are concerned with life's deepest meaning and mystery. Like Isis in search of her brother Osiris's lost organ, we are in search of the penis that cannot be imagined by medicine, the penis that leads us deep into life in all its procreativity and dynamic pleasure.

Images and Gestures Involving the Penis

Sometimes it's easier to see the greater significance of the sexual body—its soul—in certain gestures and cult expressions than its plain anatomy. Images of the phallus at Pompeii can lead us in fascinating directions as we consider the penis as an image of life's abundance. In Pompeii some of these phallic images are hung with bells and lamps, and attached to animals such as snails, turtles, mice, and lions. Animal images help animate an object, and here we get the impression that the phallus has its own vitality and doesn't need human personality to justify it.

The penis is often given wings not only because it rises and falls according to the dictates of passion but also to emphasize its animation and autonomy. As many sex manuals advise, one key to good sex is to allow the body to respond to foreplay without the interference of thought and control. Picturing the god Eros with wings gave direct expression to the idea of a flying, lofty eros and acknowledged the comings and goings of erotic desire—and perhaps its spiritual nature as well.

In another example the god Priapus pours oil on his own erect penis, clearly a sign of appreciation and honor. We might consider the use of oil in sex play not only as a means of lubrication but also as a way of evoking the ancient pagan appreciation of fruitfulness and lustiness.

In other localities, the penis might be shown attached to a man, but with enormous proportions. Occasionally in ancient art one even sees the human body sculpted as a man-sized penis. At Pompeii a man is shown lifting his robes to reveal a huge, erect penis, a gesture much used in female erotic display that we'll consider shortly.

The emotional qualities surrounding these various versions of the phallus include humor, honor, playfulness, and

 vitality. It is possible to restore these qualities to our own personal sex lives and to the culture at large, but it would take strong imagistic thinking and a deep love of life, once the veils of moralism and personalism were removed, to see past the secular penis to the sacred phallus.

Phallic Figure

A Vaginal Way of Being

Perhaps because of the "personality" complex that has seized our culture, we translate the phallus into personal power rather than into life's vitality. With this emphasis on power we simply overlook the imagery of the vagina, which is a rich soul image, full of a kind of potency that is badly needed and in small supply.

In legend, folk art, and ritual, the vagina is associated with a number of things that share its physical contours and its deeper significance. Each one of the related objects says something about the vaginal mystery, opening it up to meaning in much the same way that the penis flowers into the phallus.

In Sophocles' *Oedipus the King,* the blind seer Tiresias reminds Oedipus that in his various voyages—in the play he is often called the pilot of his boat—he found a harbor in his parents' house; that is, he found his way to his mother's vagina. The Freudian psychoanalyst Sándor Ferenczi describes sexual intercourse as the return of the penis-child to the mother's womb, which, he says, is itself at some level the originating sea in which life is born. Both Greek and psychoanalytic literature give us a strong emotional image for the vagina as a haven from the threats and cares of life, the goal of a regression toward our peaceful origins. In *Oedipus at Colonus,* when Oedipus is preparing for death, he moves from the busy life of the city to the sacred thicket in nature where only the gods and spirits are to be found, a holy alternative to his mother's "thicket" and a parallel to the momentary harbor he found with her. We might understand the tragedy of Oedipus not in personal terms but as the archetypal quest for the stilling of life's anxieties and heroics imagined as womb and tomb.

In a strongly heroic world where we are all—man and woman—expected to face our challenges, carve out a life of success, and be thoroughly independent and individual, the vagina offers a contrary objective. The vagina was seen in seeds, caves, rings, triangles, shells, flowers, and fruits—for the most part containers where life germinates and blossoms. It was also the gate and doorway, the oven, the alchemical alembic or furnace, the dolmen, garden, path, hearth, ditch, and ship. The vagina is the holy of holies, the place where the penis finds the doorway to bliss and where human life arrives after descending from eternity.

This is the realm of soul par excellence—containing, creating, warming, assuring. When my daughter was four, she was still trying to mimic her return to her mother's belly by crawling up under a billowing shirt or robe. She seemed ambivalent about entering life on its harsh terms and preferred to return to the place of safety and comfort. I feel the same when I'm traveling and seek out the comfort of a warm bath and piles of bedcovers on a cold night.

In my years of doing therapy I noticed how often both men and women crave a retreat from life into a place of safety and containment yet feel embarrassed by this failure in heroics. Yet it makes sense to find those places of felt safety and holding, whether in a comfortable home or town, in an embracing relationship, or in the sensual enclosure of sex. Even when sex is passionate and aggressive, I would think the otherworldly and eternal refuge of the vagina lies somewhere deep in the lovers' fantasies. The woman's sexual generosity lies in the profound regression and containment she has to offer as well as in the power of her expressive love. In the sexual posture of intercourse, she is the world, life itself, the great mystery of all that lies beyond and behind the heroics involved in making a life.

There are other archetypal feminine images, such as the Greek Artemis and Athena, where the accent is on future, development, strength, militancy, individuality, and personal integrity. Still, the receptivity of the vaginal harbor is of great importance to the emotions and to meaning. Our culture, in particular, both neglects and badly needs this dimension of eros and desire.

One of the deepest motivations in modern life is the assumption that life finds meaning or justification—the two are often interchangeable—in doing instead of being. It is a highly questionable assumption challenged by most religious mystical literature, and it may be behind our fear of the feminine secret and our corresponding aggressiveness toward it. We may arrive at an appreciation of the vagina only after we have considered and accepted its deep mysteries and have discovered that being fully present and secure in one's life can be the ground of creativity.

The Poses of Venus

We have a habit of encountering religious statuary and paintings as though they were illustrations of beliefs or theological ideas. Another way of looking is to see postures in sacred art as the mysterious re-presentation of a sacred act. The gestures Aphrodite makes with hands and torso in her many images point far beyond aesthetics to representations of her particular mysteries.

While I was teaching at a university in the mid-1970s, I inherited a course called "Women in Myth." It had been taught by a professor educated in anthropological approaches to religion, but I addressed the topic from a literary and psychological point of view. This was before books appeared describing the role of gods and goddesses in personal life, and so I had little precedent to guide me. Preparing for the section of the course on Venus-Aphrodite, I noticed that this goddess was presented in certain traditional poses, and I decided to study these as though they were mudras of the Buddha—gestures that had particular meanings and that expressed the nature of the archetypal reality represented by the deity.

Since Aphrodite is the classic sex goddess, her ritual and art postures offer us the opportunity to reflect on certain aspects of sex. For instance, as the classical Venus in the Museo Capitolino in Rome, she places her hands in front of her breasts and genital area. The effect is ambivalent, indicating both modesty and seduction. I have read many different interpretations of the historical background of this gesture, but to me there is allure in the ineffective attempt to cover up the body. Naturally, a goddess is reluctant to be seen by mor-

tals, and this reserve in a sexual goddess might show itself as modesty. On the other hand, Aphrodite was known for her sexual cleverness and coquettishness. A partially covered body can be more alluring than a naked one, and she may be slyly and self-consciously enhancing her appeal.

The gesture also presents two sides of sex, openness and privacy. People often go to extremes, being completely uninhibited or excessively reserved. I get embarrassed when people I don't know well start talking about their lovemaking in an ordinary conversation, but I don't know what the norm is. I'm sure that I lean to the side of reserve. When I look at the Capitoline Venus I feel

Capitoline Venus

her chaste sensuality, her sexuality made uncommonly taut in the lived oxymoron of her modest exhibitionism. She contains within herself the dual world of sexual reticence and ease.

The Capitoline gesture, in which her hands both accent and cover her sexuality, hints at the complexity of Venus's sexuality. And other classic poses reveal something about the nature of sex in even more mysterious ways.

Anadyomene

Aphrodite emerges fresh and noble from the sea in one famous pose, as in Botticelli's well-known painting *The Birth of Venus. Anadyomene* means "rising up after having been submerged." This mysterious appearance out of the vast sea shows sexual feeling, sensation, and awareness coming into consciousness from a deep source that we may locate within us or at least in some reservoir of life possibility. In the spare and punning words of the Gloucester poet Charles Olson, "she rose from the genital wave." Sexual awareness and sensation do not appear from thin air; they rise dripping from whatever primeval element is their natural home.

A poem by D. H. Lawrence about a woman bathing in the ocean is even more graphic about the anadyomene:

Oh lovely, lovely with the dark hair piled up,
as she went deeper, deeper down the channel,
then rose shallower, shallower,
with the full thighs slowly lifting of the wader wading
  shorewards . . .
Lo! God is one God! But here in the twilight
godly and lovely comes Aphrodite out of the sea
towards me.

In their search for images that will have strong appeal, filmmakers often turn to archaic imagery, and they have not overlooked anadyomene. Whether the woman is in a bathtub, or, better, just rising from it, or coming in from a swim in the ocean, or half in the sea and half out of it, Aphrodite has been evoked in a classical pose. There is no reason the human embodiment of this divine posture has to be a woman: one might be struck at the sight of a man, woman, or child coming out of a swimming pool or just out of the bath. It might be good to have a full-length mirror in the bathroom just to have a glimpse of yourself or your partner rising up from the water and to enjoy a moment of myth. A man might evoke the goddess as he steps from the shower or gets out of the bath. Even a little boy or girl standing up in the bathtub and holding her hands high to be helped onto the dry floor represents anadyomene.

Somewhat less graphically, Aphrodite rises from her source when the sun comes up in the east—she was identified with the goddess of dawn. She rises when a sexual attraction suddenly flushes up from the genitals toward the throat and into the imagination. She rises when an unfamiliar desire gradually takes shape and then seizes body and soul. She rises when a person walks into a room and you feel that until this moment of appearance he or she has been inundated in the mass of humanity. She rises when a thought of lust or sensuality comes to mind in the middle of church or during a college exam or on just rising from sleep.

I may be pulling a shirt over my head when the idea of a new project or a new sentence rises and I'm struck by its beauty, as though it were a tiny Aphrodite rising once again. Plotinus taught us that the world is full of Aphrodites. The thought of finally traveling to Italy once rose in me as I was walking to my office on a winter day. The idea for a new book will rise one day from the invisible spring that lies much deeper than my mind. It rises wet and dewy, and perhaps, but only perhaps, later it will be clothed in the hours of actual life. Many ideas rise and then sink down again into oblivion.

Anadyomene is not always welcome or terribly positive in outcome. The rising doesn't stop even when life is full, ordered, and in no need of further appearances and invitations. People may just have settled into a new home when they take a trip and find desire for moving rise in both their hearts. Prudent friends and neighbors try to talk them out of such an impractical change, but Aphrodite's appearance is rarely settling and practical. Worse, of course, a marriage may finally be enjoying a hard-won peace when something attractive rises—another person, a change of work, a shift in personality, a movement of soul.

Anadyomene is the sexuality of the continuous influx of life and vitality. In myth Aphrodite rises naked from the sea and is immediately clothed by the nymphs of the hours and seasons, an eternal and timeless beauty covered over by time and brought into all the bonds of measured life. Among the real challenges of life is the task of giving certain desires a concrete place, some time, a little money, and personal attention.

Aphrodite rises in the swelling of passions and organs in sex. If she doesn't rise, the sex falls short, and she rises only when she has been properly summoned. She comes up in craving, need, and yearning. She appears in the garments of temptation and allure, and sometimes we may be tempted to look for ways to disinvite her rather than to find her a place. But the rising of Aphrodite is life offering itself to us. As Plotinus says, she is the soul. Her appearance is the opportu-

nity for increase in life, while our challenge is to take care in
finding her a proper place.

Anadyomene suggests an alternative way of living: watching for signs of life's stirrings and risings, and responding appropriately, rather than controlling every aspect of life. We
might see that the art of living has more to do with finding
a place for the inspirations that rise from the sea of possibility than with planning and forecasting from anxiety. This latter approach manufactures a life from the ego, whereas the
Aphroditic way is to allow the ego to be the artist who looks
attentively for signs of anadyomene and finds a place for all
the soul's fertile offerings. And this too, this fundamental
way of life, is sexuality, not in any thin metaphorical sense
but as a direct and sensuous response to an urge for orgasm,
joy, and pleasure.

Parakyptousa

Another subtle pose of the sex goddess is her habit, as revealed in many sculptures, of looking from the side or indirectly. *Parakyptousa*, she was called, a word that means leaning over to look or stooping over to peep in. She is often looking the other way, and yet the impression is that she knows
exactly what is going on. Indirection is part of her seductiveness, a quality that extends to sex in general, which is full of
insinuation, innuendo, and suggestiveness. In frustration we
may sometimes wish that sex were more aboveboard and
straightforward, but this aspect of Aphrodite indicates that
something in the very nature of sex is indirect.

My Greek dictionary uses the word *peep* to define "parakyptousa," an interesting word, given its widespread use on
city streets where peep shows do a good business. We peep at

sexual epiphanies, slight revelations of flesh, and find some thrill in the peeping. But at the same time, the religious presentation of the goddess shows that she peeps too. We are revealed even as we do the peeping. Our desires and sexual inclinations show themselves as we peep at certain sights or try to hide our sexual interests.

Parakyptousa may also lie behind sexual gossip, which is a kind of peeping. What is more interesting in a neighborhood than the sexual stories that emerge about a man or a woman caught in the complexities of sex? Popular magazines depend on this deep interest in sexual peeping, telling story after story of a gay man or lesbian coming out of the closet, or of adultery among the famous. The half-concealed sexual inclination or escapade is more exciting than plain, up-front behavior.

The philosopher Plotinus says that the soul itself is Aphrodite. The soul desires us and craves union with us. The soul seduces us, whether from within, in the form of fantasies and desires, or from without, as the world slyly gets our attention. We don't necessarily get more soul in our lives by doing things in a direct way than by allowing ourselves to be distracted and enticed by the world's beauty and interest. The world is alive and has a body with private parts that can be alluring.

Aphrodite was called Peitho, Persuasion; Porne, Prostitute; Psithyros, Whispering Voice; and, of course, Parakyptousa, the Peeping One. As Aphrodite, life or the soul would like to entice us away from our commitments, our earnest tasks, our seriousness. The historian Karl Kerényi says that Hermes is life tricking us to go deeper into itself and thus into ourselves. In a parallel way, Aphrodite seduces us away from ideas, values, and habits that we may treasure. Call it an expansion of consciousness, an opening up of personality, soul making.

In a kind of dream I've heard from people over the years, the dreamer is seduced by an attractive person who may or may not be objectively alluring or beautiful. Sometimes the dreamer is surprised to discover that an unlikely person is immensely attractive—someone much younger or much older, deformed in some way, not the dreamer's type. Often, in these dreams, a spouse or lover enters the scene and either trouble erupts or the dreamer is surprised to find the lover or spouse joining the lovemaking or standing nearby approving.

These dreams may have personal and direct relevance to what is going on in the dreamer's romantic life, but they also suggest a different level of seduction. These various figures may embody certain attitudes that play a large role in one's life. As Aphrodite, life might lure us away from our current commitments—say, an idea about what is true, a spiritual or religious attachment, a political point of view, a way of ordering our everyday lives. In general, Aphrodite is not interested in habits, commitments, and orderly and long-standing arrangements. She represents ongoing life. She offers new attractions, new connections, and new passions. She does her work indirectly, her head turned away. We may wake up one day and wonder how we ever got to where we are, the seductions having been so subtle as to be unnoticed.

Life and sex are profoundly implicated in each other, so we might expect indirection in our sex lives to be matched by indirect seduction in all aspects of daily living. An appreciation for this Aphroditic side of affairs might make us less naive about life in general and deeper and keener in our perception. I've long thought that the best therapists are those who

don't expect life to be direct and obvious, but who have an
eye for the subtle lures that keep people alive and changing.
People come to therapy sometimes to protect themselves
from temptations to change, and a perceptive therapist might
address those concerns while at the same time recognizing
the soul's way of unfolding, less through design than through
a long series of seductions.

Anasyrma

Another gesture that may be familiar from life but may seem
extraordinarily odd as a religious mudra is the *anasyrma* or
lifting up of the dress. The gesture is fairly common in ancient art and has direct parallels in modern popular culture.
It was part of initiatory and religious dances and was associated with Aphrodite, Artemis, Demeter, and Hermaphrodi-
tus. Anasyrma is any gesture of shifting the dress or clothing
to reveal the private parts.

One of the most illustrious examples of anasyrma in the
ancient world occurs in the story of Demeter, the great
mother goddess who, depressed and angry, goes searching
for her daughter who has been abducted by the Lord of the
Underworld. She enters the home of Metaneira and is offered a seat of honor, but she declines. Then, in one version
of the story, the rustic old woman Baubo offers her a stool
covered with fleece, and Demeter sits down and covers her
face with a veil. She sits for a long time until Baubo cheers
Demeter up by lifting her dress and exposing her crotch.

Various sources describe Baubo as the daughter of Echo
and Pan, which may account for her earthiness and rustic vitality, and she is said to be able to make her genitals look like
a child. Her name may originally have meant "vulva" and it

may be she who is represented in statues of a woman with a large head on top of a pair of legs with genitals below the mouth.[3] Demeter's laughter is usually interpreted as a sign of her restoration, her coming back to life. This anasyrma was also a special component in the Eleusinian mysteries dedicated to Demeter and important to people of the ancient religion as a source of hope in the face of human mortality.

Here we have something of a parallel to the public phallic images, both male and female genitals taking part in the comic affirmation of continuing life. People of all ages and sensibilities travel to a liminal place like Las Vegas where they find an alternative to the demands of practical life in gambling, comedy, and skimpy clothing. Looking at the genitals is not simple prurience. It's a momentary way out of the depressing reality of illness and mortality.

In anasyrma, laughter, renewal, hope, and the continuance of life find expression, and even in modern times it is usually part of comedy, dance, and partying. The cancan is a form of anasyrma, as is the scene of Marilyn Monroe standing over a grate on a New York street, her dress billowing up around her and revealing her panties. A little girl lifting her dress for a little boy and perhaps even a boy dropping his pants to show his genitals might be simple examples of anasyrma.

I have a slight memory from childhood of a little girl in the neighborhood swinging on a swing, lifting her dress in fun and play for her gawking playmates. In *Ulysses,* James Joyce describes Leopold Bloom sneaking a peek at Gerty MacDowell leaning over to watch fireworks as her dress rises. Old-time burlesque, of course, is full of anasyrma, and one wonders if the recurring vogue of short shorts and short skirts is not a fashion statement of anasyrma.

The early church fathers, from whom we get much information about Greek customs like anasyrma, were full of thunder and hellfire as they argued for a more repressive attitude, one that still finds a place in society and in our hearts. Yet anasyrma, in the many forms it may take in ordinary life, is an example of pagan joy and may give us a hint of how we might recover some soul for our sexuality.

In the religion of Aphrodite, anasyrma is an odd kind of vision quest. It's as if we never quite get the point of life and death, and so we need to see that part of the body where life is renewed. Anasyrma may be surrounded by taboo, fascination, and ritual, but these are all signs of the shadow side of the sacred. When our city streets are made tawdry by a proliferation of peep shows, perhaps in our puritanism we have forced Aphroditic necessities into extreme modes of expression, where they are bothersome and disgusting. They aren't given a place in ordinary life, so autonomously they dominate and soil.

Anasyrma is not just the exposure of the genitals from the front, but also a special revelation of the backside, which obviously plays an important role in sex. Aphrodite was known as Kallipygos, the beautiful backside. In statuary she is shown lifting her dress and looking over her shoulder at her buttocks. In antiquity this gesture was considered a powerful apotropaic act—one that wards off evil. According to Plutarch it was used to avoid a tidal wave, and Pliny says it could be used against insects. In Germany, people resorted to it to ward off rain.

The story is told of ancient visitors to the Aphrodite shrine at Knidos who made a point to view the goddess from the back. The Marquis de Sade

Anasyrma Venus

made a hasty trip to Italy to avoid the police, going by the name Sado and accompanied by his valet. Sade said the trip was worth the few moments he had to enjoy touching the backside of a Venus he found in a remote alcove. In James Joyce's *Portrait of the Artist as a Young Man,* Stephen Dedalus is discussing Thomistic ideas of beauty with his friend Lynch when his friend confesses that he once wrote his name in pencil on the backside of the Venus of Praxiteles in the museum, a story he uses to demonstrate that art can excite desire.

The powerful fantasy lure of the buttocks and the aggression and exploitation that ensue when the sacred character of this body part is lost are the subject of Susan Lori-Parks's beautiful, tragic play *Venus.* The story is based on the fate of a Hottentot woman lured to London in the last century to show her voluptuous backside, and who was abused by audiences and by insensitive managers.

Aside from the obvious literal lessons we can take from these modern and ancient accounts of the human backside, we might also consider its metaphorical significance. We are basically a frontal society, looking ahead to the future. We don't like to look back, and yet the beautiful statues of Aphrodite show her looking backward, or backside-ward. We don't like to regress, but she finds erotic satisfaction in the back—in the background, the behind. We call it the ass, maybe to distinguish it from the head, where we locate intelligence, the ass being associated with stupidity. But perhaps Aphroditic intelligence is simply different from that of the head, and maybe it has a significant role to play.

The intriguing images of Aphrodite looking over her shoulder at her backside also suggest that in her style of awareness we can fruitfully regard ourselves as objects. This need not be either narcissistic or dehumanizing. Looking at ourselves more as objects than as subjects, we might see our thoughts, feelings, desires, histories, and temperaments more clearly as elements in our makeup. When I first began reading about alchemy in the writings of Jung, I was taken by the idea that we could regard the psyche objectively rather than subjectively and appreciate it without the usual focus on ego that is so much a part of modern psychological thinking. This focus on the backside is a similar objectification that could help rather than hinder our perspective on our lives.

We might also be led by these images to think about the backside of life: the backside of a marriage—not its frontal plans and understandings; the backside of a career or profession rather than its professed ideals and goals; the backside of a city, and not its well-lighted, glossy front. A young man full of ideals and refined ideas about love suddenly falls into a fit of jealousy, and his father smiles, appreciating this anasyrma of the young man's emotional backside.

Life lifts up her skirts and we behold her secret: that life goes on in spite of our attempts to make it work and to give it sense. This is the human comedy that reflects the divine comedy. The gods laugh at our earnestness and at our belief that life is sincerely and exactly the face that it presents to us. We can laugh now and then, as Demeter did, when life lifts its veils and gives us a comic glimpse of its beautiful and outrageous folly. Few things depict life's earthy vitality as palpably as the cancan or the striptease, and yet few things are further removed from our intelligence and our seriousness.

For generations, people have found Aphrodite in a fig or an apple just by catching a glimpse there of the form of the female sexual body. They have found this form mysterious, comic, compelling, and pleasurable. They have honored it as

a sacred ritual object, the yoni, a stylized image of the female
sex organ, and, with various degrees of innocence or depre-
dation, they have enjoyed it as an entertainment on stage and
in the movies. They pay dearly for a glimpse of it sometimes
in money and in loss of reputation. There can be no denying
its immense appeal to something deep in the imagination,
and perhaps we shouldn't ignore this image of natural vitality. We might be better off honoring the goddess with pious
imagination than denying and suppressing her with rules
and prohibitions.

In the secret, half-revealed, enticing sexual body, life breaks
through in all its glory. Aphrodite, the soul, makes its holy
and sometimes obscene gestures, whether we like them or
not. Life itself has private parts, and if we can catch a glimpse
of them, we may have come upon a natural sacrament and a
common mystery—a perception of the nature of things that
allows us to go on with deepened, lowered intelligence and
good humor.

CHAPTER 4

Archetypal Patterns in Sex

Myths, Saints, and Celebrities

ON THE SCENT of the soul of sex we have seen that the
nymph we are looking for in our sexual curiosity,
passion, and longing is felt as a presence in ordinary life. She
may be spotted in a person or a painting, smelled in a perfume, touched in a slinky fabric, or perceived by whatever
organ it is in the eye that receives color with all its emotion
and meaning. She shows herself in the beauty of a face and
in the feel, aroma, and toss of hair. She is the mysterious
background behind profound feelings and reminiscences rising from the specific organs of sex. She diffuses herself in sex
as passing memories, faint longings, and wisps of meaning.

The nymph of sex also appears in the stories and fragments of stories, the images and memories that play a subtle
but defining role in sexual experience. Sex is never plain and
simple, and like everything else in which human beings are
involved, sex is always part of a story. It is likely to be part of
the personal tale of our coming of age, our quest for an end

to loneliness, the expression of our love, and, on the shadow side, a means for exerting power or expressing anger. And so our life story may shed light on the role of sex in our lives and in our marriage. When couples tell each other their family stories, their family mythologies come to light. Each person catches a glimpse of the narrative they've unwittingly entered into by loving another.

When I tell stories about my family, not just my immediate family but my more distant relatives as well, I see fragments of my own feelings. I notice the familiar reserve about sexual matters, but I also recognize a lust for life and a deep acceptance of life experiments gone awry. Over the years, I've noticed these same themes and personalities appearing in my dreams, where they sometimes connect directly to my sexuality.

In therapy, I have always been careful to invite as many stories of family as want to appear, but I don't translate these stories into explanations for current problems. I listen to the remembered family stories for signs of the myth, the deep narrative that resonates beneath the teller's life and awareness. If the current concern is sex, I don't expect the relevant stories necessarily to be explicitly sexual. Sex is tightly woven into every aspect of life, and so stories that apparently have no sexual content may shed light on the sexuality of the person telling the story, and stories blatantly and lasciviously sexual may speak to issues that seem far distant from sexuality.

Ancient and enduring mythological motifs appear here and there in our personal and family stories. These are the archetypal patterns that give shape to our own lives. We can glimpse these archetypal figures and motifs in mythology, religion, and even recent history, and in them we might find lessons about the nature of sex and about the erotic conflicts that lie at the very base of existence.

Artemis

The Greek goddess Artemis, in many ways equated with the Roman Diana, is a figure whose aura has immense appeal to many people. Her virginity represents the purity of one who lives far from civilization's corruption, is close to animals, is at home in the woods, likes to run and sport, and favors women and young men. The androgyny in her image makes her a special patroness of those who are gay. She is usually pictured as a tall, graceful figure, quite different from the seductive Aphrodite or the bountiful Hera. Filtered through Artemis, the allure of sex is an attractive blending of purity and integrity.

Artemis is remote, preferring the wilderness of the woods to the niceties of civilization, and she is not usually found in the company of men. Rather, she is often described as surrounded by her female nymphs. Even her male devotees, like the young man Hippolytus, like to remain in the company of their own gender, and in many ways they are aloof and solitary.

Sometimes a spirit will descend upon a man or woman—at any time in life—instilling in them a strong desire for solitude or for the single life. Artemis people may feel a desperate need to be surrounded by members of their own sex or simply by friends and intimates rather than lovers. At least temporarily, their erotic desires may be satisfied by the absence of sexual behavior. In the name of Artemis, life can be celibate, solitary, pure, and self-absorbed, and yet still be free of narcissism. Artemis doesn't represent an anxious avoidance of sex, but rather a chaste way of being sexual.

Although she is the most virginal of the goddesses, Artemis is not asexual. She embodies a special kind of sexuality where the accent is on individuality, integrity, and solitude.

Her spirit can be at the root of masturbation and private erotic fantasy, giving sexuality a solitary mode. At other times we may enter sex with a strong desire to be taken seriously, our independence assured. Homoerotic fantasies, too, may turn in the direction of the whole world of Artemis.

Under her aegis, a life in sports can lead both men and women to dedicate themselves to the passion of a game. Her brand of sexuality may be attractive because she is so devoted to her own life. In myth many men are drawn by her athleticism and aloofness and, impassioned, chase after her. Apollo, smitten by Daphne and mad with desire, runs after her until she transforms into a tree; and Hippomenes races so he can be with Atalanta, another Artemis nymph. King Minos chases through hills and valleys after Britomartis. In Euripides' tragic play *Hippolytos* the young man who embodies many of Artemis's qualities is the object of his stepmother Phaedra's passion—this Artemis spirit is not exclusive to women.

We may see Artemis in a woman playing tennis, figure skating, running a race, playing basketball, or swimming. We may catch a glimpse of her in young men on a track team, hiking, or playing baseball. In men and women in training for an athletic event we may sense her self-absorption, her purity of life, and her spirituality, which often plays a big role in athletics. Society may be disillusioned to discover that its sports heroes are not as pure as expected, the Artemis myth shattered by the intrusion of her rival Aphrodite. Not all athletes are possessed by the spirit of Artemis, but she definitely has a home on the field and the court, and even in the locker room.

We may all have periods in life or just moments in a day when we need to be alone, disconnected from love and sex, devoted to an interest of our own, or simply withdrawn and remote. The myth tells us that this preference may not be an antisocial rejection of people but simply a deep, positive, even sexual focusing on oneself and one's world. Naturalists may find this spirit dominant in their lives, or painters and other artists, who become absorbed in the pure seductiveness of their work. George Sand, in many ways a follower of Artemis, dressed in men's clothes and enjoyed living in the countryside, while her lover, Chopin, found it difficult to be far from the more civilized city.

Stories tell of Artemis's aggressive ways of protecting her seclusion. Without hesitating she sprinkled waters of regression onto the head of the boy Acteon, turning him into a deer, and at the slight accidental touch of her shirt, she sent a scorpion to deal with the hunter Orion. We might expect this kind of anger in sexual liaisons with Artemis men and women and not be surprised at the unexpected combination of purity and aggression in their personalities. The Artemis spirit helps us stand up for our needs and wishes and leads us to the solitary place where our values are formed. Sex and aggression come together under many different mythic umbrellas, one of them this Artemis way of protecting individuality and personal integrity.

The stories also tell of contests between the Artemis woman and attentive males, another pattern we might see in our sexual relationships. Atalanta is swifter than Hippomenes, and only the clever intrusion of Aphrodite keeps her from besting this boastful man when he races to gain her hand in marriage. In sexual relationships, one sometimes finds oneself in such a situation, in which one or both of the partners acts in the spirit of contest.

On dates young people will often try to show their abilities at games and sports, not just to show off and win a person's admiration, but sometimes simply in a spirit of contest having more to do with preserving one's individuality in the face of love's urge to join and meld. These small rites of self-preservation may be important for the relationship and especially for sex, because the failure to remain intact in love may well show itself in sexual difficulties. In sex, people may anxiously try to preserve their individuality by holding back or setting limits or not surrendering.

In general, myth teaches us to honor and respect feelings and actions that can easily be criticized from some more socially accepted point of view. Society may appreciate openness and vulnerability and may frown upon any display of self-preservation. Since our psychology is so personalistic, we criticize lovers for engaging in contests, thinking that their behavior is motivated by an anxious ego, when myth teaches that it may be archetypal, a necessary and ultimately fruitful ritual in the course of courtship.

Flight, too, is an Artemis reaction. People often need to pull back, resist surrender, run away, keep the chase in play, and never give up. This is part of sex and not a reaction against it, a necessity and not an aberration. Artemis reactions preserve all aspects of life that are not part of marriage and partnership, such as individual ambition and achievement, personal vision, and a sense of self. In ancient rituals dedicated to Artemis people would dress up as plants and dance her special steps, honoring this goddess of pre-social, pristine naturalness. Our own efforts to remain natural and unspoiled may be seen as a continuation of this dance that celebrates the myth of purity—our own naturalness and pre-social innocence.

In spite of all of these efforts at purity and self-preservation, Artemis and her devotees have special sexual allure, the allure perhaps of a crisply dressed nurse, an awkward woods-man, an athletic young woman, or a gardener. It's not irrele-vant that in *Lady Chatterley's Lover* a woman of nobility falls in love with a rough but sensitive gamekeeper. Strong, earthy Mellors the woodsman stands in sharp contrast to Lady Chat-terley's husband, a wounded executive. The world of Arte-mis is virginal, and yet at the same time it can be immensely attractive and sexually intriguing. The love scenes in *Lady Chatterley's Lover* are filled with references to the realm of Artemis—nature, flowers, trees—and, oddly, a book that gave censors chills is rooted in the archetypal realm of emotional virginity.

A couple might like to keep their sex pure in some ways, giving it an Artemis touch that would make it conform more to their feelings and thereby increase the pleasure. Some peo-ple like to give up all reserve, expressing their sexuality pub-licly and enjoying sexual experiments in private. An Artemis couple might be just the opposite, protecting the privacy of their sex life and enjoying a degree of modesty in their love-making. While sex may indeed be hurt by traumas in the past of either partner, sometimes reserve simply reflects the nature of the couple and their deep and genuine apprecia-tion for an Artemis-like reticence.

We need the freedom to be cautious and guarded about sex, to be true to the needs of the soul for privacy. Some peo-ple may display an excessive concern about giving them-selves in sex because they don't feel free to honor their deep feelings of reserve. It might help many people to allow them-selves their sexual shyness, not discounting it as a personal in-adequacy but recognizing that indulgence and abandon are not the only kind of sexual liberation.

Jesus

Related to Artemis in spirit and imagery is the figure of Jesus, both the god-man we find in the canonical Gospels and the venerated figure of tradition, art, and legend. Because so many people are deeply influenced by their image of Jesus, he plays a special role in forming attitudes and fantasies about sexuality. It's widely recognized that Christians may have special trouble with sex, often falling into the repression-obsession pattern characterized by moralism and preoccupation. But any religion or philosophy that defines itself against the values of paganism may find sex challenging, and therefore the whole society might find some sexual relief in a reconsideration of the sexuality of Jesus.

History has given us many images of Jesus, but except for historians who try to tell us that he had a normal life, and except for a very few novelists who have portrayed him as a man enjoying an erotic life, the sources unite in presenting an image of Jesus as a typical *puer aeternus,* an eternal youth. As such he could be seen as a follower of Artemis—pure, idealistic, misunderstood, and surrounded for the most part by men.

I have no intention, nor do I have the qualifications, to argue about the sexuality of the historical Jesus, but one doesn't have to be an expert to notice a discrepancy between the Jesus of the Gospels and the Jesus who is the object of belief and worship. The former is unusually kind, open-minded, accepting, and understanding of those who are obviously confused about their sexuality. The Gospel Jesus is also intimate, emotional, physically expressive, and even sensual in many ways. The Jesus of the moralizing preacher, in contrast, is inhumanly pure and uncompassionately asexual.

A hint of Epicureanism in the Gospel Jesus appears when

he assures, through a miracle, that a wedding celebration has enough good wine. On another occasion, he gives people bread and fish, again through a miracle, not feeding starving people in severe need, but simply taking care of an audience who needs lunch. Like Epicurus, he has prostitutes in his company, and he saves from certain death a woman condemned for adultery. His heart aches at the death of his friend Lazarus, and this loving feeling is the motive for the miracle of Lazarus's return from the dead. His touch is healing and his presence full of magic. This is an image of a man who is not afraid of eros, who lives from his heart and from his body.

In the Gospels Jesus is contrasted with the moralists and legalists of his time as a man of infinite compassion. Paradoxically, the churches that profess to carry on his teaching are not known for their compassion as much as for their legalism. The Epicurean Jesus is nowhere to be seen, and eros often appears to be the chief enemy, not the chief characteristic, of his followers. The sexuality of Jesus evaporates in these rigid attitudes, replaced by anxious and obsessive suppression of eros.

The Jesus I see in the canonical Gospels is a sexual celibate or a celibate lover. He would be a scandal in our time, as he was in his own, because he tolerates so much humanity. At first glance it may seem a contradiction to be chaste and morally tolerant, but Jesus' celibacy never seems anxious or repressive. It allows him to love in an embracing way and is so comfortably part of his philosophy and style that he doesn't have to judge others for their sexual ways. Moralistic judgments always betray confusion and struggle in the one making the judgments, but in Jesus there is no sign of this neurosis that sometimes plagues his followers.

In his remarkable book *Christs,* David Miller, a former professor of mine, explores imagery of the grapevine, wine, and even drunkenness in several religious traditions, and he makes the case for seeing a Dionysian motif in Jesus.[1] The Greek god Dionysus, identified with the grape and its fermented drink, represents a life not divided between pleasure and principle, joy and emotional impoverishment. It is a profoundly erotic spirit that says yes in the face of vitality and mortality alike, and so can be felt as a kind of drunkenness, a spiritual loss of control, and a mystical intoxication. The Dionysian Jesus is like the inebriated figure in Sufi poetry who has lost his ego in his reach for union with the divine.[2]

In his beautifully complex book *The Axis of Eros,* Walter Spink summarizes this point vividly. He says Christ's message was one

> of life, of eros. . . . His rules for the constitution of perfection and for the imposition of the ideals of Paradise upon the earth were premised upon the principle that man renounce the burdens of possessions, and then "follow me." It insisted that one must "love thy neighbor as thyself," and this was something Western man could neither do nor wished to do; for all these threatening principles involved an implicit renunciation of the ego and a convention-disrupting loosening of the disordering and dionysiac forces in the id.[3]

In these two interpretations of Jesus, Miller's and Spink's, we find a Jesus who is not anti- or asexual, a Jesus whose teaching leads to a drunken state of unreserved devotion to God and to mystical enthusiasm. Referring to Old Testament instances of divine drunkenness, Miller speaks of it as "a drunkenness that made eros possible."[4] Dionysian surrender to life includes an ego-relaxed receptivity to sexuality, a willingness to let life be shaped by desire and by sexual inclination. Yet when this Dionysian spirit is linked to the compassionate eros of Jesus, it takes an unusual form, becoming an emotional oxymoron—carnal chastity, promiscuous compassion, or, in the perfect phrase of Mary Daly, pure lust.

The Dionysian spirit is usually seen as a sexually expansive force, and so it is not obvious in most portraits of Jesus. Yet, as Miller demonstrates with considerable subtlety, the Dionysian affirmation of life is strong in the character of Jesus. The theologian Rosemary Ruether summarizes the Gospel picture of Jesus in imagery like Miller's that closes the gap between Dionysus and our usual idea of Jesus:

> He sits at table with sinners. The sinful woman (presumably a prostitute) is held up to the Pharisee as a model of love and repentance. . . . Jesus lives in towns, in the habitations of friends. He does not fast, but eats and drinks (not grape juice). . . . "The Son of Man comes eating and drinking, and they say, behold a glutton and a drunkard, a friend of tax collectors and sinners."[5]

Ruether concludes that "Jesus appears to be a person unperturbed by sexuality because he relates to both men and women first of all as friends."

All figures of history, but none more so than Jesus, are transformed by the imagination of those who come after them. In spite of themselves they become objects of mythic imagination. There are by now countless images of Jesus, each defended strongly and often anxiously, and among them is the Dionysian Jesus espoused by Ruether, Miller, and Jung. This is the Jesus drunk on life, inebriated by vitality, and able to live with an intensity inaccessible to most. This Jesus knows the secret suggested by Rosemary Ruether that sex

thrives in the air of friendship. Eros and philia, lust and intimacy, can feed each other, resulting in the stimulating and
creative paradoxes of erotic chastity that characterize the Jesus of the Gospels. Later, of course, Christianity would lose
this creative, humane sexuality and become preoccupied with
the suppression of the Dionysian.[6]

In our superego-dominated world, we may wonder where
in Dionysian drunkenness we would find necessary limitations on our sexual desires. The image of Jesus suggests a way
of placing limits that derives from joy and pleasure rather
than fear and anxiety, limits determined by a positive choice
in life. Jesus seems to choose joyful celibacy and then to tol-
erate the struggles of others to establish their ways of being
sexual and their ways of finding limits.

Anyone married or living in some other kind of committed relationship can also be positive about the decision to
enter deeply into a sexual relationship. They reach far into
life and are not neurotically self-protective, and can have compassion and empathy for others as they find their own way
toward the same goal of surrender to life and their own forms
of nonrepressive limitation on sexual behavior. There is a
strong and deep-seated reciprocity between our personal effort to find a satisfying sex life and our judgment and treatment of others.

The sexuality of Jesus consists in his openness to strangers
and friends, the physicality of his healing, the sacramentality
in his approach to food, the tolerance he displays in the face
of sexual transgression, and his espousal of a philosophy
based on love. Only a worldview mired in materialism could
fail to see the sexuality in this expansive and inclusive erotic
philosophy. The sexual teachings of Jesus, told best through
his example, present a soul-centered eroticism in which

friendship and a compassionate heart are not only included but placed at the center.

We have a strong tendency to think of sex as emanating from the sex organs or from the purely physical body, but Jesus demonstrates a quite different notion—sexuality rooted in compassion and in the capacity for friendship. It is a more broadly defined but no less sensuous sexuality, in which love and pleasure are joined integrally. There is no need to import affection to what is thought to be a plain physical expression or to justify sex with love. In the sexuality of Jesus physical life and compassion are two sides of a coin. In him we find that the heart is an organ of sex, as surely and effectively as any other private part.

Hester Prynne

Another rich mythic figure of sexuality is the woman caught in adultery. We find her in the Gospel, in Nathaniel Hawthorne's *The Scarlet Letter,* and in the daily newspaper. Hester Prynne wears her letter "A" to identify her as someone who has surrendered to desire and who has broken the rules of propriety. In Hawthorne's story she is contrasted with the early American Puritans, who seem inexplicably rigid, showing little compassion or acceptance of human imperfection. We may understand Hester Prynne and her judges not only against the backdrop of the first days of America, but also as archetypal tendencies in us all.

It isn't easy to live up to our own sexual ideals or those of our community, and so we can find this tension between the weak transgressor and the demanding critic in modern social life and in our private lives. It's odd that we know privately how difficult it can be to deal with sexual desire and yet we make extreme demands on others. There must be profound anxiety behind this judgmentalism, which is perhaps a displacement onto the lives of others of our own wish for control.

We have within us also a tendency toward masochism, a degree of satisfaction in being judged and limited, and so we create institutions that give external form to the pattern. Not only do people enjoy sitting in churches being told what to do and being chastised regularly for living imperfectly, but even our self-help books tell us how to live with perfect emotional and physical health, and they are sometimes filled with veiled authoritarianism that isn't so far from that of our Puritan ancestors. What we consider expertise was once called authority, and where preachers once used the colorful language of hellfire and brimstone, our experts now speak authoritatively of emotional and physical health.

Hawthorne's analysis of sexual desire is appropriately complex. *The Scarlet Letter* begins with Hester Prynne stepping out of prison with the accusatory letter on her chest and refusing to enter too deeply into the role of penitent. She has embroidered the letter so artfully that it stands out for its size and beauty. She lets the world see it, though she doesn't flaunt it. Then she lives a life of service to her community. Her lover, Arthur Dimmesdale, in contrast, hides his sin. He has a habit of placing his hand over his heart, where his scarlet letter might have been pinned, as though he both feels the searing in his heart and covers it over. Unlike Hester Prynne he lives as though nothing had happened. His letter is invisible, interior only, and it eats away at him from within. In the end Hester prospers and Dimmesdale confesses too late to his desire and forfeits the joy he might have had. Hester's wronged husband Roger Chillingworth, bent on revenge, plays the part of the devil, and yet Hawthorne begs the reader to have compassion even for him.

The beauty of Hester Prynne's story is its portrayal of several ways sex shapes people's lives. We might all have a Hester Prynne, an Arthur Dimmesdale, and a Roger Chillingworth in our erotic makeup—one who has fallen to the charms of sex and embraces the consequences, one who tries to maintain an ordinary surface life while beneath that persona lies a heart profoundly troubled, and one who embodies the role of the wounded and betrayed avenger. Sex has a way of creating a drama of intense emotion around these characters, and most people have a taste of it at some time in their lives.

Hawthorne's tale reminds us that we can benefit from the failure of virtue that sex forces upon us. His words are precise and accurate. Of Hester Prynne he writes: "The scarlet letter was her passport into regions where other women dared not tread. Shame, Despair, Solitude! These had been her teachers." In this story the heroine is the adulteress, a woman truly shamed by her passions but who found a way through them deep into her community, her motherhood, and a life of educated, complicated virtue. Others around her failed because they refused to come to terms with sex, but she lived her entire life dedicated to her passion.

C. G. Jung says that in our sexual life we have to deal with our particular fate and dharma, the place where universal morality and our individual law come together. Hester Prynne is the great sinner, publicly shamed by her community, but she embraces her fate, acknowledges her passion, and thus finds her life. Healing of the soul begins when men and women live their earthly reality instead of their ideas and ideals.

One can easily be tempted to disown what passion has wrought in life, or to try hard to screen passion out, but these are tragic choices. I've worked with men and women who, like Roger Chillingworth, have indeed been chilled by adultery and betrayal on the part of their spouse and have responded by withdrawing from life and community. I've worked with men and women who have succumbed to adulterous passion and have disowned it without struggle by means of manipulative, simplistic, or false repentance. The betrayer says: "I'm sorry. It was a mistake. It doesn't mean anything." But the betrayed feels as though the whole of life has been torn apart, and the betrayal, whatever the conditions, means everything.

I've often felt that the betrayed party has the most obvious opportunity to go deeper into life, even though the suffering may be intense. The betrayer may be too defended against the loss of control, the influence of passion, and the shadow feeling of having done something wrong to allow deep reflection and genuine remorse. Hester Prynne is exceptional. She betrays her husband and then goes on to find her place in community and in love through the emblem of her passion and her imperfection, her colorful scarlet letter.

Hester Prynne finds her freedom after seven years of suffering, a number we might take as symbolic of whatever substantial period of time it may require for a person to find new life. She remains complex, first moving to the Old World with her daughter and then returning to Salem to live out her destined life. Earlier on, she impetuously removes her scarlet letter and senses an almost forgotten freedom, but then she puts the letter on again because she knows it is her destiny.

As part of our quest for a blemish-free emotional life, we may look for a complete absolution after having betrayed sexually, but Hawthorne preserves life's complexity by suggesting that there is no way ultimately to remove the scarlet letter, which is a sign not only of literal adultery but also of the eternally soul-shaping soiling of sexuality. Once we have fallen to passion, we have to live our lives keeping that failure in sight. Not just a mental awareness, but a full-hearted owning of the failure ushers us into our humanity. This is a kind of submission to the authority of passion that takes us deep into life, where we can engage, as Hester Prynne did, in humane community service and achieve a moral position that enhances rather than restricts life.

The illusion of moralistic perfection can be purchased at a cheap price, but deep morality lies well within the realm of passion and can be gained only after one has been baptized in the often turbulent emotions of sexuality. There, morality and vitality come together, one supporting and nurturing the other. Paradoxically, Hawthorne's novel resolves the problem of virtue and passion by bringing the two together in the life and consciousness of a woman weak enough to succumb to passionate life and yet strong enough to live her passion openly and virtuously.

The widespread hypocrisy of society today in the face of sexual passion hints that we have not learned the lesson of this remarkable story from our American literary tradition. Maybe we have only appreciated the story for its technical brilliance and not for its existential teaching. Maybe we have not realized in our intellectual defensiveness that Hester Prynne is a figure of the soul, an attitude and achievement of character to which we might aspire.

Sexual transgression is all around us, but the big-hearted conscience of Hester Prynne is difficult to find. If we merely neglect the purity, reserve, conscience, and limitations that were exaggerated in the Puritans of her day, we are not free to combine passion and virtue as she did. We can find relief in avoidance of the struggle altogether, but we won't necessarily discover the freedom and vitality that Hester Prynne won through her courage, honesty, and loyalty.

Virtue born of eros is not an achievement of intellect and will, nor does it derive from the repression of passion. It arises from an affirmation of life, a limiting of sexual behavior that is rooted in passion, not turned against it. Hester embroiders her scarlet letter the way she cultivates the implications of her surrender to passion and love. She doesn't disown what it represents, and indeed her daughter fails to recognize her when the letter has momentarily been removed. Hawthorne recognized that we become persons through our transgressions, by bringing them close to home, allowing them to etch the outlines of our character in gradual, painful realizations.

Therapy for the betraying lover does not lie in the removal of guilt and pangs of conscience, but in the deepening of remorse. No one wants to betray or be betrayed, yet betrayal is part of life and has gifts to offer, provided it is neither indulged nor denied. It may help to remember, in painful moments of betrayal, that sex has led us deep into one of its terrifying and sullying myths. Sexual betrayal is not just a personal fault, it is an archetypal narrative that from a deep, dank place shapes the underside of the soul. It, too, is an opportunity to find our humanity, to become a feeling member of the community, and to live a creative life—the kind of life modeled by Hester Prynne, the sinner.

Marilyn Monroe

In recent times another woman has appeared on the stage of American history and art bearing a scarlet monogram—MM for Marilyn Monroe. There is much difference of opinion about her motives, talents, and even her beauty, but I'm persuaded that Marilyn Monroe was the genuine article, a true avatar of Aphrodite for modern culture.

In ancient times people talked about apotheosis, the transformation of a human being into a god, a hero, or a celestial constellation. Today ordinary mortals, through some twist of fate, sometimes become stars. We still use celestial imagery to describe this transformation, and we still mean apotheosis. A person can become a myth, a great figure of the community's imagination made up of some factual biography and a great deal of fantasy. The political arena and the movie or television screen offer sufficient translation into fiction that a person can be a star and a myth even as they live and breathe and have an ordinary life off-screen.

It might be argued that no one in recent times has gone through an apotheosis of such grand proportions as Marilyn Monroe. The day she sat drawing double Ms to practice writing her new name, Norma Jean Baker began the process of becoming not only a star but a myth out of control, a goddess of sexuality. There have been other paragons of sex, but Norma Jean Baker became a figure of imagination so powerful, so contradictory, so enduring that she offers an image of sexuality that has many of the characteristics of ancient myth and ritual.

As in the case of any genuine myth, Marilyn's life story consists of extraordinary fragments, images that have found their way deep into the collective psyche: her nude calendar, tame by today's standards; her breathy song at John F. Kennedy's birthday party; her mysterious and shocking death.

She was extraordinarily aware of her calling to be a central figure in the world's sexual mythology and demonstrated a rare sophistication as she played out her role. Fortunately, we have many of her own words describing the tensions and pleasures of her place in society. Collected into a pagan gospel unfamiliar to a Judeo-Christian culture, her reflections make a kind of sacred text in the religion of Aphrodite, so close was she to the spirit that inspired her. I assume that her power came from her vulnerability, not only to the world around her but especially to the inspiration she felt within her.

The world always has its collection of sex stars, and in our time their sexuality is usually much more graphic and stark than it was in the days of Marilyn Monroe. Yet, even in her own time, though surrounded by women of renowned beauty and sexuality, she became the goddess, the myth. In fiction, investigative reporting, and biography, writers never stop trying to understand her mystery. I suspect it has to do with her loyalty to the spirit that early in her life she found dwelling within her.

She said she remembered as a young woman daydreaming about her future: "I dreamed of myself walking proudly in beautiful clothes and being admired by everyone and overhearing words of praise." Many young people might say something similar, yet in context with other reflections on her life, these words show the intensity of her devotion to the things of Aphrodite—beauty, clothes, and admiration. Vividly she hears words of praise from the future, and concretely she sees herself fulfilled in being admired for her cultivated beauty.

Later, after she had become a star, she said, "I knew I belonged to the public and to the world, not because I was talented or even beautiful, but because I had never belonged to anything or anyone else." The ancient theme of the aban-

doned child comes through in these words of a girl raised in
an orphanage, almost a prerequisite for a person about to become a myth. It isn't sufficient to hear them as a literal description of her circumstances. If Marilyn has indeed become
a myth, we can expect to see ancient patterns of mythic reality in her life and words.

An extraordinary photograph shows her from the back
standing on a stage in Korea, her hands raised upward toward the sky, an ocean of soldiers spread out before her, and
a white cross, ethereal in the background, just above her
hands.[7] This is a person open to the public, a priestess of
Venus. She played a role in the world that was a challenge to
the one represented by the cross, but this photograph suggests that the two were like stars in conjunction, two worlds
that are more intimately connected than the followers of either would care to admit.

Another time, she described the sensitivity she had for her

Marilyn Monroe in Korea

public role as a daughter of Venus: "The only people I care about are the people in Times Square, across the street from the theater, who can't get close as I come in. If I had light make-up on, they'd never see me. This make-up is for them, so that when I wave to them it will soften out in the distance across the square." What a remarkable way of thinking, so fully within the scope of Aphrodite. She was clearly a person with a genius for sex, just as some have a genius for mathematics, and she used her special form of intelligence to evoke the myth perfectly.

Truman Capote captured her role precisely: "I don't think she was an actress at all, not in any traditional sense. What she was . . . this presence, this luminosity, this flickering intelligence . . . could never surface on stage. It was so fragile and subtle, it could only be caught by the camera."[8] Laurence Olivier said that "she was happy as a child when being photographed." She lived for the image she embodied, for the ghost perhaps that could only be seen by the camera lens. It might be expected that she would have trouble with actual life and never find a man who could be a fully satisfying or satisfied mate.

One of the most enduring images of Marilyn Monroe is the classic one in which she is captured on the New York City grate, her skirt puffed up around her legs in the ancient pose of anasyrma. The fact that it is a typical image of Aphrodite intensifies the connection between goddess and movie star, and the fact that this photograph, this ancient gesture we see today in museums in the form of tiny amulets, has become so identified with her and has been reproduced countless times—all of this classic, mythic material demonstrates that Norma Jean was a woman possessed, a woman who responded to an unusual call to serve the deep imagination of the world.

Many writers have tried to solve the puzzle of Marilyn
Monroe without considering her genuine mythic presence in
a society that needed her. Our rejection of the pagan sensibility leads us to place sex in a category far removed from
genuine piety and seriousness. In this hollowed-out world,
Marilyn Monroe continues to be a reminder of the vitality
and allure of the repressed myth. She is not just a sexual person, as many of our contemporary sex stars are. Through
her genius for remaining true to her inspirations, we can find
in her the sensuality and creative illusion that we crave but at
the same time reject.

We could learn many lessons in the arts of sex from her,
lessons that in most cases would probably contradict the
avowed values of the society. Marilyn, for example, has been
accused, even by her most sophisticated biographers, of
being narcissistic, and yet her words suggest something different. Her concern for her image is part of her myth. It may
have taken more courage from her to remain focused on her
self and her image than it takes to complain about her narcis-

Marilyn Monroe in
The Seven Year Itch

sism. I believe that narcissism is due, anyway, to neglect of our persons, and so in reaction we insist on ourselves or display ourselves ineffectively. Biographers seem puzzled by Marilyn's comfort with her body and with nudity, but her sexual ease simply demonstrates the depth of her identity with this myth that still challenges us.

We might learn from Marilyn to find and honor that spirit in us that is fundamentally sexual. The dancer Margot Fonteyn said of Marilyn that her body movements produced "a delicately undulating effect like the movement of an almost calm sea. It seemed clear to me that it was something of which she was not conscious; it was as natural as breathing, and in no way an affected 'wriggle,' as some writers have suggested."[9] I don't know if Margot Fonteyn was aware when she wrote this that in ancient times Aphrodite was identified with the sea, but I do know that many people dedicated to the Aphroditic spirit often embody it unselfconsciously.

For most of us, Aphrodite is one sanctuary of meaning and vitality among others, but we can learn from Marilyn how to bring that spirit forward in our lives and in that unexpected way find soul. She is a mythic figure who entices us even now to read her words, watch her movies, enjoy her impersonators, and glimpse her spirit in our daily lives. She beckons us into a realm that she perfected and we neglect. Like Marilyn we could become intelligent about sex, not from outside the sexual realm but from within it. We could realize that there are ways to be sexually brilliant, sexually talented, and sexually soulful. We can be educated in sex, not just in its physiology and psychology, but in its own special ethos.

CHAPTER 5

Sexual Fantasy and Dream

The Role of the Erotic Imagination

WHEN A MAN or woman gazes at the body of another, whether in sex, in the movies, in a magazine, or in the privacy of a daydream, it isn't readily apparent what is going on. For many this gaze is so alluring that it seems to answer a strong need, not just a passing fancy, and sometimes it can be overwhelmingly compulsive. For others it is a scandal. But then, compulsion and scandal are often closely connected. Both reactions indicate that the sexual gaze has strong emotional power and is mysteriously and fundamentally meaningful.

Sex is so stunning and powerful that the sexual gaze would seem to have something in common with the religious gaze. Contemplating a holy object is a central element in many religions. Catholics revere the moment in the Mass when the priest holds up the bread and wine so it can be seen by everyone present. Up until Vatican Council II changes, bells were usually rung during this holy moment in the Mass. When I was a child, the church also had a special rite of blessing called benediction in which the consecrated bread was placed in a portable shrine, a monstrance, from the Latin word *monstrare,* to show, and offered for gazing and contemplating. In a cloud of incense after hymns and prayers, the priest would lift the host for all to see it and to be blessed by it. It was a simple and beautiful rite centered on sheer showing and looking.

Some scholars believe that in their central ritual of the Eleusinian mysteries the ancient Greeks would spend days in fasting, procession, and sacrifice in a rite that culminated in the priestly display of a grain of wheat and maybe in ritual or theatrical intercourse. Buddhists contemplate the image and gestures of the Buddha, often depicted in towering statuary, and Hindus have elaborate and varied rites, *puja,* centered around their sacred images.

I don't mean to suggest any sacrilege in making these comparisons. The act of showing and the corresponding response of gazing in contemplation and blessing in religious ritual may shed some light on the powerful role of sexual imagery and the overwhelming need to see the human body and sexual activity. If there is any substance in the common sentiment that sex is sacred, it would seem appropriate to explore that sacredness in religious terms.

In religion the role of images and icons and the veneration of images is extremely complex. There have been emotional and divisive arguments about whether or not images serve the religious life, and most religious people are careful not to worship the images as such, finding idolatry abhorrent. Still, the veneration of images in religion is widespread and often forms the very core of religious life.

The image may be understood as a representation of the

deity, a means of contemplation and worship, and so statues may be clothed, bathed, dressed, and even offered food. In many instances they are beautifully made, often according to ancient rubrics; they may be towering in size or made with jewels and precious materials. Usually they deeply impress the one who is gazing and therefore nurture the spirit of piety and adoration. Some devotees believe that when a statue or painting is made perfectly, the spirit of the deity enters into the statue, and the person who presents himself before the image receives the benefits of that spirit.

Sexual images seem to share some of these qualities of the religious image and the contemplative gaze. Of course, for many religious people sexual fascination is the opposite of the religious spirit, but in some traditions where sex is considered sacred, it isn't much of a leap from honoring the image of a saint to venerating an image of a sexual god or goddess.

Considering sexual imagery for its deeper purposes, my interest is not to find ways to eradicate it but to look for its *telos*, its deep necessity. It doesn't do us much good to maintain public disapproval of sexual imagery while private appeal to it is so widespread and compulsive.[1] Highly educated and deeply spiritual people are sometimes drawn to pornography, like Paul Tillich, who, his wife tells us, would sometimes place a sexy magazine inside one of his theological tomes. In the other direction, Erica Jong describes Henry Miller as "the most contradictory of characters: a mystic who was known for his sexual writings."[2]

Images of Aphrodite and Venus, as well as other deities, hint at the human body's mysterious iconic quality. Today without thinking about religion people go to darkened theaters and small booths, or sit before a television or computer screen, and become deeply absorbed in imagery depicting the naked human body or sexual acts. We know that both of these sights were part of religious rituals in the past, and it may be that the sacred is indeed camouflaged in these ritual-like situations.

In modern life sex is one of the few numinous areas we have left, numinosity being the aura of awe and mystery usually associated with religious feeling. We have destroyed the mystery of the planets and stars with our telescopes and roving machines. We have diminished the numinosity of nature through our countless studies and exploitation. But fortunately we have not yet reduced the power of sex to stir deep desire and to compel the contemplation of images. Maybe it is a saving grace that the human body can still evoke the overwhelming desire to gaze and even the deeply felt need to insist on taboo.

The Body as Icon

The looking that goes on in sex is not mere seeing. We are not looking for information, we are not looking at the human body the way a physician would. It might seem that we are looking for the sheer pleasure of it or that we are interested in raw physical gratification. But the compulsion is too strong to be explained away in purely physical terms. The soul is clearly involved, and in some mysterious way sexual looking has enormous meaning to a great number of people. To see what is going on in this compulsion we may have to penetrate through our moralistic judgments and ask, as openly as we can, what deep longing drives us to this gaze that is so compelling and so rarely fully satisfied.

Why do people want to watch others make love on a

stage? Why do they want a camera's close-up of organs and penetrations? Why are magazines printed and sold every day filled with the same views, the same acts, and the same situations? Desire and pleasure play a central role in the quest for the sexual scene, just as the wish to heal might move the physician and the hope for religious awareness might drive the churchgoer. What do we see when we gaze at the human body erotically? The answer to this question is elusive because sexuality itself is blessedly still a mystery.

Contemplation is a religious word: the numinosity that surrounds sex and gives it its emotional charge calls for religious categories. The language we usually use for sex is too physical, too idealized, or too vulgar to touch its numinosity. Sometimes it seems that we use clinical language for sex to distance ourselves and maybe to protect ourselves from its power, and vulgar language may have the same effect.

In monastic practice, contemplation is distinguished from prayer by its meditative quality. It is a receptive attitude whose purpose is union with divinity. The medieval Christian mystical teacher Meister Eckhart often refers to the object of spiritual contemplation as naked divinity: "the soul's naked being finds the naked, formless being of the divine unity, which is there, a being above being, accepting and reposing in itself."[3]

This divine nakedness may give us a hint about the numinosity in human nakedness. A powerful aura surrounds the well-painted, well-photographed nude and may give a certain halo to a lover in the flesh as well. Unclothe the human body, and we are granted a glimpse of the nymph, the Aphrodite that gives life such pleasure and satisfaction. If the sexual body were not numinous, people would not be hypnotically drawn to it, nor would religion be so concerned about its propriety.

At one level gazing at pictures of nudes, whether or not they are involved in sexual activity, may be an attempt to see naked reality in the most absolute terms. Why would such a gaze be so compelling unless it had a fundamental attraction and purpose? The photographer Edward Weston, famous for his images of plain, unclothed men and women, often reflected on his work in these broad terms. In a journal entry of 1930 he describes how a good photograph requires a model's "revealment," the photographer's realization, and the camera's readiness. When these are all in place, he said, "the very bones of life are bared."[4]

In his celebrated book on the nude, Kenneth Clark tells the story of the Knidian Aphrodite, created by Praxiteles in the fourth century B.C. The story was told that the people of Kos, who had commissioned the statue, rejected it, and so it was moved to the island of Knidos, off the Asia Minor coast. It was set in a sanctuary full of fruit trees and surrounded by grapes. The goddess is shown naked, about to step into a bath, holding in her left hand the garment she has just taken off. Her lips are parted and her right hand covers and emphasizes her pubic area. According to a surviving story of a visit to the shrine by devotees, one person threw his arms around her neck, and all who sought a view of her backside had to enter the shrine through a locked door in the rear. Clark concludes the story with a telling remark: "No one questioned the fact that she was an embodiment of physical desire and that this mysterious, compulsive force was an element in her sanctity."[5]

Clark makes the same disclaimer I find myself stating time after time—it's difficult in our culture to appreciate how this Aphrodite could be the object of religious veneration. But if we could arrive at that point we might turn Clark's statement around and see that sanctity has a role in sexual imagery. Gazing erotically at the human body, we are contemplating the mystery of our own nature as well as the mystery of our passionate longing toward union in absolute terms. The body is indeed a temple, not simply for its beauty and value, but because it houses the holy mystery of human existence. By approaching it, gazing at it, even being frozen by its allure, we engage in profound wonder, full of fascination and pleasure.

It is as though the sexual gaze answers the most fundamental of questions: Who am I? How did I get here? What am I supposed to do? The answers are contained in the body, if only we knew how to look. Not knowing, we look hungrily and without full satisfaction. Some people complain bitterly about our looking, and maybe they should. Any true religious act requires taboo as a way of preserving its sanctity.

Sexual Contemplation

In a movie theater or at a stage show, the objects of lustful gaze are likely to have no personal relationship to the ones who are looking. Some find this arrangement depersonalizing, and it clearly has its denigrating aspects. But in the best of circumstances this sexuality may be impersonal rather than depersonalizing. It may point beyond the men and women showing their bodies to the Aphrodite that is the soul, the nymph invoked by the sexual or pornographic rites.

Contemplation is sometimes described as a generic state of consciousness: one simply contemplates. But it also makes sense to contemplate in certain definite ways, such as contemplating nature, our homes, art, or a piece of music. In this same way it is possible to gaze on the sexual body and be

drawn into a particular kind of contemplation—sexual meditation.

I recall once walking down a street and noticing a young
man on the opposite side. A beautiful young woman passed
him, and as he was looking at her he walked straight into a
telephone pole. This is contemplation. I was having dinner at
a restaurant with a woman once who couldn't take her eyes
off our handsome waiter and finally spilled sauce all over her
dress. If we ever lose this capacity for absorption in sexual
fantasy, we will be another step further from the soul that defines us as human.

Edward Weston states his philosophy in language that
echoes William Blake's celebrated recommendation to see
the whole world in a grain of sand: "I have come to realize
life as a coherent whole, and myself as a part, with rocks,
trees, bones, cabbages, smokestacks, torsos, all interrelated,
interdependent—each a symbol of the whole. And further,
details of these parts have their own integrity, and through
them the whole is indicated, so that a pebble becomes a
mountain, a twig is seen as a tree."[6]

The torsos in Weston's list suggest that images of the naked
body may be perceived as intimations of life as a whole.
Gazing at the naked body, we are exploring the nature of life,
the mystery of a human being, and the secrets of all bodies—
the body of the world, the body politic, bodies of water, the
body of a book, and, in a phrase from D. H. Lawrence, the
body of God. The world's body often reveals itself as a source
of pleasurable gazing, as when you notice the moon in the
sky at a particularly splendid moment or a waterfall in a forest. In an equally captivating way, human nature stands revealed in the drawing of a breast or in the literary portrayal
of eyes or hands in the moment of love.

Our challenge is to really see, to look penetratingly and amply for a perception of the world that lies within and beyond the obvious. To contemplate an image is to become absorbed in it, not just to scan it at a distance. Sex inspires the gaze, peek, glance, and stare, all of which are specific ways of being present to an image, and in the realm of sex presence is of the essence.

It is also part of human life to be seen, to be the object of desire. Men and women alike generously show themselves to the gaze of lovers, some to the gaze of the public. Marilyn Monroe may live in anyone, and even though her presence as an archetypal figure may be disturbing, she may also fill our lives with soul in the way that only the sexual nymph can. The exhibitionist demonstrates that there is something in human nature, neurotic or not, that enjoys being seen, especially sexually.

If we could hear the word without any institutional or denominational nuance, we might understand that in our compulsive sexual curiosity we look at the erotic body religiously—with deep devotion and with a transcendent goal. Through the body we are seeing something of the soul and therefore of the mystery of life itself. The compulsive aspect of sexual gazing betrays the fact that our looking is not deep enough. When we honor a holy icon we know we're in the presence of the numinous. But in our secular society we have lost an explicit awareness of the sanctity of sex. We think of it in purely human terms, as far from religion as possible, and therefore our looking is not right.

Our sexual gaze is full of numinosity, but we have no language or artful ritual for this kind of veneration. Perhaps our colorful slang and the tendency to surround the sexual gaze with the light of a brilliant Las Vegas show or the darkness of a movie theater are concealed attempts at ritual, but the soul requires explicit devotion. The splitting in our culture of body and spirit has repercussions so profound as to be almost unimaginable. Sex lies at the very base of our identity and at the core of our need to escape loneliness and discover joy. By so effectively secularizing it, we suffer an enormous chaos and emptiness at the very base of our existence.

Sex in Dream and Fantasy

The religious veneration of images may also help us appreciate the confusing appearance of sexual imagery in our dreams—both our diaphanous daydreams and our opaque dreams of night.

Most people have sexual dreams throughout their lives. These dreams may disturb that element in us that tries to control sexual desire. I was on a national television program once, discussing dreams and recommending the practice of telling our dreams to a spouse or intimate, when the well-known host said, "Surely you wouldn't tell all your dreams to your wife." The audience laughed, knowing that some dreams are not only graphically sexual but may involve behavior and partners that might be a scandal in the context of ordinary life.

In a dream I once heard, a man is making love with his wife and sees that his penis is long, narrow, and straight—like a pencil, he says. He feels uncomfortable, but his wife lavishes his penis with affection and obvious pleasure. The man told me the dream with some discomfort and said that in the dream he felt embarrassed. I didn't ignore the other figure in the dream, his wife, who sees nothing wrong and, in fact, seems to enjoy the shape of his penis. Quite often it is a figure other than the dreamer who tells us how to take the dream.

The man was a writer and artist, and so it didn't require a great effort to focus our discussion on the sexuality of his creative work, not that this direction offers the only sensible approach. He talked about his feelings of inadequacy in not having a solid station in life, in not providing well enough for his family, and in not having realized the expectations of himself he had as an artist. In the pencil-penis his feelings seem to have been well condensed, and in his wife's sexual adoration we saw evidence of his capacity to accept and love himself.

We can take another lesson from this dream: dreams of sex are not always explicitly about sex but may have to do with a broader kind of love and longing, with eros in the deeper sense. Such dreams also may show how thoroughly sex is implicated in other areas of life, especially if we consider qualities of sexuality like desire, pleasure, sensuousness, and even taboo.

Our sexual fantasies, too, have a great deal to do with our search for meaning, direction, and individuality. Fantasies of sex obviously draw many people into intimate relationships, married life, and parenthood. They may entice us out of a bad marriage or away from a relationship that has lost its vitality. In a stable and generally happy relationship, sexual fantasies may help keep desire itself alive and at work.

Eros serves the soul by leading it on through desire and pleasure, and the objects of our desire are not always as simple and obvious as they may appear. Sexual fantasies may call forth new life in the guise of new sexual experiences, and so the motive for repressing these fantasies may not be as much moral sensitivity as fear of life's irrepressible abundance.

Many times in therapy I have seen a person with a broad smile and a look of satisfaction on his face just after he has convinced himself of a new way to repress his desires. It isn't easy sometimes to distinguish between neurotic gratification and deep pleasure.

Sexual fantasy wakens, points, and motivates. It is a form of education that teaches us the direction in which our soul's desire leads through the testimony of the pleasurable sensation occasioned by specific erotic images. A young man once told me about a series of dreams he had had in which his lover was having sex with one man after another. The images stirred up excruciating jealousy in him, and more than anything he wanted the dreams to end. Two years after these dreams, he was living with someone else in a satisfying relationship and his former lover was happily married. His earlier dreams that had his lover involved with other men seemed to be ahead of his life, and his feelings of jealousy seemed to show his resistance to fate.

I once had a dream in which I was flying through the air in circles, hanging onto a rope that was in the shape of a figure eight. A friend I admired was hanging onto the opposite end of the rope, and together we were enjoying our dance in midair. My friend was older than I, established and fairly well known. I had this dream shortly before my own work began to be noticed, and so maybe it expressed a certain level of equality I was beginning to achieve with that person. On the other hand, I can also see it as part of a long series of flying dreams in which I had trouble taking off and landing. Here, I am at home in the air and have a reliable partner. We're hanging onto infinity (the lateral figure eight), the whole works, the universe, in our ungrounded, unworried delight.

I don't think that this dream necessarily has a direct relationship to my friend. I see it as an enactment of the condition of my soul. It settles some of my fears about being too flighty and airy in everything I do, in my work, in my life, and in my thoughts. I discover in this dream the mysterious truth that one can have companionship and live joyfully in the elemental air, in the ungrounded space of imagination. The dream addresses the very theme of this chapter—the validity of the imagination, unrooted and disconnected from life. The dream image could be painted like a tarot card, having no direct relationship with me but standing as a fertile universal image for an unnamed mystery.

This dream is vaguely erotic and reminds me of the many dreams I have heard from men and women involving tender moments of lovemaking with unknown or improbable lovers. Just as I found myself oddly but joyfully connected to a friend, many people enjoy but are puzzled by the lovers they team up with in dreams. One key to these dreams may be to consider the various worlds the lovers represent. My partner in the infinity dream was a work colleague, and so the dream hints that the context of this air-dance is work.

Eros and the Interior Life

I've also heard versions of a dream from several people in which the dreamer finds himself in a bedroom with a partner, wishing to make love. Unfortunately there are several people in the room, as though in a formal gathering or reception, and the would-be lovers have no privacy. Eventually the crowd leaves and the lovers find themselves alone, only now the room is brightly lighted and they want some darkness. The dreamer finds the light switch, but it doesn't work, or there are so many buttons he can't find the right one, or when one light goes off another comes on.

There are many elements in this common dream: the conflict between the wish for privacy and darkness, the obstacles of the crowd, and the tricky control switch. It isn't easy to find the interior life free of crowded ideas, soothingly dark, or easily under control. This dream could be society's myth, pointing to our difficulty allowing ourselves to have a soul and to enjoy an interior erotic life. It also relates to an idea we considered earlier, that darkness is a means of giving ritual quality to sex.

The same theme is echoed in the story of Eros and Psyche, in which Eros demands that Psyche come to bed with him in total darkness. When Psyche gives in to the temptation to see her lover and brings an oil lamp into the bedroom, Eros goes away. Experience would seem to corroborate that eros wants darkness, privacy, and secrecy, both in our literal bedrooms and figuratively as part of the intimacy lovers share. Love and the soul flourish in a deeply interior space, free of the ideas and judgments of the world, in a place of their own.

This aspect of eros and sexual love is illustrated, too, in the tale of Tristan and Isolde, who enjoy their love for a while in a remote cave. The couple has to travel across barren land for two days before finding the cave, an ancient place that had been used by giants of old who, according to the author of the story, there "had their hiding place when they wished to be private and make love."[7] The cave served a similar purpose for Tristan and Isolde: there "they did exactly what their hearts demanded." After they were discovered by King Mark,

Isolde's husband, who saw them through a window, the author remarks, "Never again in all their years would they be so private as they were then, nor did they ever again have such a good opportunity for their delight as they then had."

Love and sex need to withdraw, at least momentarily, from society, from both its physical presence and its moral and intellectual interference. Love seeds and blooms in a private place, a place where the soul comes to the foreground and busy life recedes into the background. Our inclination to be private in sex may be motivated more by the need of the soul than by a concern about embarrassment. It may be important to keep sexual memories private, too, to take care about how much you tell anyone, even a physician or therapist, about your sexual past—although obviously I'm not talking about holding back information that another might need for their physical or emotional health.

Lovers often have periods in their courtship when they keep their affections to themselves, recognizing that the soul in these tender days needs something of a hothouse or a cave in a faraway land for the germination of love. Sex can also be kept private out of guilt or as a way to manipulate circumstances—the shadow side of the lovers' cave.

These dreams of sexual privacy demonstrate the larger idea that sexual dreams come in many varieties; it would be a mistake to see the sex and miss the nuance. Waking from a sexual dream, we might consider all the details and think less about sexual excitement and more about the specific way sex is presented in the dream, noticing in particular the role of desire, the kind of pleasure offered, and ways in which propriety might be transgressed. In privacy dreams, for example, we are invited to reflect on the need in sex to be free of

the harsh and oppressive demands coming from moral institutions. De Sade presented a similar idea in his fiction when
his libertines sought out underground, bolted, thick-shielded
chambers where they could indulge their fantasies. The soul
obviously has a place in the light of life, but it is also a space
unto itself, a cave where significant things happen that may
never see the day.

Contemplating the Goddess

Whenever I see men standing passively in small groups before magazine racks filled with pictures of men and women
in various levels of undress and sexual pose, it seems obvious
that they are wrapped in contemplation. As I peruse volume
after volume of sexual literature written and published by
women, I sense a powerful longing to restore to sex its full
body and soul. We crave the very thing that we repress—our
need to explore and contemplate the mysteries of powerful
desire, intimate intercourse, and the drama of erotic encounter.

I'm reminded of a dream I once heard from a young man,
one I refer to elsewhere in my writings, in which he found
himself lying on the floor in a throne room, looking up between the legs of a mother goddess who was seated on the
throne. Completely absorbed in his vision, he felt that blessedly the whole of life's activity had stopped to allow him this
absolute pleasure. Compulsion is too weak a word to describe his need to have this vision. I felt I could see this scene
replicated in his life in subtle ways, in the many signs of devotion he showed to the various women in his life and in his
habit of being a highly compassionate and nurturing maternal figure. The strong inhuman, mythological tone in his

dream also seemed to be mirrored in serious difficulties he had with food, children, and women in his tendency to be all-mother, outrageously sensitive and adoring, and unconsciously brutal.

This dream was pornographic in a certain sense, and yet it was obviously a ritual act as well. At the time it made me wonder if every recourse to pornography is not an enactment of this dream, a ritual return to a god or goddess who is appropriately approached in a sexual manner and whose presence is to be visually contemplated in a rather humble, if not humiliating, posture. Do those men at the magazine rack act guilty and try to hide because they fear society's disapproval, or is there a sense of shame about having to succumb to the goddess, give up the rewards of propriety, and submit to a necessary ritualistic contemplation? Do they feel the shame of being a human being, drawn by a powerful lure to the very goddess whose existence and claims on them they deny or neglect? Are they doing on the street what my client was doing in his powerful dream?

Sexism is intolerable at personal, social, and political levels, but it has deep roots in the unwholesome way we live in this world. The ultimate sexist attitude is not simply denigration of women, but an absolute neglect of all that is embraced by the images of goddesses around the world. Sexism is the expression of a divided and constricted way of life and a deep rejection of the goddess in our lives. Achieving political equality for women, as necessary as it is, is not enough. Maybe contemplation and the holy gaze are themselves gifts of the goddess whom we have repressed and whom we now adore only in our dreams and compulsions.

Making the Religious Soul of Sex Present

One of the most remarkable sites of sexual fantasy on earth, in some ways connected to the pornographic newsstands, lies in a small village in central India called Khajuraho. Between the early ninth century and the beginning of the twelfth, a number of relatively small, beige and pinkish temples were built there on high terraces. The main entrance to most of these temples faces the rising sun. Each temple is unique in design and dedicated to a specific deity. There is a statue or symbol of the divinity in the interior of each temple in a sanctuary that represents the cave as the source of life. Only the Brahmin whose task it is to perform the sacrifices is allowed in the sanctuary.[8]

On the facades of these temples are many sculpted figures representing battles, dancing, daily activities, beasts, and various kinds of ornament. On many of the temples are erotic scenes showing every form of lovemaking, including intercourse between a man and a mare. Everywhere are images of jeweled, rapturous, curving, graceful bodies, including couples in tender embrace.

In his memoirs Jung tells of his travels to India in 1938, when he saw similar images at Konarak. His Indian guide explained them as the means of reminding unenlightened young people of their dharma, the law of their lives. First they must deal with their sexuality and then find their spiritualization, he said. Jung was doubtful that young Indian people needed to be reminded of their sexuality, and he was especially incredulous when the guide mentioned that he and Jung had attained a certain level of consciousness and were above that sort of thing.[9] But Jung seems to approve of the idea that we have to deal with our sexuality as our karma, as the stuff of which we are born and made. Erotic images keep people from being spirited away in their religious practice.

There is much more to erotic images than the reminder to fulfill our ordinary lives, but the point should not be lost. One reason pornography is so inescapably present in our culture may be that in many ways we are a society of the spirit, not only in a religious sense, but in our ignoring the sensual life before us while pursuing culture-building, analysis, understanding, and a highly controlled, technological future. We may need to enter more fully into our karma—our family life, the needs of our bodies and hearts, and our ordinary lives—or sexuality will continue to press upon us as an emotionally charged complex antagonistic to meaning rather than complementary, a threat to ordinary tranquillity rather than a comforting source of it.

In his preface to a picture book on Khajuraho, Alain Daniélou mentions the "mysterious presence" one feels in the erotic statues, and he quotes an ancient Dravidian poem, the *Manimekhalai,* where a sculpted figure on a temple explains himself: "When Maya, the heavenly architect, after keeping a long watch on me, sculpted this statue in my image, the likeness was so great that I felt obliged to inhabit it."[10] This extraordinary statement on the numinosity of images offers a deeper perspective on erotic images in general: they contain a spirit that is potent and important for a vital life. They are disturbing in the way they burst through our moral bindings and intensely spiritual in spite of their obvious carnality.

When a religious statue has a sexual theme, we may conclude that it houses a sex spirit, and the point in approaching such a shrine might be to take some of that spirit home to vivify our daily lives. Alan Watts, whose books of the 1960s advocate a sensuous approach to spirituality, commented on

the Sun Temple at Konarak. He reminds the Western ob-
server, who typically divides thought from sensation and
finds meaning only in the rational mind, that Indian yoga is
a "purification of the senses from their bondage to con-
cepts."[11] It would be a mistake, in Watts's view, to translate
this erotic imagery into ideas and symbols, since their very
point is to keep us engaged sensually and erotically.

Watts points out that the couples are not "going to bed"
but are dancing. They are not nude; they wear crowns, neck-
laces, bracelets, and bangles. They show us, without explanation, how sex is a ritual and not an animalistic act, a yoga of
ecstasy and not a mere necessity for the survival of the
species. In the West, he says, we don't realize that we have a
need for ecstasy. I would also add that in these extraordinary
Indian sculptures we discover that beauty, grace, rhythm,
and form are essential to sex, and that they reveal the potential in sex for spirituality.

Watts describes sex not, as scientific studies often state, as
an "outlet," but as an "inlet." It is not a release of pressure
but a holding of pleasure, where the goal is not orgasm but
sustained sensation. Giving ourselves plenty of time, preparing a place, adorning our bodies, and creating a spiritual milieu, an arena bigger than ourselves and our "relationship,"
might pull off the veils that have shrouded sex in the shadows
of biology and psychology during the recent modern period.
We can restore the mystery grasped so palpably by our ancestors who built temples to eros in realization of our absolute and unforgiving need for enchantment.

The erotic images on the temples of India have a special
grace, but we could add to them the sexual themes in Greek
and early Mediterranean art, the churches and pagan centers
of the British Isles and Europe, the estates and streets of

Pompeii, the paintings of Japan, the sculptures of Africa, the sacred sexual images of Peru. Around the world religion and sex have come together to create graphic images of sex that sublimate it creatively by granting it a spiritual context and purpose.

I have been warned by friends who know Indian culture and religion well that I probably cannot grasp the real meaning of Indian erotic religious art. The Indian people, they tell me, generally do not see the lingam—the stylized male sex organ—and the yoni as sexual at all, but as representations of life itself or of the great ineffable sacred mysteries of religion. I'm sure this warning is wise, and yet I still wonder if a much broader, deeper, and mystery-filled Western notion of sex might not bring us closer to the unspeakable mysteries of Eastern erotic imagery, shedding some light on the strange non-Indian preoccupation with pornography.

It is difficult to imagine in our current context, but maybe one day we will arrive at the point where we can have graphic erotic imagery around us and not think much about human sexuality or feel a compulsion to stare. We may be able simply to enjoy erotic images and to see through their surface sexuality to the fundamental, creative eros at their core. Then we will have discovered the deepest secret of sex, that it is life itself, precisely in its holiness rather than its secularism.

Images That Offend and Disturb

It would be unrealistic and incomplete to present only the positive side of the sexual imagination, for it's obvious that such images can also offend and disturb even those of us who consider ourselves broad-minded. Erotic images can be unsettling in many ways. We may find them simply too graphic and harsh, like a Robert Mapplethorpe photograph. Some are clearly sexist, coming down hard on one side of the power struggle of the genders. Some seem to have no heart but to show only body organs. Some are associated with violence and sacrilege. Some are merely inane and silly.

It is simplistic to claim that erotic images are always beneficial and that anyone who finds them objectionable is moralistic and narrow-minded. Certain sexual images can shock, embarrass, and unsettle, and they inspire outrage. The completely open-minded sex connoisseur may be as much defended against the shadow of eros as the moralist is against the vitalizing power of sex. As any advertiser knows, beautiful and ugly sexual images are potent, and they have a powerful impact on people of all moral persuasions.

In the story of Eros and Psyche, as part of its deepest initiations the soul has to snatch some of Persephone's beauty cream from her underworld boudoir. The story seems to say that the beauty of death, the shadow elements in life, and a certain amount of negativity all have important roles to play in the educated and sophisticated life. Years of practicing psychotherapy have convinced me that ordinary people may well have to pass through ordeals that take them into shadow areas exactly suited to their karma.

Ancient poets frequently remarked on Persephone's beauty, and yet in the Orphic hymn to her she is described as "horned." Full of contradictions, she is the sweet young girl picking spring flowers with her mother and later the terrifying bride of Hades and thus the mistress of hell. The Orphic hymn praises her saying:

> You are life and death to toiling mortals,
> O Persephone, for you always nourish all and kill them
> too.

This ambivalence or contradiction is present in erotic imagery as well. For some, this imagery is a way of playing, a diversion or entertainment, while for others it marks the downfall of civilization. For all her darkness, Persephone or Aphrodite or whatever deep spirit keeps graphic sexual imagery thriving is indeed a powerful force, the dark side, perhaps, of all the positive sexual imagery in religious mysticism and iconography. It is not a question of one being good and the other evil. Because of the narrowness of our current vision, all we have of sexual imagery is Persephone's dark side, the kind lacking altogether in innocence.

Those men standing at the magazine and video racks or searching the Internet or placing an intimate commercial phone call or phoning for an escort, and those women enjoying books on sexual fantasy or patronizing male stripper clubs represent us all in our desperate attempt to find our needed sexual ecstasy and the spirituality of the senses.

If indeed our compulsiveness and anxiety around pornography are due to fearful repression, then recommendations for all of us are fairly clear. We might reflect on our prudishness and our hypocrisy. Do we in fact protest too much against those very images that have a powerful appeal to us? This question is appropriate not just for those who make broad criticisms of sexual imagery, but for each of us as we try, throughout our lifetime, to weave our sexuality into the rest of life. Can we enter more energetically into life by lifting our sexual repression, without losing our important sexual inhibitions and privacy? Is it possible to enjoy the sexual gaze—as those who see and as those who are seen—without literal diminishment of our persons? Can we be sexually creative and free and at the same time sexually moral?

Deepening Ourselves as Sex Objects

Feminists have rightly complained about the humiliation involved in the pornographic gaze. We may feel objectified and depersonalized when someone stares at us on a subway or bus; how much more so when the gaze is sexual. On the other hand, there is a kind of looking that is not distancing and not humiliating. It is an intimate erotic gaze in which you, as object, agree to be a stand-in for the god or goddess. It can be uncomfortable, especially if we're taught that it's humiliating to be made into a sex object, but it can also be pleasurable and ennobling.

The very sacredness of sex may be due to our glimpsing in our beloved the vast world of meaning and value that lies behind the facade of ordinary life. "Life is a door to existence," says Georges Bataille, and through the loved person we find deliverance. Sex is also a doorway to a level where life is lived with extraordinary immediacy and presence, a model for what is possible when eros leads the way.

If we are depersonalizing and deanimating our world and ourselves in this age of analysis, then instead of trying to intensify the subjective, it might be better to find a soulful way to treat things as objects and even to be an object. But how do you gaze soulfully and how do you become an object of sexual gaze without losing your soul?

When I present myself to the gaze of my lover, I am making a gift. I'm letting down my tools of self-protection and my defenses, exposing myself not just to an eye's perusal but to a soul's reflection. I am being seen not just in my physical stature, but in my very being. The intense feelings involved in disrobing, the inhibition as well as the pleasure of self-exhibition, are due not merely to physical conditions but to subtle emotions and states of soul. It's an enormous thing in any life to be made visible, to be revealed.

We live in a world where objects have been deprived of their souls, and the last thing we want to is become lifeless objects ourselves. But even the things of the world want to be seen and touched, and the most ordinary objects of daily life have soul. We can bring soul back into mere objects by the way we make them, treat them, and respect them. The same is true of ourselves as sexual beings. We can discover the depths of our own gazing and the importance in sex of looking and watching. And we can recover the value and pleasure of being the object of a mystery-filled sexual gaze.

It may be important to have occasions for sex in daylight or outdoors, to have appropriate leisure and privacy for looking, to dress revealingly and provocatively at times. It may be helpful to have paintings and photos on our walls to open us to the subtleties of gazing and to invite the spirit of eros to enter.

Today, many think we need to teach couples how to be sexual with each other, but I want to emphasize a deeper project—discovering the depths and heights of sex, its inherent and unsentimental sacredness, the spirit and soul within the mechanics, techniques, and paraphernalia. We have to invite the spirits of sex into our bedrooms, or else sex will remain a secularized, egocentric, narcissistic, and exploitive endeavor, even in the midst of our supposed sexual enlightenment.

It's up to us to push through the symptomatic, depersonalizing gaze to have a vision of the mystery that is sex, but I would never expect a complete solution to the problem of erotic imagery and pornography—a perfect balance, a full integration, a pleasing amalgam. Life doesn't work that way in any sphere. The best we can hope for is a constant creative dialogue so that the pornographic doesn't become debilitating or neurotic, and the more innocent erotic imagery is not lost amid our fears about the pornographic. Aphrodite herself was once called Porne, patroness of prostitutes, a sign that pornography is more a mystery than a problem and that hiding behind its evident noisomeness is a dark beauty, the Persephone in sex. Aphrodite was also identified with Persephone herself and called Persephaessa,[12] a mythological way of saying that the lure of the sexual image has deep roots and spiritual transcendence.

For many years I have had a painting in my bedroom depicting the great Hindu god Krishna. His face is blue, and he is surrounded by the women cowherds, the *gopi*, who are his playmates. His right hand is on the breast of one of them, who I assume is Radha, his favorite. Playfully and enticingly he attracts the young women to him, as divinity draws human souls to itself. Yet he remains elusive, unpossessable, passionately desired but ever out of reach, as divinity can never be contained in the human realm.

Living with Erotic Images

Suppression, oppression, and repression are not constructive ways to deal with anything, including objectionable sexual images in movies, books, and magazines. In connection with pornography, how do we "go with the symptom" and find a way through it rather than around it? One obvious way would be to cultivate the practice of erotic gazing, deepening the ways in which we look at the world and at the human

Lucas Cranach (the Elder), *Venus*

body, although each person and each culture finds its own way of evoking the beautiful and the meaningful in its public and private life.

In terms of specifically nude and sexual images, the realm of art is full of inspiring paintings and sculptures for the project of giving image to the nymph. The most impressive nude I've ever seen is the Lucas Cranach painting of Venus now at Canada's National Gallery of Art in Ottawa. Placed at the end of a long hall, it reveals itself slowly to the viewer's gradual initiatory approach. Her small, tilting head gazes at you with its classic sidelong glance. Her arms and legs are long and her torso slight. Her gestures are seductive but reserved. Ornate jewelry keeps her from being completely nude, and a classic diaphanous fabric wraps around the middle of her Gothic body lifted in ritual anasyrma.

A nude is not simply a nude. The most subtle aspects of gesture, body shape, color, and ornament enrich the body with fantasy, so that the belly is indeed a continent in this geography and an upturned wrist like the Cranach Venus's is a seductive invitation to the gazer. About Cranach's nudes Anne Hollander, widely known for her enlightening books on costume and dress, notes the typical transparent gauze that conceals nothing. They are "as specifically erotic as fur" and "create significant nudity out of mere bareness." They also depict "a gust of wind or a delicate touch moving across tender areas."[13] In Cranach's female and male nudes I see psychological complexity, an awareness on their part of their nudity and their naked presence in the world around them — a perspective that wouldn't hurt any of us as we try to be transparent persons in a complicated world.

Seeing the Cranach *Venus* in Ottawa was one of the thrilling moments of my life, and I'm aware of her presence there, although I haven't returned to visit her in several years. The painting is not just beautiful, it's a shrine to all that beauty evokes, especially the spirit of Venus-Aphrodite, who gives life charm. She makes all our struggles worthy of our efforts and, as the poet William Burford has suggested, tones down the heavy spirits associated with death and mortality. I can deal with the dark challenges of life with a measure of peace, having seen the Cranach Venus and having been touched by her deep beauty and mystery.

Anyone can bring the spirit of Venus into their home. The earliest images of Venus we find in history are simple forms, and we can similarly paint or sculpt the slightest hint of a human body with a bulge here and a curve there on a piece of paper or a lump of clay. We can follow the Indians and place a simple lingam and yoni of our own design in or near our home, to remind us of the fundamental secrets of life represented in sexual images. Venus is classically at home in the garden and it isn't difficult to find a garden sculpture of her. Surrounded by flowers and shrubs she is in her element, with a piety not unlike similar sculptures of the Madonna or the Chinese Quan Yin.

A friend of mine once found an old piece of sewage conduit and placed it upright in his garden. He chose it for the simple beauty of its texture, shape, and color. Friends made appropriate jokes about it being a phallic image. I saw it as an ancient way of giving home to the sexual spirit, appropriately in a garden, and also appropriately associated with the sewer.

We can equally find the spirit of Venus in paintings and sculptures of the nude male, because it is the nudity, not necessarily the gender, that elicits her erotic spirit. The great classic male nudes, like the Hermes of Praxiteles and the bearded

god of Histiaia, tease us into contemplation of muscle, posture, proportion, and penis, each one of them mysteries that
touch upon our most personal emotions and desires. Donatello's quirky *David* sends the imagination off in many directions. Without evocative images we would have no means to
meditate on our sexuality, our bodies, and the erotic passions
that keep life in movement and make it worth living.

Anyone can hold as precious certain meaningful erotic images and give them a place of honor in their heart. In spite of
the moralism about sex that surrounds us, we can realize
that the pleasure erotic art offers is far from immoral; it is a
taste of immortality that can be woven into other aspects of

our spiritual lives. Erotic art reveals the
beauty and pleasure potentially present
in all of life, so it inspires us to take our
desires seriously and to follow the in-
centives of pleasure.

Donatello, *David*

CHAPTER 6

Priapus the Scarecrow

The Comic and the Vulgar in Sex

T HE BEAUTIFUL human body that painters and photographers love to show us in myriad ways is an approach to the body largely influenced by the myth of Aphrodite. From another point of view the body may look odd and even grotesque. Without an airbrush and special preparations and angles, the ordinary human body when photographed or painted may look more curious than beautiful, and with a little artistic license we can even make it freakish and shocking.

Some religions have done just that: they have isolated the sex organs, exaggerated them, and stylized them. The Greeks and Romans, for example, took the male erection, made it disproportionately large, and put it on a small, lumpish, bald, ugly-faced man, creating one of the most unlikely of deities, the garden god Priapus, who speaks to us in an ancient poem:

Why do you laugh, you silly slut?
Not Scopas' nor Praxiteles' touch

Made me, nor was I polished much
By Phidias. Some poor rustic cut
This body from a block of wood
And said: "You are Priapus. Good."[1]

Something of the essence of Priapus emerges in his being
carved from a block of wood. The slang "wood" for the erect
penis no doubt arises from a similar fantasy of the male erection.

We are so far from the religious sensibility that could find
divinity in a figure like Priapus, indeed in the aspect of life
that he governs, that we have to be satisfied with mythological and poetic interpretations of him. He stands squat and
obscene at the far end of paganism from us, and we can't see
religion in him, although our ancestors seem to have been
sharply aware of the depth and universality of his world.
Maybe they were earthier than we are and, paying more attention to the body and its idiosyncrasies, could appreciate
this lusty, impertinent figure.

Priapus, like any god, had his prayers, rites, and images,
but, unlike other deities, the images surrounding him had little socially redeeming value. Professor Rafael Lopez-Pedraza
tells of evidence he once found demonstrating that a woman
in old Greece baptized her child in the name of Priapus. [2] It's
difficult to look at images of this figure, so ugly and obscene
as to be used as a scarecrow in gardens, and imagine dedicating your child to his brand of spirituality. Indeed, it's difficult
to use "Priapus" and "spiritual" in the same sentence. But in
our fabrication of a certain kind of moral life we have lost
a valuable sensibility that flourished in paganism. What we
consider a scandal, the Greeks and Romans believed to be a
holy mystery.

I don't want to overstate the negative case for Priapus, for many other religions have figures in their mythologies and rites that are obscene and phallic, such as Coyote and Koko-pelli in North America and countless minor figures in religions everywhere on the globe. Still, Priapus takes us to a far end of the sexual spectrum, where our reaction might well be either to laugh or to be offended. He introduces us to the soul of sex in a way that is easy to reject as an aberration or as having nothing to do with spirituality—the comic and the vulgar.

According to mythology, Priapus is a son of Aphrodite, not so surprising since she was worshipped as Aphrodite Kal-liglautos, the goddess with the beautiful backside, and, as we have seen, was also known as philiommeides, or lover of the genitals. She is not embarrassed by the body, and she bears a son who makes a point to accent the phallus and the but-tocks. If we are to have a rounded education in things sexual, we have to appreciate both ancient and contemporary fasci-nation for the body, and especially for the sexual parts.

What kind of spirit fathers Priapus is not so simple a mat-ter. Mythology gives us four alternate fathers: Hermes, Dio-nysus, Adonis, and Zeus. These four tell us that even the little god Priapus is a complex figure whose meaning branches out in several directions. Sexual humor, vulgar conversation, tastelessness, and bawdiness play various roles in the making of a life and the establishment of a culture, each represented by Priapus's various fathers.

Hermes

Hermes is himself a phallic god, clever, witty, and sexy. He plays a role in the tale of the love affair between Aphrodite and Ares, god of war, in the Odyssey. Helios, the sun god, informed Aphrodite's husband Hephaestus about the affair, and in response the divine craftsman made a net of iron and spun the fastenings like a spider web, encircling the couple's bed. Later, when Hephaestus arrived on the scene, Ares and Aphrodite lay in the bed, caught tightly in the net. The wronged husband complained bitterly to the other gods, who laughed but still determined that Ares was seriously at fault and should pay for his deed.

Looking on, Apollo asked Hermes if he would be willing to sleep with Aphrodite in that web of steel. Hermes answered: "Lord who strike from afar, Apollo, I wish it could only be, and there could be thrice this number of endless fastenings, and all you gods could be looking on and all the goddesses, and still I would sleep by the side of Aphrodite the golden."[3] Spoken like the father of Priapus!

Hermes is remarkably complex and subtle. Inventive, tricky, and gifted with language, he is the guide of souls to the underworld and a major figure among the Olympian deities. He has a great deal to do with meaning, but not with logic and reasoning. He is nature plain, unadorned, expressive, and serendipitous. When a person sneezed, a friend might call out the name of Hermes, the way we might say "God bless you." When someone's belly rumbled or when someone unexpectedly passed gas, Hermes was present.

Hermes retains considerable dignity, but his son Priapus is more the spoiler of all that looks dignified in human life. Priapus was connected to the Dionysian rite of small neighborhood revels, the *comos,* intended to disturb the peace and poke fun at society's values, a ribald custom from which we get our word "comedy." Anyone who has ever heard a stand-up comic knows something about the way Priapic humor pokes fun at high-minded society: pratfalls, crotch grabbing, mooning, and jokes about the sex organs. Some people are entertained by such bawdy humor and some are offended, and both are proper responses to this divine freak.

Because we take morality so literally, it may be difficult to appreciate that being offended is a natural human response. With Priapus we are arriving at a point in our treatment of sex where we can't maintain the moral high ground, where we are invited into an area that is full of pleasure and meaning and yet at the same time can be outrageously offensive. Some people, for instance, may find off-color jokes revolting, while others may be offended but not let that stop them from laughing. Still others are true sons and daughters of Priapus and simply enjoy the comic, earthy side of sex.

One of our more Priapic comedians once grabbed her crotch during the televised singing of the national anthem and horrified citizens across the country. Like Priapus the scarecrow, she was chasing away the winged creatures of spirit, the angels who find it difficult to live close to the body, especially the sexual body, without benefit of a shield of purity and propriety. In this case the birds of patriotism and civic propriety had come to roost in the garden of an athletic stadium—sports are close to religion for their spiritual purity—and were put off by the woman's Priapic gesture. I don't mean to say that we should not be offended and should not complain in such circumstances. That may be our role in the mysteries. Personally, I am not one to readily enjoy Priapic humor, but occasionally I can sink far enough into my humanity to appreciate the jokes.

The soul of sex reaches beyond the taste of any one of us, and so we have to enter what may be unfamiliar and uncomfortable ground if we are going to get a sense of it. The rigid moralist has to relax his habit of judging, and the libertine has to find it in himself to be offended. One gets the sense sometimes that sex educators would like to enlighten us so thoroughly that shame would disappear and we would become completely comfortable with every aspect of sex. Maybe sex should always be uncomfortable in some areas. Like religion, sex is *tremendum et fascinans,* incredibly alluring and yet at the same time overwhelming in its sheer vitality and emotional power. Sometimes it may offend our dignity because it is more than human, not less.

In his role of scarecrow Priapus frightens away all kinds of winged spirits—our lofty thoughts, our airy ideas, our flighty opinions, and our otherworldly aspirations. It's difficult to land our spiritual sensibilities on the extended phallus of a garden statue presenting Priapus's erection, and it isn't always easy to be a spiritual person and at the same time appreciate earthy pleasures. Our challenge is to see how this outrageous spirit plays a role in the serious business of the soul and how it adds to our exploration of the soul of sex.

The erect phallus represents the appearance of life in all its lustiness. It signals the resurrection of life, coming back into vitality after a flaccid period of quiet or even after a failure of vitality. When I was a boy of thirteen an old man who lived across the street from me died. The family called for my mother to help, and she brought me along. In the neighbor's house we found the man lying on the floor between his bedroom and bathroom. He had apparently died in transit. Several women and children were walking around crying and anxiously wondering what to do. My mother was saying a rosary, leading some of the family members in prayer. But no one commented on the old man's erection, his penis standing tall in his pajamas as he lay cold on the floor. I was transfixed by it, led to many thoughts, as the hail marys droned on. I wondered if the erection had to do with his arrival in heaven, or if death makes us so utterly relaxed that the blood rushes to this erotic center of the male body. This memory confirms for me now that Priapus is indeed the power of life, which couldn't thrive if it weren't equally intimate with death.

We need our stand-up comics telling their bathroom jokes and favoring the private parts in their stories. They are children of Aphrodite and Hermes, using body and language to keep us alive, down to earth, not vaporized into our spirituality or into the practicalities of daily life. It may not seem a noble calling to be the scarecrow of society, but in fact we do honor our comedians, like George Burns who told story after story, year after year, with a cigar his only prop—a cigar is never only a cigar—confessing all the time, well into his nineties, to his love of sex; and Benny Hill, surrounded by women in bikinis, falling on his backside in scene after scene of Priapic romp; and Rosanne Barr taking up the ancient craft of Priapic comedy with intuitive faithfulness to its bawdy humanity.

When people laugh at farts and banana skin pratfalls, Hermes is always in the room, guiding us toward the underworld, toward our own death, by reminding us of our mortality and our earthiness, teaching us that to be fully alive we have to become closely acquainted with death in all its varieties of failure, embarrassment, and lack of control. At the same time, this affirmation of death is a celebration of life. As a source of meaning and vitality, Hermes is the god of writers and comics, of business leaders and politicians. His spirit fathers the Priapic life, and some versions of the myth claim Priapus fathered Hermes—sometimes there is more meaning in a good dirty joke than in a Sunday sermon. It's also significant that young children, usually much closer to the soul than their parents are, appreciate the Priapic and can laugh uproariously at the mere mention of a butt, pee, or poop.

Samuel Beckett favored physical comedy, and all of his writing shows a deep appreciation for Priapus. *Krapp's Last Tape* opens with Krapp standing still in profile with a banana sticking out of his mouth—a Priapic image that sets the stage for Krapp's review of his life on tape, where he finds that most of it was crap. In his early novel *Dream of Fair to Middling Women,* just recently published, Belacqua, the main character, makes a statement that echoes Priapus and the Marquis de Sade: "'The human bottom,' he proceeded, 'is extremely deserving of esteem, conferring as it does the faculty of assiduity. . . . The Greeks, I need hardly tell you, entertained a high notion of its beauty; and the celebrated poet Rousseau worships in the temple of Venus Callipyge.'" [4]

I assume that assiduity, persistent attentiveness, is mysteriously related to the body part affectionately known as the ass. This interesting little word comes from the Latin *asinus,* donkey, the animal that epitomizes stubbornness, thickheadedness, and dumbness, but it is also related to the word "arse," meaning ears, backside, or tail. Stupidity and the hind quarters share something in common, perhaps a decent distance from the brain and all of its overestimated capacities.

According to Ovid, when Priapus approached the sleeping virgin goddess Hestia with sexual intent, he was given away by the braying of an ass. The Egyptian god Seth was pictured in Hellenistic times with the head of an ass and was identified with the Greek Typhon, a figure of lustful excess and violent disorder. [5] When we call someone an ass we are evoking the spirit of Priapus, evoking his low, dim, and highly questionable intelligence. Everywhere we hear dumb sexual jokes and dumb sexual conversations and see dumb sexual magazines and movies—all celebrating the spirit and the contrary wisdom of the asinine Priapus.

The Priapic aspects of sex invite us to an odd kind of sensitivity. Priapus has nothing to do with Apollonic mental brilliance or affection, but that doesn't mean his way is not valid or doesn't possess an intelligence of its own. Priapic earthiness is as deeply human as maternal affection, and saves us from an excess of sentimentality. In that way, the Priapic may be full of soul and, for many, an effective way to fulfill their humanity.

Priapus keeps us honest. Exploring and explaining nature and human life so industriously, we become excessively mental in all areas of life, including sex. We are industrious about making sense of life intellectually, but in the process we lose heart, soul, and courage. Maybe these important values can only emerge from an earthier perspective, the kind we find in the odd figure of Priapus.

The North American trickster figure Coyote has certain Priapic qualities. As anthropologist William Bright has written, "Coyote . . . is an insatiable glutton, a gross lecher, an inveterate thief, liar, and outlaw, a prankster whose schemes regularly backfire."[6] Although Priapus is not a trickster, Coyote does share with him the questionable virtues of lechery and phallicism, and it's worth noting that to the people who tell Coyote's stories he is not a devil, not a figure of evil, but a reason for laughter and the object of an odd sort of reverence. The anthropologist notes that Pueblo people recognize that non-natives would judge Coyote moralistically, and so they find ways to keep him out of sight. In their own communities they know how to appreciate his humor and his sacred role in the nature of things.

Professor Bright tells a story of Coyote that might help us see some value in Priapic sexuality: Coyote is drinking water from the river when he falls in—the comic, accidental fall so typical of Priapic humor. He notices young women down-river on the shore and decides to transform himself into a piece of driftwood. Then he floats down the river. The women pick up the pretty little stick, and then realize it could be Coyote. They toss it back into the water, but it's too late, and soon they both find themselves pregnant.

The pretty little stick is not unlike the phallic erection found on garden statues of Priapus or on herms and posts dedicated to his father Hermes, erections convenient for hanging up hats and coats. It also echoes Priapus's claim to be essentially a block of wood.

In the driftwood story the image of Coyote, as Professor Bright notes, is unusually light and pleasant. It portrays the phallicism in nature and a getting pregnant that is not literal. This pregnancy is a fullness that comes from innocent curiosity. When we approach life with innocence—enter the river of life—we may well encounter its tricky, somewhat dangerous, and inseminating capacities. In the comically phallic Coyote we may find new life.

The trickster Coyote could give a fascinating sex education class that would turn our sexual values upside down. He would challenge our pieties about propriety, morality, and affection, purifying these necessary human values of their rigidity and inhumanity. He would show that they have an underside where their opposites also have a fertile role to play in life, as in another Coyote story that Professor Bright tells.

Old Coyote and Old Coyote Woman lived on one side of a hill, and Old Beaver and Old Beaver Woman lived on the other. Coyote suggested that he and Old Beaver go hunting and bring their rabbits to the other's wife. Old Beaver woman sang a song asking Coyote to come and make love with her. But Coyote didn't get a single rabbit. The next day Old Beaver went hunting and killed so many rabbits he could hardly carry them. He brought them to Coyote Woman and made love with her. She cried out, and Old Coyote said, "Old Beaver don't you hurt my wife." But she answered, "Shut up Old Man Coyote, I am crying out because I like it." When they had finished, Old Beaver Man said to Coyote, "We won't have bad feelings, you know this was your idea." So they all remained friends forever.

This story line is simple, but the traditional stories of Coyote play an important role in the spiritual education of Native Americans. They are not moralistic but consider the complexities, reversals, and subtle ethical demands that come up in ordinary human life. Often the tricky Coyote is bested in his own schemes, but life goes on. His humorous stories celebrate the beauty and vibrancy of life even in the face of misfortune, and they honor the role of failure and the breaking of ego in a life free of fussy seriousness.

The task is to capture Coyote's native honesty and his life-affirming spirit. The friendship between Old Coyote and Old Beaver is an important, saving element in the story, as is the pleasure-loving attitude of Old Coyote Woman.

Coyote is clever, but he doesn't have a big ego. As in the case of most clowns, his craftiness often backfires on him and, as in this outrageous story of wife swapping, he becomes the victim of the joke. The fact that they all remain friends at the end suggests that from the Coyote point of view there is no need to moralize sex but simply to allow life to take its course, to have its way with us and overcome our intelligence. In this respect, Priapic stupidity is a form of holy ignorance. The dumb, off-color joke and the cloud of unknowing may have something in common.

I would offer one caution about celebrating Priapic ignorance: as in the case of any soul figure or theme, it is one thing to let that theme flow through life and leave its mark; it's quite another to identify with a figure and embody it quite literally in your own person. I've known people over the years who literally and misanthropically lie, cheat, and grovel in the lower regions of sex, justifying their style consciously as Hermetic or Priapic or just living out the role without any reflection. Some people are just plain dumb, which is not at all the same as cultivating a Priapic stupidity full of heart and irony. The holy fool is not a plain fool; he is a subtle spirit that can enliven a person or a culture. When our foolishness is literal it is deadly, but when it is holy, it invites soul in to animate our lives.

Dionysus

Dionysus is another father suggested for Priapus, and the two were sometimes identified with each other, according to Walter Otto, who has written on Dionysus. The fig tree was sacred to both gods, a tree with both phallic and vaginal significance—wooden penises were made from the fig tree, and the fruit is commonly seen as an image of the female sexual anatomy. As Otto carefully phrases it: "The swollen fruits with their juicy blood-red pulp must always have conjured up thoughts of secret significance."[7] Otto also points out that the phallus was described as the friend of Dionysus, but that in vase paintings the god stands out in his dignity from the wild satyrs around him, who are extremely phallic and raucous figures. As in the case of Hermes, the father is grander and loftier than his son, the earthy Priapus.

Dionysus was the god made visible in the juicy grape that grows from the vine and in the sap that trickles out of trees. To taste the Dionysian spirit, we also have to live in such a way that our sap flows and the juicy fruit appears on our branches. Both sap and juice can ferment, making a concoction that dims our rationality and liberates our capacity for fantasy.[8] In the Dionysian spirit we live more from imagination than thought, or with thought steeped in imagination. Classicist Norman O. Brown, inspired by Freud, describes the Dionysian sensibility as rooted in a body intelligence. James Hillman, the Jungian analyst who founded archetypal psychology, would change that to an intelligence shaped by the soul's fantasies. The Dionysian style is more like the body than the mind—fluid, instinctual, and immediate. Our culture values being in control, knowing what we're doing, and being able to express what we're experiencing and feeling, while the Dionysian attitude has more abandon in it and more adaptability.

In their rituals the Greeks honored Dionysus by displaying large wood phalluses called wagging ones and by carrying baskets in their processions filled with small wood penises. These detached phallic ritual toys were treated as holy objects in the play of ritual.

Today people sometimes complain of pornography's focus on the sex organs as though they were objects unrelated to the person. Paradoxically, our culture, though dedicated to impersonal functionality in business and commerce, is offended by any hint of overt depersonalization in sex. Ancient religions often detach the phallus from the body, like the ritual lingam and yoni in India, and treat this separated part as a celebration of the organ and its rich religious symbolism and not as emotional castration. In these cases subtracting the person from the phallus or yoni doesn't lower but raises the value of the organ.

The Dionysian reality gives birth to and provides a context for the Priapic spirit. Dumb sexuality is not an essential part of the Dionysian sensibility, but it is closely related. If we wish to transcend the artificial rules and structures that we've strapped onto sexuality—anxiously defined gender roles and the like—then we may have to learn to celebrate sex rather than explain it and worry about keeping it emotionally healthy. We might also find ways to express our appreciation of the sexual body, instead of forcing it into secret clubs and confined neighborhoods and unpleasant shops.

As it is now, we separate propriety from the Dionysian. We see this division in our cities, where wild graffiti spoils our clean neighborhoods and public transportation. We see this split where rows of sex shops and theaters contribute to the decline of a neighborhood. We see it in our own behavior when our leaders in all areas of life, from politicians to ministers, preach sexual purity and practice promiscuity.

To reach life-giving, mind-shrinking Priapus, we have to come down off the pedestal of sexual aloofness and admit to the sexual sap that flows through us. Whatever forms such an affirmation might take would restore archaic ritual celebrations of life's exuberance epitomized in sex.

Euripides' play *Bacchae* opens with two old men, Tiresias and Cadmus, preparing for the Dionysian rituals by dressing in women's clothes. The Dionysian attitude does not stumble over gender. It appreciates all kinds of gender identifications and preferences, giving equal validity to all. It also seems to be quietly in the background of cross-dressing, an archaic ritual with serious meaning for society. We could all, men and women influenced by a society burdened with order and control, metaphorically put on the other gender's clothes and find a fresh, ecstatic way of life.

One of the most beautiful motifs in classical art is the maenad, the woman who follows Dionysus. She is shown with her head flung far back in a frenzy of abandon and loss of self. Whatever this head suggests of feeling and attitude depicts precisely what the Dionysian spirit is like. Whatever it takes to get our head in that posture is our way of entering the liberating Dionysian modality. As Emerson says in an inspired passage from his essay *The Poet* and in pure Dionysian fashion: "The poet knows that he speaks adequately then only when he speaks somewhat wildly, or 'with the flower of the mind'; . . . not with the intellect alone but with the intellect inebriated by nectar."[9] Our thinking has to loosen up and our rationality become less tense and rigid. Our thoughts could flow and be juicy instead of coming out in dry chunks and formal patterns.

This Dionysian surrender to life in its art and its unconsciousness fathers the Priapic life, mythology says. In Priapus, we are in the garden, our sexuality unusually exposed, the birds of our high-minded and lofty values chased out, protected and private, in a state of excitement and vitality. We are far from the reasoning mind and yet paradoxically closer to an important kind of knowing that in ordinary terms we think of as instinctual or bodily.

Our culture needs its maenadic exuberance, the use of our heads for abandonment to life rather than control of it. The flowing, saplike, Dionysian style of life intensifies the sense of drama, a key element in the historical Dionysian religion. Following Dionysus's lead we can allow ourselves to be many characters in the theater of our lives, taking both masculine and feminine roles, for the Dionysian is essentially either multigender or beyond gender. We can live ecstatically in the sense that we allow the ego to recede and the imagination to take the lead. We can give ourselves to the constant invitations of life and the intuitions and inclinations of the heart.

In a profound way, this is a sexual style of life, for we would live the way we make love, allowing the body to dictate our actions and offering our passions and desires a central role in all that we do. It is easy to make the Dionysian impulse into a mere reaction against the dry rationality and abstraction that is so prominent in our world. Then the Dionysian would indeed be literally orgiastic. But if it is treated as a quality of soul, it will not be merely literal and will add a necessary ingredient to our lives that could also be intelligent, proper, socially graceful, and ordered.

The Dionysian spirit affirms life and allows it to happen, even if we don't understand what is happening, and it is this abandon and trust that give rise to the strange saving grace of Priapus. Priapic imagery gives a sense that life is full and exciting. Where Priapus reigns, Dionysian happiness is a real possibility.

Adonis

A story much loved in ancient times tells of another figure associated with sap, Adonis, revered as the lover of Aphrodite. He was the son of Myrrha. She deceived her father, the king, and slept with him, and then when she discovered that she was pregnant, she prayed to become invisible and was turned into the tree that now bears her name. The myrrh tree emits a spicy sap, and Adonis was born from her like sap pouring from a tree. The child was so beautiful that Aphrodite hid him in a chest and gave it to Persephone, queen of the underworld, for safekeeping. When the boy grew into a handsome young man, the mistress of the underworld didn't want to give him up. Zeus declared that the boy was to spend a third of the year alone, a third with Persephone, and a third with Aphrodite.

Every year, it was said, he was gored by a boar while hunting, perhaps one incited by Persephone, and so he would go off each time to Persephone in her realm of death. Among the Greeks, courtesans customarily made terrarium gardens in ritual memory of him and in acknowledgment of Aphrodite's tears at his death. Kerényi observes: "In eastern shrines they gave themselves to strangers. Whoever did not do this must at least sacrifice her hair to Adonis."[10]

A classic puer, Adonis attracted both the goddess of love and the goddess of death by his beauty and sweetness. Since this sweet young sappy man was also reputed to be the father of Priapus, mythology here invites us to consider a connection between Priapus and youth. A student once told me that if she ever wanted sex with someone without any personal involvement, she would choose a young college man who could keep coming to life sexually and who could satisfy her at a purely physical level. This is one way to see the puer aspect of Priapic sex—the emphasis on the extraordinary, potent youthful penis seeking sexual satisfaction almost blindly—as well as the female side, the eternally youthful woman who seeks endless sexual pleasure without emotional attachment.

Narratives and rites associated with Adonis have strong sexual themes. The Greeks used myrrh as an aphrodisiac, and Adonis was seen as an image of wild sexual abandon. Recent studies of Adonis portray him as an adolescent sowing his wild oats, a lover of Aphrodite rather than the purer and more settled goddesses Artemis and Demeter. Like his gardens, which die quickly in the summer heat, he lasts only a short time, remaining immature and falling short of the full life of a husband and citizen.

But the story of Adonis has deeper implications as well. Life itself can be youthful and potent, offering the pleasure of its vitality, even when that pleasure is brief and passing. Adonis sexuality is not as serious as sex in marriage, but it has its place with the goddess who represents the joy of full sensual existence (Aphrodite) and the goddess who embodies the deep interior of the soul (Persephone). This kind of sexuality somehow spawns Priapus, child of Adonis, not such a responsible and serious figure himself.

People sometimes complain that sexual humor is adolescent and sophomoric, but the traditional stories about Priapus teach us that it's all right to be less than mature and serious in sex at times, to tell bad jokes, and to entertain irresponsible fantasies and desires. Medicine, education, psychology, and other professional spheres would like us all to be serious, loving, and responsible about sex, but Priapus offers some relief, scrawling a humorous and perhaps obscene truth on a bathroom wall. Recently in my travels I came upon a restaurant bathroom where patrons were provided with a blackboard and chalk in a convenient place. Here, I thought, is a restaurant manager with Priapic sensitivities.

Of course in a time of AIDS, rampant ill-timed pregnancies, and other deadly serious social problems associated with sex, we have to be responsible and thoughtful, but when the encouragement to responsible behavior turns moralistic and loses its shadow, then our cautions are not effective. We need both the adult voice of responsibility and the adolescent voice of the raging hormone if we are to find the soul of sex, which is ultimately the only thing that is going to keep us safe.

Mythology provides images of sex that go against our usual ideas of what is valuable and responsible, and in doing so it allows us to gain an appreciation of the more superficial level of existence personified by Adonis. To call it superficial is not to say that it is unimportant or that it lacks soul. Quite the opposite, we may sometimes find the soul more easily in those areas that are more earthy than sublime and more ordinary than remarkable.

Zeus

The fourth father suggested for Priapus is Zeus, the great leader of the gods and goddesses. When Zeus nods his head or laughs in agreement, it's as if to say "god wills it." If Zeus not only approves of but fathers Priapic sexuality, that affirms its clear necessity and value. The fact that Zeus is one of the fathers urges us to consider as deeply as possible the role of Priapus's sexual style in all of life, for Zeus rules everything and everybody. His domain is the all; as the ancient *Homeric Hymn to Zeus* says in his praise, "he is the best and greatest of gods, far-seeing."

If we are farsighted, we might see that sex in its plain earthiness, without any transcendent elaborations, can give any life a degree of soul, humanizing us and helping us meet each other in our most fundamental humanity. In most areas we strive to avoid mistakes, improve, become smarter, and transcend. Priapus is interested in none of these. Like Coyote, he is merely a piece of wood that some rustic whittled. Sometimes the search for soul amounts to a quest for the ordinary life—taking pleasure in daily tasks, good neighbors, children, satisfying work, and ordinary sex with someone you love. Interest in the extraordinary tends to be ambitious, self-seeking, overly energetic, and dehumanizing—an attitude full of spirit but not usually rich in soul.

Zeus's patronage implies necessity, which might be a good perspective on Priapus. In the nature of things, Priapus is not beautiful and seemly, but he is necessary. His kind of sex plays a role in society and in the life of the individual, even if he lacks nobility. In fact he is usually more embarrassing than meaningful. Yet precisely because he can't easily be placed among the noble things of life, he enjoys a mysterious, creative presence, and there is in his nature even a hint of the sublime.

Priapus and the Soulful Relationship

For individuals and couples this odd Priapic philosophy gets translated into sexual playfulness, joking, and a certain trust that lovemaking can keep a marriage or a relationship soulful. Having good sex doesn't mean that a relationship is deep and stable, but we might do well to trust the attitude of Priapus as much as experts who pride themselves on their enlightenment and intelligence. From the Priapic point of view it may be fine to be sexually inept and fumbling, as long as we remain earthy, willing to be foolish, and of good humor.

The typical modern couple wants to do things right: communicate well with each other, pursue their own interests and vocations, raise children in a way that will not make them neurotic, and enter therapy at the first sign of confusion. But it is also helpful for couples to laugh at themselves, to enjoy simple and sometimes meaningless pleasures, to be simple and even dumb at times, to play, and to enjoy their children's natural and uncynical scatological humor and unsocialized ways of talking about sex.

If Priapus offends you, as he offends me and most people, then you may be sensing the edge of your capacity for life. People talk lightly and eagerly about personal growth, but the expansion of soul entails a stretching of sensibilities that may be painful and disturbing. Under the aegis of Priapus, personal growth has no sentimentality, and it may be focused on enlarging life at the bottom, not at the top.

Imagine growing by becoming less certain and less informed, getting in touch with your ignorance and foolishness rather than your intelligence, and learning to allow sensation to dim rationality. Imagine personal growth as a matter of becoming more humorous and more earthy, and emotional health as being in touch with the body and given to pleasure.

Professor Lopez-Pedraza says that Priapus gives a mythological context for the freakishness that is part of everyone's personality and all cultural life. With our preference for Apollonic virtues of adjustment, prudence, moderation, and hygiene and without an appreciation for what Priapus represents, we lose a significant dimension of our humanity.

An adequate cure for this loss of humanity comes from an unlikely place: from our own creative, unique, and livable embrace of Priapus, perhaps in the form of rediscovering the ordinary concrete life, living without excessive intelligence and information, succumbing dumbly to the demands of body and soul, and deepening our connections with others through instinctive play and good humor.

CHAPTER 7

The Mystic's Orgasm

Eros in the Spiritual Life

ONE SPRING day when I was in Rome, a friend took me to an old church, Santa Maria della Vittoria, and led me past the sacristy and through several doors until we arrived at a Bernini sculpture of St. Theresa. We stood and contemplated this famous sculpture for several minutes, noticing, like many others, that her mystical swoon is hardly distinguishable from orgasmic rapture. In his intriguing book *The Evolution of Allure*, George L. Hersey makes some pointed comments on this sculpture, taking note of the angel about to thrust the arrow of Christ's love into her breast, which he is just uncovering. The angel's clothing is coming undone and St. Theresa is in a passionate state. Hersey quotes William James, who said of the saint, "Her idea of religion seems to have been that of an endless amatory flirtation—if one may say so without irreverence—between the devotee and the deity."[1]

Just as Priapus gives image to the valuable lower regions of sexuality, mystical literature from around the world describes the human encounter with the divine in sexual terms. This sometimes surprising imagery says something about the passion involved in religious ecstasy, but it also points to how the highest levels of spirituality are made accessible through sex.

Christianity is filled with metaphors of sex used to describe the relationship between ourselves and God, or, to put it more broadly, between ourselves and the mystery that is the context of our lives. The *Song of Songs* from the Old Testament is just one source where the divine-human relationship is pictured in graphic erotic imagery:

Bernini,
St. Theresa in Ecstacy

Let him kiss me with the kisses of his mouth!
  For your love is better than wine,
Your anointing oils are fragrant,
  Your name is perfume poured out.[2]

The Sufi mystical poet Rabi'a writes: "Each lover is alone with his love. Here, I am alone with you."[3]

The sculpture of St. Theresa points to the ultimate fulfillment to be found in a certain kind of exalted intercourse between the human and the divine. The mystical possibilities of sex flow from a similar surrender sex asks of us: surrender to passion, to another person, and to the life mysteries that sex often ushers in.

It's common to point out the sexual nature of being forceful in a penetrating way, but we don't hear much about the sexuality of being open and receptive. Perhaps our deeply ingrained sexism has blinded our culture to the eroticism in vulnerability. The arrow about to penetrate St. Theresa certainly looks like a phallic image, and "weapon" is an old slang term for the penis, while her rolled eyes and open chest unmistakably portray some kind of orgasm. She is about to be struck by the penetrating shaft of divine potency, and she takes the appropriate attitude of utter openness, in the process becoming God's lover and a saint.

To be sexual is to be open to many kinds of penetration—love, intimacy, influence, teaching, example. We love—and sometimes fall in love with—our teachers, experts, doctors, nurses, and therapists. Our openness to their professional attentions carries over to their persons. We make ourselves vulnerable and perhaps overlook the sexual implications of that vulnerability, finding ourselves shocked at the nature of our response to someone in the helping professions. One look at the posture and expression of St. Theresa should quickly educate us to the sexuality implicit in the purest forms of openness.

There is a shadow side to mystical vulnerability, of course. As with anything, we can substitute an inadequate object for our openness. Vulnerability can be symptomatic, neurotic, and literally wounding. I have worked with many men and women in therapy who seem excessively and painfully open to the influence of others. Theresa's arrows might alert us to the actual injuries that desire can cause, and make us less naive about being vulnerable. At the same time a more profound openness to life's invitations may be the remedy. Like cures like: a deeper and different kind of openness might heal our habits of being too vulnerable to inappropriate and inadequate objects of devotion.

In India the relationship between the devotee and the god is represented as a sexual one, and in other religions as well, including Christianity, union with the divine finds expression in sexual imagery. In the *Cakrasamvara-tantra*, a sacred Indian text, the god says:

> My female messengers are everywhere;
> They bestow all the spiritual attainments
> By gazing, touching, kissing, and embracing.[4]

We have been led to imagine sex as purely physical and therefore beneath our higher aspirations, but the Tantric sacred texts, Sufi poetry, and Christian mystical writings convey a religious insight that sex is also implicated in our purest spiritual efforts. Gazing, touching, kissing, and embracing all have a place in the spiritual life, where they mean something different from human love and yet are continuous with it.

During my childhood and adolescent years in Catholic

schools I was told regularly to keep sexual images out of mind. I was warned obsessively about the dangers of impure thoughts, and I concluded that if I had to confess them to a priest each time they appeared, I'd have to live within easy walking distance of a confessional. I was made to feel guilty about these images and was never taught that they might have a positive place in my imagination. They were evil, pure and simple.

I can see value in the spiritual warning against being consumed with sex. It can be overpowering. Sexual compulsion is at work everywhere around us. But setting limits on one's preoccupation with sex doesn't have to be accomplished by repression or psychological defense. A sensitive and artful ego could find limits without becoming generally anti-erotic or suspicious of sex.

Our sexual lives have much to gain from a relaxing of both the compulsion and the excesses. I think this is what C. G. Jung had in mind in the inspired passage from a letter he wrote Freud in 1910, where he envisioned a renewed Christianity with a positive relation to eros, which would be able

> ever so gently to transform Christ back into the soothsaying god of the vine, which he was, and in this way absorb those ecstatic instinctual forces of Christianity for the *one* purpose of making the cult and the sacred myth what they once were—a drunken feast of joy where man regained the ethos and holiness of an animal.[5]

When we divide sex from holiness we may feel that sex is separated from our high spiritual aspirations and even from our intelligence. At the same time religion becomes a sexless mental exercise in dry understanding and the splitting of theological hairs, instead of a passionate engagement with the mysteries that surround every aspect of life. If religion were to restore its lost capacity for ecstasy and not separate itself so far from sex and the passionate life, we might enjoy the spirituality in the most charming and physical aspects of sex, including the erotic gaze, touch, kiss, and embrace, and both religion and our sex lives would benefit.

For this reason I place special emphasis on Bernini's artistic interpretation of St. Theresa, on Sufi erotic mystical poetry, and on Tantric teachings and imagery. Although we don't understand the full mystery of these profound amalgams of sex and spirit, we can still be inspired by them to find our own ways toward erotic ecstasy in religion and genuine piety in sexuality. Without an awareness of the religious base of sex and the erotic nature of religion, our sexuality must necessarily remain inhumane and incomplete, because, as paradoxical as it may appear, a religious sensibility is the absolute foundation for a humane and humanitarian life.

It's often assumed that men and women allow sex to be the brightest shining light in their universe, at least at periods in their lives, simply because they crave certain physical sensations. People talk about wanting novelty in sex as though a new partner or a new position is satisfying only at a purely physical level. But what if we granted ourselves an added level of humanity, and sex a new degree of meaningfulness? What if what we're searching for and to some degree finding in sex is not purely physical? What if it transcends psychology as well, so that not even interpersonal relationship or human love would adequately explain the intensity of our desire and the importance of these passions in our lives?

Religion is one of the human passions and the bedroom a room of mysteries. It's a place where we change clothes—an ordinary daily ritual that is full of fantasy and thought. There we sleep and dream, and there the soul comes out of hiding and into awareness. There we ritually realize the erotic sensations that shimmer through our limbs during the day and keep the imagination focused on desire. Deep, sacred sentiments and actions permeate our ordinary lives, and sex is no exception, as it serves the soul and points us upward toward a transcendent goal.

In sex an inner life of strong emotions and vivid fantasies meets with a real person to create a moment of exceptional intensity when life is full and reason is dim. It is a time when play is paramount and yet when nothing could have more serious implications. Even when sex is not ecstatic or perfect, it takes us to a level far from the mundane. Gaze and touch induce a kind of trance, an altered state of consciousness, a realm of imaginal sensations and events, a separate reality.

The soul craves such excursions from literal reality, and so it is no mystery that sex is so compelling and enticing. But it is the soul, and not some inanimate body, that feels the hunger and can't resist the appetite. An altered state like sexual trance is not empty. Much goes on during this excursion away from daily living, though this special activity accomplishes things in the soul that may be quite different from what we aim for in ordinary life. In sex we may subliminally discover many truths about our partner, ourselves, our relationship, passion, and life itself.

Hints of the Sacred in Sexual Language

Sex serves the spiritual life by taking us away from the purely temporal plane for a momentary taste of eternity. To catch a glimpse of the eternal within ordinary sex, we can look closely at our sexual vocabulary to find hints about the role of the spiritual in sex. When we arrive at a point where the depth, indeed the religious and spiritual dimensions of any activity, have been lost, we can sometimes pick up traces of ancient religion in the history of our secular words.

The *American Heritage Dictionary*, for example, defines orgasm as "the highest point of sexual excitement, characterized by strong feelings of pleasure and marked normally by ejaculation." Here we have the small suggestion that sex takes us high. It is a peak experience that points us in the direction of the spirit. In this definition, I would avoid the word "normal" and substitute "usual." Usually orgasm involves ejaculation, at least in the male, but not normally, as though it might be abnormal not to ejaculate.

Although the definition is almost entirely physical and materialistic, we could take the words "excitement" and "feelings of pleasure" as expressions of soul states and then amend the definition further. Orgasm would be the feeling of transcendence that comes over a person in sex when pleasure is intense and the body accordingly convulses in delight, and this sense of reaching out beyond ourselves may feel like a moment of spiritual bliss.

The *Oxford English Dictionary* defines orgasm in cool terms as "the height of venereal excitement in coition." Here we get two interesting words—venereal and coition. Venereal is the adjective form of Venus. Unintentionally, the dictionary leads us to imagine orgasm within the scope of Venus, as a feminine experience, divine and not merely human, mythological as well as physical. We can consider the spirituality of Venus and imagine orgasm within that religious framework, not forgetting that the worship of Venus was genuine religion.

Coitus is also a curious word in the sexual vocabulary. The

Merriam-Webster Collegiate Dictionary defines it as "the natural conveying of semen to the female reproductive tract," giving the impression that the word refers to the act of the penis "having gone into"—*co-itus*—the vagina. But the word was used in the sixteenth century for any kind of union, even a simple conversation.[6] Besides, most people would probably not think of intercourse first as the depositing of semen, but rather as the pleasure of bodies joining together, and maybe even as the union of souls in that coupling.

One thing is clear: we are in need of a dictionary not entirely dedicated to the materialism and secularism that dominates the culture. One could even imagine a soul dictionary redefining all of our words with attention to their sacred core and their rich fantasies throughout history.

Getting back to "orgasm," the word comes from the Greek *orgas,* which has the following fruitful meanings that I take from the Liddell-Scott *Greek-English Lexicon:* a well-watered, fertile spot of land; a rich tract of land sacred to the gods and goddesses, particularly Demeter and Persephone; growing ripe; swelling with lust and being in heat; and being eager, ready, and excited. For the ancient Greeks the noun *orgeon* referred to a member of a religious association or even a priest.[7]

The rich history of this word invites us to imagine orgasm as a swelling of the body and the emotions, and also as a moist peaking of excitement. Renaissance medical books described Venus as the goddess of the moist aspects of life, indicating that her spirituality is close to life, to the body, and to the spirits of nature.[8] Most people, I think, would describe sex as emotionally juicy rather than dry. To have an orgasm is to reach a high point in spiritual experience, but it is not a dry peak. The history of the word suggests a natural ripening of fruit rather than a fiery flash or mental brilliance—a crucial difference, because the body and the emotions are not divided then from our experiences of transcendence.

This image of saplike swelling applies to sex. Its spirituality is organic, close to the ways of nature, and not separate from the ordinary and the natural. The name Venus comes from a word for desire and sex,[9] so the spiritual sense of the word appeared out of its ordinary meaning. Venus rose from sexual intercourse like the spirit of sex rising from our familiar experiences of sexual fantasy and lovemaking, just as Venus is sometimes portrayed emerging from the sea.

In art Venus herself is sometimes pictured with an apple or some other fruit, not only because the fruit may look like the sex organs but because sex itself is intimately connected to nature's bounty. Demeter and Persephone are mother and daughter, the spirit of earth's abundance and goddess of life's underworld, patroness of daily life and presider over the mysteries of the soul. Orgasm elicits both of these mysteries—physical joy and the soul's pleasure.

The Greek dictionary also describes orgasm as a sacred place, the *temenos* of Demeter or Persephone. Orgasm carries us to a place that is not in the human realm, a place apart, where religious ceremonies are held. Literature talks about mystical rapture and sexual rapture as though the two had much in common, and rapture, of course, means to be taken.

Today we usually imagine sex from the point of view of Demeter, whose realm is one of actual bodies, their nourishment, and their good condition. The many books that give instructions on how to be emotionally and physically healthy in sex express this Demeter myth. Some authors and scholars try to expand our notion of sex by talking explicitly about "the goddess" in Demeter terms. We have yet to see an equal interest in Persephone, the soul of sex, the underworld of fantasy, deep feeling, and religiosity that has a great role to play in sex. Reliving her myth, we experience sex as a rapturous and ecstatic seizure of consciousness. In her religion we are stunned by an underworld mysticism, full of physical and emotional sensation, an enriching but overwhelming loss of self and recovery of soul.

If we were to give Persephone a place in sex we might also find a way to appreciate the depressive side, the melancholy that may accompany a sexual relationship or appear unexpectedly during or just after making love. *Post coitum omne animal triste est,* goes an old saying—after sex every animal is sad. As queen of the dead and the underworld, Persephone also allows us to consider the deepest and darkest feelings and thoughts that come to mind around sex.

I've worked in therapy with several people who complained that while having sex with the person they loved madly, they would suddenly be flooded with fantasies of former lovers of their partner. While these fantasies were quite clearly connected to general feelings of jealousy that plagued them, I felt the fantasies were not just pathological but served an important purpose. I saw these jealous images as coming from Persephone, from the misty and often negative world of the soul's hinter regions, where soul work takes place in ways that on the surface do not look healthy. Sometimes they deepen a person's thoughts about sex, transforming innocence and in a constructive way making the appreciation of sex more complex.

Persephone, queen of the lower world, deepens the awareness and emotions of those she haunts. We might also remember that Persephone's downward path is a form of mysticism, for the spiritual life can be profound as well as transcendent, and sex in particular is an effective way to find the mystical depths as well as the mystical heights.

Spirituality in the World

To appreciate the soul of sex, we may have to accomplish several things rather foreign to our current tastes and values. First, we have to learn how to enter the realm of the senses with abandon and trust, giving up our need to understand as we go down into sensation. Second, we have to discover the nature, workings, and validity of mystical experience, an equally difficult task in a culture that believes only in the existence of that which it can measure and prove. Third, and perhaps most difficult of all, we have to appreciate that these two tasks are inseparable, two sides of a coin, each a prerequisite for the other. Spirituality and sensation not only are not enemies, they feed each other. Sensation can be an effective way out of ego, and therefore it serves spiritual goals.

There are many ways to deepen our appreciation for the sensual and mystical elements in sex. Sex has several archetypal roots, fundamentally different ways it can be experienced and interpreted. As Hillman remarks in his theory of psychological polytheism, "Each god loves according to his fashion."[10] This observation could also be reversed: every love and lovemaking has its own god or goddess. We have already considered several mythical figures who shed light on sexuality. We could explore further the Dionysian, Pan-like, Jesus-style, Saturnine, Sapphic, Priapic, Artemisian, Adamic, Coyote, Druidic, Celtic, Shakti, and Venusian experiences of sex. Beyond classical mythologies, we could look to fiction and discover Lady Chatterley sex, Madame Bovary sex, Leopold Bloom sex, and on and on. A clever person might even describe Bach sex, Mozart sex, Stravinsky sex, and Grateful Dead sex, using music as a way to distinguish the archetypes.

In recent years many have written about the goddesses of

the Greeks, and especially about Aphrodite, as an image for women, but I would like to take a slightly different approach and consider the possibilities of a spiritual life for men and women that is shaped according to qualities traditionally associated with Venus. This is not quite the same as finding the goddess within you or simply making an archetypal or mythological description of her. My emphasis here is on the spiritual life filled out and colored by the reality that the Greeks and Romans evoked in their prayers, songs, stories, and rituals.

Spirituality is both immanent, meaning not separate from everyday life and the natural and fabricated world, and transcendent, moving ever farther away from ordinary experience toward the perimeters of our individual lives. In the name of spirituality people meditate, pray, read, travel, search out teachers of vast vision and learning, and dedicate themselves to idealistic values. In the sophisticated spiritual life, immanence and transcendence are never separated; one finds holiness both within oneself and at the very edge of one's world.

Most people today think of spirituality in an ethereal sense. When they meditate, they want to remove themselves as far as possible from the body and the material world. They hope to transcend the limitations of time and space, knowing all about life and death, the heretofore and the hereafter. They would like a perfect value system, and they imagine a perfected world. Without the guidance of a sophisticated tradition, spirituality can become ambitious and can sever a person from his community and environment.

Marsilio Ficino was a highly spiritual man, a priest and a philosopher. As he accomplished in his life what few have dared—a reconciliation of paganism and Christianity—Ficino cultivated a spirituality that is integrally engaged with life and yet at the same time transcendent. The blend can be glimpsed in Edgar Wind's following summary of Ficino's attitude: "For Ficino the world was 'full' of a god who transcends it: *Iovis omnia plena* [all things filled with Jupiter]. He therefore worshipped God simultaneously both beyond and within the creation."[11]

Venus Spirituality

Ficino spells out different varieties of spirituality, and he uses traditional astrology as his chief means of sorting them out. Within his astrological scheme, Venus plays an important role as the source of a particular kind of spirit, and he links her spirit to that of Jupiter and the Sun, calling these the Three Graces, a trio we could loosely identify as God, nature, and sex. He makes the interesting remark that for studious people in particular, while Jupiter and the Sun are of great value, they need Venus to keep from drying out.[12]

I would apply Ficino's observation to our own situation as we try to establish a vital spiritual life in a secular age. We look around us and see a materialistic world. We conclude that the spiritual life must be something apart and completely different and unrelated. We slip into a dark, quiet church to get away from the noise and bustle of the city. We sit and meditate at a lonely spot remote from human commerce. We read books, attend lectures, and go to church to cultivate an otherworldly spirituality. Many people long for out-of-body experiences, a goal that would not be of much use to Venus.

Our spirituality can become dry as we look for it in teachers, gurus, and books and move away from the daily life of business, work, play, family, home, and nature. For us, it may seem absurd to look for spiritual rewards at the workplace, but for Ficino, every aspect of life has its own kind of spirituality. His high regard for Venus and her humanizing work in the soul suggests that sex, her main concern, also has an important part to play in the spiritual life.

We have seen that sex takes us to a special place of feeling and imagination that is at once ordinary and extraordinary, deep in the body and yet at the same time transcendent. This overlapping area is sometimes called liminal, on the threshold, and religious experiences are sometimes described in contemporary religion studies for their liminality. These threshold experiences, described vividly in the books of Carlos Castaneda, are moments of exceptional value to the soul and the spiritual life. In them, both time and space are rendered extraordinarily sensitive to spiritual influence.

Victor Turner, an influential anthropologist of religion, developed this notion of liminality as a way of gaining insight into ritual and other aspects of religion.[13] For example, Turner describes rituals in certain communities where conventions, rules, and roles are temporarily disregarded. The liminal person, say someone undergoing a rite of passage, is betwixt and between, unusually open to influence and change. Therefore, as Turner says, liminality is "frequently likened to death, to being in the womb, to invisibility, to darkness, to bisexuality, to the wilderness, and to an eclipse of the sun or moon."[14] Alcohol and other drugs take us away to a liminal place, as do amusement rides, the theater, and movies.

In ancient literature, we find that experiences like these are particularly nurturing to the soul, implying that the soul's activity is primarily, if not always, liminal. We might see sex as a liminal ritual, giving us the opportunity to escape from what we usually call reality to a place that is neither ordinary nor completely extraordinary, where we are most ourselves and yet out of ourselves.

Oils and perfumes, privacy, music, special dress—all of these accoutrements of sex help evoke the sense of liminality or threshold. What happens in this liminal slice of consciousness speaks directly to the soul and only indirectly, if at all, to ordinary life. There we speak in ways we might never think of in ordinary hours, and we do things entirely appropriate to that place and yet unthinkable in other contexts. Sex establishes a domain that has its own language and customs, as well as its own purposes that may be focused on the relationship, oneself, or the spiritual life.

Drawing out the inherent spirituality in sex may involve surrendering to a full emotional as well as physical orgasm. It might mean being extraordinarily generous in lovemaking or allowing the sexual relationship to pour out into the rest of life in a spirit of love, pleasure, and intimacy. Negative attitudes toward sex can subtly interfere with liminality, because this special level of sensitivity requires a high degree of openness.

The quality of our sexual experiences may depend on the ability to find the elusive but available middle place that is fully physical and fully spiritual, given over to passion and yet meaningful and expressive. Our sex may be too mechanical or even excessively sweet. Good sex requires that we leave ordinary reality behind by entering as deeply as possible into sensation, imagination, and passion.

In his unique study of Aphrodite, Paul Friedrich, influenced by Turner's work, describes Aphrodite or Venus explicitly as a liminal goddess.[15] He points out that unlike the many Greek deities who keep their sexual distance from mortals, Aphrodite could be the lover of any god or mortal. He concludes, "By seducing mortals and providing a transcendent image of such seduction she mediates between the human and the divine in a way that gives man exceptional intimations of the immortality he can never attain."

Here we have another hint about the spiritual nature of sex—it can give us intimations of immortality. Sex takes us out of ourselves and stops time. The degree of intimacy involved is unimaginable when compared to our usual social etiquette, as sex takes relationship to a level not even approached in social interaction. It's no wonder that sex has been employed in religious ritual for millennia, since it provides an obvious, powerful metaphor for relationship with the divine.

Sex with a human lover points to and participates in a deeper kind of intimacy, a more than human connection to the ground of being. In the Renaissance Neoplatonic view ordinary life is the starting point in a journey to the highest possible levels of mysticism. This easily applies to sex, in which our liminal partner is a go-between whose openness to passion transforms him or her into an angel of sorts, a representative of the spiritual order. Through our partner we glimpse something that human creativity can't manufacture.

As we enter sex, the circle begins in deep sensuality, the deeper the better, and then opens up to the peculiar emptiness and self-forgetfulness of erotic passion. We lose ourselves in the oblivion of sex and find our soul in the spiritual place that is accessible through openhearted passion. This is Venusian spirituality, a transcendence of self achieved through intense, pleasurable union. At the same time, as is usually the case in religion, mystical transport leads us back into deep involvement in life and community.

Sexual Spirituality

We can address the issue of sex and spirituality from two directions: we can look for sexual ways to be spiritual and for
spiritual ways to be sexual. The first step, and the minimum,
is to avoid dividing body and spirit, and the best way to accomplish that goal is not to even think in these dualistic
terms. Not only sex, but everything we do, every object,
every event, no matter how secular it may appear, has spiritual significance. If we live by this non-dualistic philosophy,
then sex will naturally remain tied to spirituality, but if we divide body and spirit in any part of life, we may expect problems with sex.

There are many valid ways to be sexual, and it would be
simplistic to suggest that only when people share deep love
and affection is their sex meaningful. Still, love and affection
offer an obvious and direct means of assuring a spiritual dimension in sex. Love and intimacy are not ordinary human
achievements; they are both extraordinary, especially in a
world where it appears difficult for couples to find and sustain a deep relationship. Today, because of our prejudice in
favor of the mind, we may think of spirituality as an intellectual activity centered on belief and the pursuit of knowledge
and skills, or even vision and values, but the religious literature of the world suggests overwhelmingly that spirituality is
primarily an act of love.

Thomas Merton emphasizes the "law of love" and observes that "married love can be a fulfillment of this profound love, a spiritual act of obedience to God in freedom
and in joy."[16] It takes courage or madness to leap into a marriage and to set severe limits on our life with a lifelong vow,
and yet this commitment to marriage and to a particular way
of being sexual draws on our deepest emotions, demands

unimagined trust, and pulls our entire life into a certain web of meaning and style, to the point that everything in our past, present, and future is affected, and all in the name of love. How much more profound and transcendent is this gift of love compared to a much less expensive outlay of intellectual attachment to what we perceive as truth.

The opening of the heart in personal affection plays an important role in the development of a spiritual life. I have been in monasteries and other spiritual communities where people are obviously full of virtue and good intentions and where they live their celibacy with honesty and joy, and I have been acquainted with other spiritual communities where sexual experimentation is the norm, where sex is everywhere and affection difficult to come by.

Our capacity to be sensuous and affectionate might be the key to resolving tensions between the spiritual life and sexuality. The highly spiritual person will have to realize at some point that you do not become spiritual by suppressing sex but by transforming its expression. Around the world monasteries are known as the keepers of culture and resources of beauty in architecture, writing, painting, sculpture, and books. In all these products we sense the presence of Venus and witness her role in sustaining and applying the spiritual achievements of meditation, prayer, and the common life. Monasteries are also known as places of gracious hospitality, yet another sublimation or alternate expression of sexual passion.

In the monastic example we can look at the incredibly beautiful and rich illuminated manuscripts, the extraordinary architecture, and even the fine wines and breads as the spirit of Venus, powdered and tinctured into these sublimated forms without loss of joy or pleasure.

How do we make our spirituality sexual? By being persons

of deep affection and with all the possible individual variations on the expression of that affection. Like the monk in his or her monastery, we can find ways to make our affection visible and felt. We can be affectionate toward our friends and neighbors and in such simple ways sexualize the neighborhood. We can be outrageously affectionate toward our lovers and spouses and thus give the world the model it needs for living from the heart. We can nurture our affection for animals, things, and places. All of this affection brings into human community a vision, a point of view, and a philosophy discovered in our most sublime meditations and readings. It is the anima soul to the animus intellect, the heart-spouse to the mind-lover, the visible body to the hidden spirit. It is all liminal life, completely sexual because of its affirmation of Venusian values.

The natural release of affection is the beginning of sex and, as affection's origins are sublimely spiritual, sex can flow directly out of our spirituality by way of love. The task is to recognize that the spiritual life is rooted in love, not merely in understanding, and then to cultivate affection and sensuality as part of our spiritual practice. Spiritual literature sometimes gives the impression that love is important but rather abstract, perhaps too universal to be felt. But Neoplatonic philosophy suggests that spiritual love is inseparable from human love with all its affection and sexuality.

Affection is the process of making love sensual, and so it may lead directly toward sex, giving sex the soul it needs so as not to become aggressive, manipulative, and empty. "Affection" comes from two basic Latin words *ad*, to, and *facere*, to do, and so it means *to do to*. When affection is lost, we are indeed done to, but when it is present we *do to*, bringing our lives and hearts to bear on our neighbors and our world, offering a spirituality of the heart, not only of the mind, to a culture starving for heartfelt attention. Affection is a doing kind of love, not a thinking one.

People involved in spiritual activities often become judgmental and intolerant, perhaps because the higher one goes in the spiritual life, the more removed one becomes from ordinary human foibles and struggles. The spiritual vision may be so pure, clean, and clear that the human condition may appear paltry. Therefore it makes sense in the spiritual life to give special attention to the graces of Venus, to marry our lofty spirituality with the grounding affections that are never far removed from our sexuality. In this way we avoid the dangerous condition in which sex is severed from our lives by our intense absorption in the spirit. In the best of worlds a robust spiritual life provides the catalyst for transforming our sexuality into a life of beauty and community.

The Spiritual Body

Affection is one effective way to resolve the dualism of body and spirit. Another is to use the body itself to attain a transcendence of ego in a Venusian kind of yoga or spiritual practice. The beauty of the world and the physical beauty of a loved one can lead us to spiritual heights. All we have to do is use our bodies and our senses in a spiritual practice that is sensitive to Venus's values, especially her beauty, pleasure, and sensation.

I have had several occasions in my life to stand in the presence of a Venus—Botticelli's *La Primavera* in the Uffizi Gallery, the Lucas Cranach Venus in Ottawa, the Capitoline Venus—and to meditate on her mysteries. In Rome, I stood alone in a musty hall a few inches from the famous Venus and felt her holiness and sensuality blend so fully that I couldn't separate my feelings of religious awe from the erotic presence of her body.

Standing before the beautiful Roman presentation of the goddess I became aware of the complete interweaving of body and spirit and the ancient and holy reconciliation of mysticism and sensuality. The healing of these divisions in modern life would go far to resolve many of our social and political problems, because the body and its beauty keep us humble and humane.

Without sensuality our religion becomes dry and aggressive. Without deep spirituality our materialism grows hollow, unsatisfying, and compulsive. Religion and materialism find resolution and fulfillment in the soul of sex, at that crossroads where we discover that these two potent forces are not antagonists at all, although they captivate us and often make us lose our reason. They head toward the same goal and can be joined in common purpose. When spirituality and sexuality come together, like yin and yang, like husband and wife, we discover our lost security. We find the vertical life, the electric axis on which deep sensation runs into lofty spirit, the essential complement to our horizontal pragmatic lives and the source of deep satisfaction and spiritual comfort.

CHAPTER 8

Eros and Morality

Sexual Ethics and Emotional Freedom

Oscar Wilde once said that the best way to make children good is to make them happy. Usually we think of goodness and morality in sterner terms as alternatives to happiness and pleasure. Morality often appears as a chain around sexual delight. The problem may be that we are accustomed to imagining morality from a purely spiritual point of view as a way of limiting rather than enhancing sexuality. If we were to think of the soul of morality instead, we might see morality as contributing to life's pleasure and thus providing a positive element in a fulfilling sexual life.

As a society, we have made remarkable progress in technology and in many other areas, but unfortunately our moral education remains seriously undeveloped. We still express our moral opinions with raw passion, belligerence, bias, and almost complete lack of compassion. In our many moral positions we are divided and pitted against each other.

We speak hypocritically and judgmentally about our fellow citizens who have been caught in their own moral confusion, and we are quick to punish and imprison. In the spirit of the times we are harsh about crime, and we don't believe any indiscretion merits privacy.

In this highly uncompassionate milieu, it isn't easy to be morally comfortable with sex. Moral reactions around us are full of anxiety, and as individuals we pick up on that tension. We tend to think negatively about morality, seeing it in direct conflict with our deep, perhaps unspoken desires. Especially in the area of sex, which is insistently and mysteriously linked with morality, we may bounce back and forth between strong desire and strong inhibition, unable to find a middle place where passion and virtue can join in a relaxed and creative way. In the midst of this moral anxiety and confusion, it is difficult to find sexual joy.

Morality is not just an instrument of inhibition and not just a means of control. It has a creative role to play in the complex workings of the psyche, and at its best it makes a positive contribution to sexual pleasure. Our sex lives would improve if we could come to peace with long-lasting guilt, establish an ethical way of life that we can live with, and enter a continuing process of moral deepening. We can give our morality the same degree of sophistication we enjoy in other aspects of our lives.

The Psychology of Sexual Morality

Over the years of practicing therapy, I came to recognize a special kind of sadness in some of the people I worked with. They felt subdued by what could be called moral depression, a constriction of the spirit. They lived with a sensation of heaviness and had difficulty finding joy in life due to a deep-seated habit of forbidding themselves certain pleasures and satisfactions. Often these people just couldn't find the sexual comfort and delight they craved.

We have seen that eros may take many forms and that it is a spirit, a moving and inspiring influence, that, tradition says, feeds the soul. The portrayals of eros in sacred art as a young man with wings show its spirited nature, its ability to lift the heart, and its capacity to animate and quicken. As James Hillman has written so beautifully in his book *The Myth of Analysis,* wherever eros stirs, the soul comes to life. Unfortunately the converse is true as well: whenever we put a lid on eros, the soul feels deprived of breath and life.

One particularly poignant case of moral depression comes to mind. A man in his mid-thirties complained that he couldn't get his life on track. He was an exceptionally creative man, sensitive and friendly. He had established his own business related to the arts, but he always felt overworked and on the edge of financial disaster. When I met him, he was living with a depressed woman who, it seemed to me, wanted to have full control over his life. They had been together for several years, but they had never had a happy sex life. By the time I saw him, he had given up any hope of sexual satisfaction and was concentrating on keeping his business solvent.

He told me his life story many times. His father was a minister, an Arthur Dimmesdale character who had a secret in his past. The son thought it had to do with a sexual indiscretion with a member of a former congregation. The family never discussed the incident, but his father talked as though sex didn't exist, and he seemed to live in a cloud of shame. The young man's mother gave all her energy to protecting her husband and she, too, refused to talk to her son about the great guilt they carried in their marriage.

The guilt this mother and father held close to their hearts

translated into a stern, passionless moralism and into children who stumbled along in life, failing at their work and their intimacies, not knowing the nature of the obstacle to their happiness or to their sexual tranquillity. The young man I saw week after week was suffering under a self-imposed family curse. He was rebelling against his father especially, and yet his entire life seemed tied to his parents' conflict, which was a tight bundle of moral and psychological anxieties smothered in a fog of guilt. The son I knew broke all the sexual rules his father had laid down, but he didn't find any freedom in his rebellion.

From the outside the minister and his wife looked like models of moral virtue, but from the inside their morality was complicated by their inability to deal emotionally with sexual transgression. All their children were deeply depressed. One had attempted suicide. It appeared to me that someone in that family had to find the courage to sort out their moral ideas and years of guilt to see how much psychological wounding had gone into the making of their ethical rigidity and rebellion.

It is difficult to acknowledge the powerful longings and desires of the soul, which often cause us to break family rules and betray social expectations. When morality is exploited as the means for keeping desire in check and for covering up outbreaks of love and longing, the result may be a special kind of depression that shows all the signs of an imprisoned heart and bound eros. It is a steep price to pay for the illusion of innocence.

Every moral decision, every moral position, every moral argument is riddled with passions, fantasies, and emotions so steeped in cultural, family, and individual histories that their roots can never be fully known. If we think of morality in simplistic terms, ignoring the psychological issues involved, we will continue to act out our moral confusion instead of developing into people of compassionate and positive ethics.

Unless morality rises up from deep reflection, it will be nothing more than a set of psychological defenses camouflaged as ethical principles. Joyful sex requires that our morality be mature and alive. It would be worth every effort to examine ourselves for the guilt and worry that may dwell in our more inflexible moral positions, so that we might recover the soul in both our morality and our sexuality.

Moral Duplicity and Complexity

Morality is as complicated as life itself, and when we fail to appreciate that complexity, it may show itself symptomatically as confusion or as an odd but revealing duplicity about moral issues. You don't have to be psychoanalytically trained to notice that some people protest too much in their moral outspokenness. The very intensity and rigidity of their objections to sexual behavior betray their interest in it. Sometimes moral duplicity shows itself as a simultaneous flight from sex and an unusually intense preoccupation with it. Sometimes it is revealed in shocking reversals of moral character.

A woman in her fifties once came to me for therapy. She had been brought up in a moralistic home and for many years had simply mouthed the moral clichés she had heard often as a child. She tried to live up to those impossible expectations, but some lust for life kept her unsettled. She felt depressed and lonely and had an overpowering desire to get her life moving. But she was at an impasse. She wanted more of life and thought of making a radical change, especially now that the years were passing swiftly. It was now or never, she often said. She was determined to make that shift, but every time she came close, at the last minute something always kept her locked in fear.

One day she came to me and said that she had finally fallen in love with a real man. The person she described sounded like an equally depressed and confused person, but someone with a mirror version of her moral scruples. He was tough, sadistic, and self-serving. He had been in trouble with the law most of his life, and he was always scheming for ways to make an illegal dollar. He was a visitor from hell, a Hades to the woman's Persephone, a man who represented all the values that had been rejected by her family. Sex with him was rough and dirty, but she found joy in it.

Almost overnight this woman's moralistic structures collapsed. She had planned on an orderly shift in values, but what she found was a complete and immediate breakdown. She assisted her lover in his dangerous activities and became familiar with his underworld friends and associates. For three years she lived in that world. Fortunately she survived with only a few beatings and the loss of all her money. Eventually she came up from that dark place, not to return to her former life, but dedicated to finding a new way of living that fell in place only after much thoughtful risk and effort.

As a therapist I encountered several other men and women who led meticulously moral lives for years, usually modeled on values of their families, but who eventually went through a rapid change. Jung called this flip-flop *enantiodromia,* an extraordinary reversal in which a person suddenly shifts to a new and unexpected topsy-turvy set of standards. It is one way, not the recommended one, to leave simplistic childhood morality behind and fashion adult values. It is also another symptomatic sign of a lack of moral complexity.

As we become adults we usually become critical of certain family values, while others remain lodged unconsciously in our feelings and thoughts. Generally I cherish the education I received in Catholic schools, but I don't want to perpetuate all the values I was taught there—parochialism about religion, anxieties around sex, or the repression of individuality, for example. It's interesting for me to notice that these three themes appear often in my writing. I make moral issues out of these values that I reject from my past. One way to deal with misguided moral influences is to reconstruct them for your adult life, even if that process takes years and a great deal of effort. Again, in therapy, I have witnessed men and women in their fifties and sixties struggling to be individuals with their own moral guidelines, but still afraid of family judgment or the loss of family approval and affection.

Because morality has a complicated and deep psychological connection, sorting out our moral attitudes is an emotional project. For years we may have used certain moral principles as the means of dealing with passions and desires, but as we mature, we may realize that a more sophisticated approach is now appropriate. The shift is usually not easy. It may entail a new relationship to the family and even a uncomfortable shift in our very sense of who we are.

The Symptom of Moralism

On the public stage and in private life sex is often in a battle with moralism. The two have an odd-couple connection, which, I suspect, has deeper roots than the simple felt need to keep sex under control.

Moralism is morality without soul. It is morality as a symptom, a neurotic complex that obsesses us and clouds our judgment. It isn't really morality; it is a failed attempt to be deeply moral. Establishing a comfortable moral way of life is part of the task of soul-making. It is a deep, positive process necessary for a life in tune with nature, self, lovers, friends, and community. But we are not born with a moral scheme perfectly in place, and it is not something that can be taught easily. Morality is alive and always changing. Its development goes hand in hand with the maturing of our lives in every area.

Since we are all in various stages of development and none of us perfect, we all have elements of raw, unrefined moral ideas and emotions—we all have areas where we are moralistic. Everyone has to go through a series of alchemical processes to transform moralism into deep morality. The world cannot be divided simply into the moralists and the freethinkers.

Some complexes are not easy to deal with— say, an inferiority complex that affects everything we do. We may try to get rid of the complex, and we can see the harm it does, but it may take years of struggle to make any headway. The same is true of moralism, except that in this case we have the added difficulty that we don't see moralistic attitudes as needing work or as in any way psychological. We take our moralism literally, and so there is an added screen around it making it difficult to perceive.

A psychological complex is a bundle of feelings, memories, thoughts, desires—all kinds of psychological material—tied together under a particular theme and mood. Complexes are autonomous, they seem to have their own will and drive us to feel and act in certain ways. Jealousy can be a complex, as can fear of flying. Complexes are negative in tone, but they are the raw stuff of the soul that needs to be refined to the point where it can be woven into the whole fabric of life and personality.

The complex of jealousy, destructive and dangerous as a symptom, can be hammered into personal strength coupled with vulnerability. Fear of flying might eventually be transmuted into an adventurous and imaginative life. The problematic symptom is narrowly focused and excessively concrete, but the refined version is subtle, positive, and compatible with the rest of life.

As a complex, moralism may contain fears about being sexually pure and fundamentally acceptable. We all want to be accepted and approved. But this need comes up against sexual passion, and sometimes the two may seem to be entirely at odds. From the moral complex we try to control our sexuality, but the spirit of repression simply hyperactivates the sexual passion and directs it along inappropriate lines, because it is not woven into the whole of one's thought and values. As passion increases, the moral complex becomes more entrenched and more negative. We may focus our growing frustration on ourselves or on some other person or group, or maybe even on humanity in general.

The moralistic complex may be hidden under a veneer of irreproachable facts and reasonableness. For instance, whatever scientific or medical value they may have, our current attitudes toward smoking, fatty diets, alcohol, and drugs are embroidered in scarlet, like Hester Prynne's letter. The moralism in our tirades against these things suggests that something else is going on other than simple concern about our health. Drugs, fat, and smoke may carry anxieties that have little connection to our expressed concerns.

We are all moralists to some degree, some obviously more so than others. We can be moralistic about anything. Students in a rather posh school once complained to me that I had polyester in some of my clothes. There may have been good reason for their complaint, but I felt "natural-fiber moralism" in their comments, which were too judgmental and superior to be helpful. In many cases, people pride themselves on their moral tolerance and remain blind to the many moralisms operating in their own lives: environmentalists are often moralistic about business; vegetarians can be moralistic about meat. Some people, of course, seem to be moralistic about everything.

A complex or symptom points to what is lacking, and so paradoxically we can look to the symptom to find the direction in which we need to go. If we are feeling moralistic about some aspect of sex, sensing the need to limit sex in some way, the solution is not to overcome the inhibition but to take the lead of our feeling. We may find positive ways to diminish the importance of sex in relation to the rest of life. Demonizing what we need to limit only makes the complex more demanding and more negative.

In many cases moralism may be nothing more than the unfinished search for a meaningful and honest moral life. That is why it is not always advisable to trust the ethics of a rigid moralist—his morality is not rooted deeply or established with confidence and certainty. Moralists may present their views as though they were solid and thoughtful, but that certitude often reveals itself as being shallow and diffident. The overbearing sureness with which it is asserted betrays its fragility.

People find illusory moral strength outside themselves— in numbers of like-minded people, in authoritative writings and experts, and in sentimental appeals to family traditions and cultural habits. As people get older, they find comfort in long-held moral guidelines. As they see more of life, they hold its loose ends together anxiously with familiar but inadequate codes of conduct.

Especially in certain periods in life, the sexual emotions can apply a great deal of pressure, and moralism may be a tempting solution. It doesn't take an effort of thought or any personal struggle. It is a ready-made, off-the-rack means of control, and furthermore it makes us look good. We can feel superior to others who are being dirtied by the passions, and we can enjoy the illusion that everything is under control.

In any life the sexual nymph may refuse to lie still and take orders. She may rise unexpectedly in the shape of forbidden desire or simple interest. We never know where she will take us, and so we are tempted to put her in chains. The only alternative is to take a chance on life and to have faith in ourselves.

Soul the Mediator

A spiritual element is important in moral decision making, since it is easy to have our judgment swamped by the feelings of the moment. On the other hand, if the principles are so dominant that the feelings get no hearing at all, then spirituality becomes nothing more than the tool of repression. When soul and spirit are blended, we work our way toward an ethical decision by allowing our principles and our desires to interplay with each other until a suitably complicated solution has been reached. The result is an ethical outcome that is neither repressive nor merely self-serving.

Spirit is typically concerned with facts and principles. Soul is led by nuance. It looks for guidance in image, poetics, and implication. For example, a married person strongly tempted toward an extramarital affair may discover that she needs some kind of freedom, but not necessarily sexual experimentation. On the other hand, she may come to understand her sexual longing as an invitation finally to be freed from an oppressive relationship. It may take time to sort out the morality of a decision involving the passions.

If she were to dismiss the new desire as a temptation to be resisted at all costs, she would distance herself from her soul and perhaps feel depressed and aimless because of that distance. By remaining close to her desire and yet not acting precipitously, she comes to know her soul better and may catch a glimpse of her deepest needs, and then she can act confidently and responsibly.

Over the years I have had a very small therapy practice, and yet when I recall instances like this one, in which a man or woman has had to search their hearts to discover the nature of their desire, I realize how frequently we must all enter this place of soulful meditation in search of a moral decision. Married people have to consider deeply the meaning of the commitment they have made to their partners, their responsibilities to their children, and their ethical duties toward their own lives. These allegiances are never simple, and they often seem to contradict one another. People feel torn and brutalized by all the emotional influences that go into moral reflection. Even after all this battling, the outcome may never be clear or without remorse.

In a course I once taught in Canada, a man stood up and addressed the class poignantly: "If you have ever been divorced, you know what agony means. You are not the same person you were before the divorce, and you will never take a decision lightly again." He was clearly speaking from the continuing pain of his own experience, describing a personal education in the heart.

When a significant moral decision is full of soul, it is an initiation, a rite of passage. Former naiveté gives way to the wisdom of felt experience. Morality makes us honest. It deepens us. It asks all the courage we have and gives back in wisdom and character. A moral decision in the sphere of sex deepens our sexuality and, paradoxically perhaps, intensifies sexual pleasure.

Sex and Conscience

Since highly spiritual morality is usually based on principle and belief, a soul-centered morality may look vague, emotional, and relative in comparison. But the soul, too, can hammer out a tough kind of morality that in the long run is more demanding and more deeply placed.

Soul is not just raw emotion and fantasy. It has its own reliable sources of insight and values, the most potent of which, in the moral sphere, is conscience. The spiritual side of conscience is presented in ethical ideas and principles, while the soul side appears in empathy, compassion, and remorse. Eros and conscience are often in close dialogue, one urging us on sexually, the other surveying the situation for its wisdom and appropriateness.

Conscience is a daimonic guide. The Greeks used the word daimon for unnamed spirits, felt and sensed as a definite presence. The daimon could be encountered in nature, or it could make itself known internally, as a voice or a simple presence. The muse that inspires and guides the artist is a kind of daimon, as is the strong intuition that protects us at critical times. When we feel inspired, motivated, and passionate about something, a daimon is at work.

Daimonic conscience may appear as a voice we hear inwardly, telling us to avoid a certain behavior or urging us on. Conscience may play a role in remorse, as we stew over regrettable action and feel the sting of self-judgment. It may slow us down as we prepare to do something questionable.

Conscience is a valuable tool in the quest for a moral life, but since it is an inner voice and presence, it requires a good listener. These days most of us live our lives focused mostly on the external world. We are not terribly sophisticated about the inner life. We are interested in making new gadgets, but we don't spend much time developing inner technologies like imagination and intuition. With our attention directed outward we may miss the warnings of conscience, or, given the lack of faith also characteristic of our time, we may trust reasoning more than intuition. It's usually easy to overrule conscience with a convincing argument.

It is common to think of conscience as a negative influence, something that reins us in and keeps us out of trouble. And this sense of negativity, which is a problem in morality in general, may incline us to dismiss the development of conscience. It may not seem inspiring or all that helpful. I often hear about workshops where people can develop their psychic and intuitive abilities, but I have never heard of one devoted to conscience.

As I get older, I become more aware of the value of my intuitions. I still find myself overlooking them day after day, but whenever I give them their due, they turn out to be helpful. I get the feeling that my life has increased in some way as a result of this attention, and that I have powers at my disposal now that I previously neglected. Because sexual fantasy seems to just swarm with life and move in many directions, conscience can be a major help in sorting out all that material and clearing up sexual confusion.

Conscience is a special kind of intuition, and in the inner life it is important to distinguish the various presences that influence us. It may have several faces, and indeed several voices. Because it is a presence that has been with us for most of our lives, we should be able to recognize it when it appears and then to feel more secure in giving it a hearing. At the same time, we can always get better at heeding it and being guided by it.

As with any guiding daimonic presence, we can be more or less attuned to it. The word "lax" is sometimes used in connection with conscience. Some people have a relaxed attitude toward this guiding voice and others are scrupulous in heeding it. We do well to develop a good relationship with conscience, so that we can benefit from its regular guidance and form a moral life with its help.

As in all matters of the soul, inner dialogue, conversations with friends, reading, and the influence of models of conscience can all educate us in our morality. Whenever I read about people I admire going to jail for their convictions about matters that I believe are important, I am challenged in my morality. These good people are teachers as well as agents of change. Their consciences lead them into courageous acts of moral education for society, and it is clearly our job to be good students and to take that education to heart.

The love of life associated with a strong and hearty conscience can only add to the sexual joy life has to offer, since the affirmation of life is the best context for sexual fulfillment. Sex cannot be separated from the rest of life without being wounded, and one of the best ways to prepare for sex is continually to develop a strong conscience and a thoroughly moral way of life.

We may be tempted to think that sexual freedom comes from disregarding values and morality, but that idea makes twisted sense only if we have a limited idea of freedom and a negative idea of morality. In the deepest sense morality is simply the confluence of interests of our own nature with destiny, nature itself, and community. When this kind of morality is in place, sex prospers.

Erotic Morality

An alternative to moralism and inner division is morality with soul, erotic morality. The very phrase "erotic morality" may sound like an oxymoron, a contradiction in terms. We usually imagine eros and morality to be opposites. Then, because eros is the principle of vitality, when we are behaving and thinking morally we get depressed and life becomes colorless. When it has no roots in eros, the very pulse of life that draws us forward, morality has a deadening effect that tends to spread through families, marriages, and communities. People who choose to live life in its fullness have no choice but to test the limits of accepted morality and often transgress them.

Strongly affirming life, being in love with nature and our own selves, we may be inspired to do everything to protect the world and those in it. Many extraordinary people have given themselves to safeguarding family and community, not out of moral principle but out of love. The whistle-blowers, the conscientious objectors, the civilly disobedient, the imprisoned idealists are often misunderstood and condemned by moralists, and yet their ethical generosity far transcends the limited effect of the tame morality of principle.

What could be more sustaining of good sex than such a powerful love of life? Responsive exuberance translates into action on behalf of others, and so it has within it a certain sexual charge.

Love and moral conviction hold together powerfully in two letters from the battlefield. Major Sullivan Ballou wrote the following words to his wife, Sarah, before he was killed in the Battle of Bull Run in 1861: "Sarah my love for you is death-less. It seems to bind me with mighty cables that nothing but Omnipotence could break; and yet my love of Country comes over me like a strong wind and bears me unresistibly on with all these chains to the battlefield."[1]

Another letter was left at the Vietnam Veterans Memorial wall. It was written by John Campbell in 1985 to his friend Eddie, who had served in his company and had been killed on the battlefield: "If your name on this wall makes it harder to send guys half way around the world to die, then maybe it wasn't a total waste. I love you, brother. I pray some day we can welcome each other home."

Our moral life needs to be grounded in love, or else it will root in something else, because it is always based in some kind of emotion and imagination of life. It can be deeply angry and anxious, or it can blossom up from a simple sense of duty based in love. Sex need not be inventive, wild, unimaginably sensitive, frequent, or full of charm or beauty. But it does require a deep moral vision if it is to address the soul with full sensuousness and vitality. Morality will be full of heart if it isn't narrowed into an angry dismissal of the erotic life and its passionate sexuality.

To improve our sexual lives we don't need new techniques or new electronic and mechanical aids. We need a transfor-mation in the way we imagine the point of our lives: whether to live narcissistically toward the fulfillment of our own com-plicated fantasies of pleasure, or to live generously with an open heart and appreciation for a lively sexual imagination. Love and imagination go together and they generate moral vision jointly. They foster a sensitivity that breathes life into sex and joyfully discovers the limits that define it for those involved, without subjecting it to deadly repression.

If we allow sex its soul, which means that sexual fantasies and desires are not always to be taken literally, but as poetry and image pointing to something larger, then we can accept that every sexual fantasy is valid and makes sense. No desire needs to be repressed; it needs to be entertained, considered, and discussed. As a therapist, I spent hours with men and women talking about their sexual desires and the conflicts they raised. In my mind, these discussions were exercises in soul-making. We were taking raw sexual desire and reading it the way you might read a Shakespeare sonnet—for implication, innuendo, pun, indirection, and suggestion.

If we approached life less literally our morality might be worn more lightly and might oppress us less. Morality should be joyous, an affirmation of life rather than a denial. Sex is not always as literal as we make it out to be, and it isn't necessary to act concretely on every desire or to act out every fantasy. The majority of sexual fantasy and desire points to the erotic dynamic in life and not to actual sex.

To be free of our own moralism and its accompanying guilt, we would have to acknowledge that the soul has its own sexuality, made up of images, feelings, values, fears, and longings that need only rarely find enactment in life. For the most part, fantasy is fantasy. Desire may look carnal, but it is more likely connected to the unfolding of the soul.

If we were to take our desires seriously, but not always literally, we would be guided toward the tranquil life, a life full of creative activity perhaps, but free of a highly emotional contest between moralism and sex. Moralism might turn into morality, where eros is not the enemy.

Keeping in mind the soul of sex, we might describe sexual morality as the careful weaving of desire and passion into every aspect of life. It is based in trust in one's soul, which, when known intimately, is the only certain guide to sexual conduct. This trust cannot be sentimental or naive. It has to be shaped by the bitterness and remorse of our sexual history as well as by its joy and hunger, and by our knowledge of life and the world.

Erotic morality reaches deep into the heart and into the community for guidance. It allows time for wisdom to be revealed. It doesn't define itself against desire or pleasure. It is woven tightly into a whole fabric of values rooted in an affirmation of life and a love of one's own soul. It is comfortable and in no way exploits or condemns.

We discover this erotic morality by knowing our life story well, owning up to our prejudices and negative influences, and embracing our past wounds and failures. Eros was known as bittersweet, and it is only in the bittersweet embrace of life that we can find our way to pleasures that complement our moral sensitivity.

CHAPTER 9

The Joy of Celibacy

Subtle Expressions of Sexuality

THE CREATIVE link between eros and spirituality reveals itself in the way we live our lives and in everyday encounters. Many people choose to live celibate lives, either for life or for a period of months or years. Many others find themselves celibate because of fate and circumstances. They may be divorced or widowed, or they may simply not have found a partner, or they may not want a sexual relationship for themselves because of their age or temperament. Although these lives are celibate, they may also be completely sexual. We may breathe soul into our days with a simple and subtle kind of sexual purity, an empty space in a crowded world of sexual preoccupation and yet a space that is not formed by repression and is not outside the realm of the sexual.

As I reflect on my youthful experience as a monk, I understand my own celibacy at that time not as a denial of sex but as a different way of living it. Although I didn't have sexual experiences in the usual sense, my life was full of intimacy, community, beauty, pleasure, body, desire, and even passion. I didn't feel the absence of lovemaking as self-denial or negatively as a loss. Willingly I chose to live a celibate life, and it had such emotional rewards and provided such a rich sense of meaningfulness that I didn't feel deprived.

What I learned from those twelve years of celibacy is that sexuality is deeper and more subtle than we usually imagine it. I certainly never thought of myself as asexual or repressed. My sexuality was fully alive and present to me in my fantasies, in my sense of self, in my emotional relationships, in my discovery of a rich and fascinating world, and in my work. Not having a lover was a small gap in an otherwise rich life of sensuality, desire, and fantasy.

I'm not saying that religious celibates all feel this way or that I would have continued to enjoy this kind of sexual celibacy for many more years or that the experience was without conflicts and self-questioning. I'm happy to have left that life and to have explored a different kind of sexuality. But those special years broadened my ideas about sex, and the intuition that inspires this book has to do with a sexuality that is not always literal, a sex life of the soul that doesn't necessarily include the body or an actual partner. This kind of sexuality is not amorphous and vague. Nor is it merely metaphorical. It is admittedly subtle, but it is also deep and all-pervasive.

The word "celibate," from the Latin *caelibs*, bachelor, primarily means unmarried. "Chaste" means morally pure and has the connotation of abstaining from sex. There are two ways to be celibate and chaste. One way is to remain unmarried or not to have a lover. Another is less literally to weave the spirit of celibacy into life whether one is married or single, and to cultivate the spirit of chastity or sexual purity, whether one has a sex life in the usual sense or not. From this broad point of view, which faithfully represents the soul of sex, celibacy and chastity may have fertile roles to play in any kind of lifestyle.

The Problem of Wanting to Be Normal

Today it may be difficult to appreciate both celibacy and chastity because we assume that it is healthy to have an active sex life, and unhealthy and maybe even abnormal to do otherwise. Most sexual advice you find in magazines and books is aimed at active, successful, well-functioning intercourse. You don't hear much about the value of not functioning or not being interested in sex, and I have never seen an advertisement for a videotape promoting sexual purity and reserve.

One defensive way to deal with our powerful and uncontrollable sexual feelings is to try to feel normal. We clear up our sexual confusion by reducing the wide range of sexual possibilities to a very few. Everything that doesn't fit within that range we consider abnormal and in need of therapy, treatment, or even punishment. But the comforting illusion of normalcy is bought at a price. Sex is not simple for anyone, and when we force it to fit anxious categories of health and normalcy we, the keepers of those categories, suffer under them as much as do those who don't believe in them.

Critiquing the very idea of normalcy, James Hillman points out that it is a repressive idealization that misrepresents the way things are. In our fantasy of normalcy, he says, we want to be either statistically average or approaching our ideal.[1] It's strange that in a society that prizes individuality, so many long to be average and then feel unhealthy if their lives stray from the norm. Sex is remarkably individual and one never knows where or when one's sexuality is going to turn. Sex is so directly tied to the ever-quixotic soul that it is as unpredictable as life itself.

The need to be normal can also be intimate and personal. Many of my clients in therapy would come to a point where they would ask anxiously: "Am I normal? Does anyone else have these thoughts and wishes that I have?" But the soul isn't only normal. It may be comforting to feel normal, but the most interesting and creative developments in life often push us toward eccentricity.

The biographies of many outstanding creative men and women turn on the individual quirks of their sexuality — Emily Dickinson's softly sensuous and mystical solitude, Woody Allen's shifting liaisons, Leonard Bernstein's bisexuality, Madonna's sexual explorations, Cary Grant's image of normalcy personified in spite of his many affairs and marriages, Oscar Wilde's and Michael Jackson's sexual ambiguities, and George Sand's celebration of androgyny.

Our individuality is nourished in the deep and formative abnormality of our soul's autonomous longings. This is not to say that we should celebrate our abnormal tendencies in reaction to the pressure to be normal, because this approach would simply maintain the division between the normal and the abnormal. We might better take both, the normal and the abnormal, less literally and find ways to keep the two connected to each other. The desire to be normal is a valid one, but it need not be used as a means of repression. It is complete only when, at the same time, we also appreciate our abnormal or unusual desires and traits.

The desire to be normal may get in the way of our appreciating celibacy, but it also interferes with all aspects of sexuality. In most people sex refuses to be shackled by our defensive wishes to fit the norm. It goes its own way in spite of our intentions and efforts. In fact sex may offer deep satisfaction only when we abandon any hope of being normal, when we discover that our sexuality will be complete only when we stop protecting ourselves from strong erotic desires that drift away from social expectation.

As we find our way out of artificial divisions in thought and emotion, we often come up with new language that better expresses the new experiences. Hillman writes about necessity in this way, a word I have found helpful over the years for speaking of those yearnings that may be painful and objectionable but that demand our acquiescence. We might also consider more individual ways to be sexual, discovering not only the joy of sex but the joy of celibacy as well. Some things may remain merely acceptable or livable. All of this language, free of judgment and bias, suggests a way to acknowledge seemingly contradictory claims and helps us out of the dichotomies and oppositions that can keep us stuck.

We are all influenced by psychological language and may tend to think clinically about our intimate lives. Psychologists and psychiatrists find the categories normal and abnormal useful, but we private citizens don't have to use the words in a technical sense. If we feel abnormal because we don't have an active sex life, we can choose to enjoy our individuality rather than worry about being unhealthy. Some people hate to be normal, but they, too, can translate that feeling into the sense of being at one with the human race. The spectrum from normal to abnormal is simply the range of possible human individuality and commonality. Our individual position on that scale is unique and may change radically in the course of a lifetime.

Celibacy as a Life Theme

I am married to a person who, much like myself, loves being married but also has a strong desire not to be married. Both of us, at least in our feeling and in the stories we tell about ourselves, would do fine if we lived alone or celibate in a community. I don't pretend to understand myself in this area, but my guess is that if I were still living in a celibate religious community, I might look upon marriage, as I now occasionally do on celibacy, as an attractive alternative. I resolve any contradiction in my feelings about marriage and celibacy by being fully and willingly married, while at the same time taking advantage of opportunities for momentarily satisfying my need for celibacy by cultivating its spirit.

Celibacy can be taken poetically, having real effect but not made into a literal way of life. One can feel momentarily unmarried, or in certain circumstances unattached and dedicated to chastity. In this sense celibacy is the subtle sensation of being solitary and also having the special attitude that comes from not, at the moment, engaging in an actual sex life.

My work, for example, sometimes takes me to places far from home where I spend days at a time living in hotels. I find hotel living, on a short-term basis, quite satisfying, in large part because I return to many of my experiences as a monk. The atmosphere is relatively quiet, and I have the chance to spend time as I want to. I can work at any time, and I can arrange my space in a style that is close to that of the monk. I leave my hotel-monastery to give lectures or sign books or talk on the radio, and in those situations I'm treated as an individual, not as a married person. And this is all quite pleasing for a brief time, although I must confess that, except for missing the monk's life now and then, I prefer traveling with my whole family.

My point is that we can all weave the celibate spirit into our daily lives. We can be momentarily and situationally celibate in attitude. We have to know individually how much time we need for daily celibacy and what style of celibacy is most satisfying—whether it is simply being alone, being free of sexual flirtation, or being taken as an individual rather than as part of a couple. A five-minute celibate walk, a celibate lunch alone, or a temporary celibate community with a group of same-sex friends might suffice. We might discover the unexpected pleasure in spending time with someone who might otherwise be a potential sex partner but enjoy the celibate qualities of our time together. In all these cases, celibacy means enjoying the spirit of not being sexually active.

The Spirit of Celibacy in Sex

The many people who live a celibate life for one reason or another are not necessarily asexual. They have the opportunity to sublimate their sexuality, again in the alchemical sense—translating it into close friendships, or dedicating themselves to pleasure, beauty, and art and to engagement with the world. The soul of sex is not to be found only in the act of love but also in a life motivated by a broader love and extended pleasures.

Living a full sensuous life with friends, intimates, and

things, and indulging in pleasurable activities is an erotic life, and it may well fulfill whatever sexual needs the soul has at a particular time. An unmarried person or anyone without a lover might consider the importance of giving themselves all these qualities of sexuality even though lovemaking is not an option. I don't see these things as substitutes for sex, but as bona fide ways of being sexual, especially as they address the subtle erotic needs of the soul.

The word "bachelor" originally meant farmhand, and a spinster, of course, was one who spent her time spinning. We can leave behind any sexist and pejorative implications in these words and see that sex transforms into a life of culture. These words now connected strictly with a celibate lifestyle used to have the broader connotations of tending fields and working with fabrics. Going even further into the imagination of these words, I see two mythological figures full of meaning—Aristaeus, the original farmer, beekeeper, and emblem of personal excellence, and Athena, the goddess-weaver who creates and sustains cultural life. These figures help us appreciate the cultural and creative possibilities in a celibate life.

Sex finds natural expression in loving, passionate, active attention to the culture of one's own life and the culture of society. Sexual desire can be satisfied in creative engagement with the world, as long as desire, passion, pleasure, and other qualities of sex are brought into the enterprise. Men and women without a sex partner can be profoundly sexual, taking as their guiding spirit the great goddess Athena, one of the rare virgin goddesses, who is responsible for strong, imaginative, comprehensive culture building—who weaves culture and life into a brilliant tapestry. Aristaeus was honored as the one who brought us up from brute survival existence to gentle, civilized refinement. From both archetypal perspectives excellence, art, craft, and social involvement make life rich and rewarding, directing the passions toward intimate and sensuous contact with life.

The Spirit of Celibacy in Marriage

In several profound ways being not married is an important aspect of being married.[2] Married people need not lose the sense of who they are as unmarried persons. I may make most of my life and work decisions as a married person, but in some areas especially I am alone. I may have to know for myself what I need, and that may not be acceptable to my partner, or it may demand so much of my individuality that it would be impossible to get there with my partner. I may have to go through some experiences not as a married person, but as an individual, and that calls for a certain kind of celibacy—not a literal lifestyle but an attitude and deep fantasy about my world and my relationships.

My wife has many highly sophisticated spiritual practices that she developed long before we were married, and I simply don't have the temperament to participate in most of them with her. I have tried at various times, but they just don't speak to me. She maintains her practices in our home, but she does so for the most part as a single woman. I, too, do some things that have been part of my life for several decades, and my wife can witness them but she can't really participate in them.

I play the piano as a celibate. No one shares this with me, and no one really understands its importance or the nature of my pleasure. I also read some things celibately. Some of the books in our home are mine, some of them my family's.

Mine speak to me as they speak to no one else I know, and my wife's speak to her with an individual precision and delight. I don't know anyone who takes the same kind of pleasure I do in reading a Samuel Beckett novel and a woodworking magazine on the same evening, and I can't enter much into the books and articles on painting technique that fire up my wife. Most books and activities we enjoy together, and we may read in the same room, and yet some areas are individual, and we enjoy the marriage as much for those celibate moments as for the times of mutual sharing.

Being an individual without attachments or companionship offers many emotional rewards, and these satisfactions don't have to be sacrificed entirely when we pronounce our marriage vows. Having lived in a monastery, I know the emotions and thoughts associated with celibacy, and I feel something similar as a married person. If I meet a person who is attractive or who clearly wants a certain kind of intimacy with me, I feel my marriage vow very much like the vow of celibacy. I'm not available, and that is my choice. I don't feel deprived or repressed. I feel the limitation provided by the vow, but in that limitation I sense genuine freedom and joy. Oddly, this sort of celibacy seems to be an essential part of the married life. Both may require subtle experiments, conversation with a spouse, and a philosophy of life that appreciates the mix of marriage and solitude.

There is another side, a shadow if you like, to this kind of celibacy. Depending on the circumstances—the phase of life you're in at the moment, the quality of your marriage, and inexplicable emotions and inner developments—it may be excruciatingly difficult to be celibate, and the joy and freedom of it may be entirely absent. Married people often face the problem of being attracted to somebody else, and the attraction can become so strong that the person feels her very existence as a person is at stake, and in no time she may find herself in an emotional triangle that seems to have no acceptable resolution. As a therapist dealing with such situations I have often thought that temptations against the vows of both celibacy and marriage may signal important and powerful developments in the soul. The only way out or through the challenge may be a deliteralizing of the temptation. We can ask ourselves, in terms that go beyond the literal relationships involved, what the triangulation of emotions is all about. If we simply gave in literally to all new invitations to intimacy our lives would be torn apart and would never find security and grounding.

Some people who have been enjoying a sexual life limited by marriage or celibacy suddenly feel powerfully drawn by a desire to be promiscuous. Sometimes these feelings remain within the realm of fantasy and dream, but often people act on them and only gradually begin to reflect on them. Then they may feel guilt or regret and become confused.

The fantasy of living a rich, wild, unreserved promiscuous sexual life may visit anyone, sometimes at the most unexpected moments. The thought may be deeply disturbing, because one doesn't know if the yearning in this fantasy will be satisfied without actual experiment. Here the subtle idea of sexual purity and a celibate attitude may be helpful, not to repress the difficult stirrings of the imagination, but to sufficiently complicate the situation so a workable solution can be found.

About one third of the people who came to me for therapy over the years arrived in a state of deep anxiety over the impossible conflict of wanting to keep their marriage intact and yet feeling crazy in their love for a third party. Typically one sensation was notably absent amid all the confusion—the feeling of personal integrity and individuality. Celibacy as a sense of self unrelated to another person had all but disappeared, and in its absence came a sense of being out of control, blind to any possible resolution of the conflict.

In these situations I would never try to help a person resolve the conflicts directly and immediately. The anxiety and heroics that arise when we attempt to stay in control and be reasonable in the face of irrational developments often deepen the impasse. I did look for the figure of the celibate, the one who was neither married nor tempted, the one whose joy was to live apart from both the spouse and the new lover. This was a triangulation to match and mirror the triangle causing so much emotional suffering. Recovering the lost celibate sense of oneself enlarges one's experience and offers options when life has been imagined too narrowly.

Everyone a Celibate

Spiritual celibates model a potentially creative way of life that any of us could try. It is made up of integrity, individuality, and solitude, complemented by an intense experience of community. This is the monastic situation, but it could be a model for a marriage, a workplace, a friendship, or a family. In all these areas we might find a place for solitude and personal integrity along with the intimate pleasures of community and friendship, and it might require some degree of celibacy to achieve this satisfying combination.

Community and individuality are separated in many people's lives. They are striving to be individuals, and at the same time they are lonely. To some extent the culture as a whole struggles with this problem—the insistence on individuality, which presents itself as narcissism, and the breakdown of community.

We could learn from these experiments that the spirit of celibacy, joined to a certain simplicity in lifestyle, can help bridge the gap between individuality and community. By comfortably finding a place for individual effort, without any need to stand apart aggressively from others, we can exercise our creativity. We can better accept our deep needs for privacy and personal integrity. At the same time, we will appreciate the benefits of genuine emotional involvement in community.

Bringing the spirit of celibacy into ordinary life requires subtle discernment. It may be necessary to pay close attention to the dictates of the heart, to know when it's appropriate to act celibately and when to be explicitly sexual. Men and women in therapy have said to me that they wonder if something is wrong with them when they don't feel a desire for sex. Many factors can influence such feelings, among them the heart's need for a celibate life to restore a strong feeling of individuality.

Celibacy also heightens the eros in other areas of life. The celibate spirit reins in sexual desire, allowing it to be transformed or sublimated into less literal forms, such as love in community, pleasure in nature, and excitement in work. When the qualities characteristic of sex—intimacy, pleasure, body, desire, orgasm—enter into other areas of life, those areas become eroticized in a real way, not just metaphorically, and our sexual longings are fulfilled then at another level, increasing the pleasure and taking away some of the pressure for sexual satisfaction from our partners and lovers.

You can detect the spirit of celibacy when it is alive in a group of people anywhere, as at your workplace or in your neighborhood. Parties and gatherings may be celibate, or, on the other hand, they may be occasions for flirting and orgy. I don't mean to offend Aphroditic necessities and imply that flirtatious gatherings are bad or harmful. I simply want to note the difference. A party that is celibate in this sense can be immensely enjoyable and involve no repression or moralism. At a time of widespread sexual confusion, when we feel the pressures of both repression and obsession, it may be helpful to see that celibacy has a place. There is nothing wrong with you if you like a community in which individuals are not always on the make, but where each person is treated simply as an individual and not as a potential sex partner.

The Castle of Chastity

Chastity means sexual purity, a state or feeling of innocence. This sense of self may be accomplished by living celibately, but it can also be a quality of married life. It carries a sense of innocent and pure-hearted reserve. Sex naturally takes away a kind of innocence, and that loss can be disturbing. Sexual experience can also make one feel soiled. Sex marks a transition from innocence to experience, but without some measure of innocence it may be difficult to feel good about oneself. A great deal of sex can bury the feeling of childlike purity that, for many people, is a precious part of the personality. In therapy, I have encountered men and women who wish they had never had sex, had not been married so many times, or hadn't had so much sexual experience with so many different people. They felt that through sexual excess they had irretrievably lost something precious.

The origins of the word "chastity" hint at some of the emotions it contains. It comes from the Indo-European *kes* or *kas*, which means to cut. This root gives us "castrate," a literal way of cutting off from sex, and also "castle," a fortification or a separated, cutoff place. The image of the castle highlights certain aspects of sexual purity. In the condition of chastity we are removed from a certain dimension of life by means of psychological distance and fortification, and perhaps even by aggressive self-protection. Castles are romantic structures, but they were built for warfare—thick walls, deep narrow windows, bowmen's outlooks, guard walks, moats, drawbridges. With attitudes of defensiveness, aggression, distance, and thick layers of protection, a chaste person may resemble a castle.

Sometimes chastity has to be defended with vigilance and militancy, and it isn't always easy to distinguish between strength and defensiveness. Friends and acquaintances may be stung by a person's attempts to remain single and sexually uninvolved, and they may complain. But on reflection they might recognize that chastity usually requires a degree of toughness and self-defense.

In history, the word "chaste" has been confused with the word "chasten," which means to chide or discipline, and it is true that chastity can have a masochistic element in it. The absence of certain pleasures can be a burden, even if its purpose is to make life full and rich through restraint. A person living a chaste life may suffer the lack of sensuality as a deprivation and may need to turn to other pleasures so as not to feel deprived.

Sexual purity has a place in the most sophisticated life. It can strengthen a sense of personal integrity, restore a feeling of fresh innocence, and help with a renewal of life and personality. I have witnessed several men and women, used to a full and active sex life, suddenly blossom during an unusual period of celibacy. As the monks knew so well, sex can be distracting. One can gather some of the benefits of celibacy without being negative about sex.

The Ripening of Innocence

The wish to start life over and not get involved so early or so intensely in sex may be a personal one for a man or woman who has had many sexual relationships, but there is also an archetypal dimension to it. Something deep in the human heart would like the chance to start over, to be renewed in a fundamental way, and to reacquire the gifts of virginity.

One of the more striking rituals practiced in ancient religions was the annual submersion in water of the likeness of a goddess to signify her renewal. Just as in many religions a neophyte plunges into baptismal waters or at least has them poured over the head, so the goddess can be renewed, begin a new life, and recover her original innocence in the holy waters of ritual. In Greece, Hera, the absolute archetype of the married person, was honored with an annual rite of cleansing in the spring Kanathos so that she could be revered as virgin and wife. Before each lovemaking Hera was a virgin—an image we might keep in mind for ourselves, men and women.

This powerful image of the goddess wet with the purifying waters of renewal teaches an important lesson about the soul's sexuality. We can never go back to childhood innocence literally, but the soul is not bound by literal facts. It can be restored, its virginity renewed. Our attitude, our way of life, our sense of ourselves can all return in a certain way to the starting point. And we can cultivate this psychological virginity, this purity, even if we are sexually active.

It might help to distinguish between naiveté and innocence, or between an original innocence related to lack of experience and a more mature innocence that exists simultaneously with sophistication and maturity. This latter kind of innocence is an achievement in which we become wise to the ways of the world without falling into cynicism.

Religion provides an extreme version of this archetype in the holy fool, who knows that one should be wise and prudent in life, but who chooses a persona of naiveté that is betrayed by an underlying wisdom. The fool also avoids the cynicism of those who surrender to demands to be realistic and to flee innocence and its vulnerabilities. The world may treat innocence as though it were foolish, but religion gives us a way of appreciating foolishness that is deep-seated and aware.

When innocence is spoiled, we may lose not only our sense of personal purity but other qualities as well. A person who laments having had so much sexual experience may be longing for a life in which sex isn't so dominant, so encompassing and perhaps soulless as to leave wounds and scars. We may feel the loss of a greater self, wider experiences and interests, more and different people in our lives. The sense of loss itself gives some indications of how to respond to this sexual dilemma: by broadening our lives, expanding our interests, connecting to a greater variety of people, and relinquishing the persona that found the promise of salvation in sex.

"Innocence" means not being wounded; it doesn't mean not having had sex. We recover innocence by not allowing ourselves to be wounded so much, giving up our habitual masochism, and feeling the strength needed to live a creative life. All of this amounts to a real renewal and might well be accompanied by a deep feeling of newly won innocence.

In the modern world children are losing their childhood innocence early. Some parents, recognizing the value of a pure and lengthy childhood, protect their children as long as possible from the loss of innocence that may occur through sex, trauma, or the complexities of modern life. But the culture as a whole seems to be unaware of the importance to society of a long and pure childhood, just as it has lost its appreciation for celibacy and chastity. Parents on their own can't safeguard the innocence of their children. The community necessarily has to be involved, but for its participation it has to value innocence and purity.

Once again, sex cannot be separated from the way we live in general. If we are cynical in business and in politics, if the media present a public life of hypocritical values, and if we don't believe in our stated ideals, then these shady attitudes will doubtless affect our sexuality. We won't be able to find the innocence that we so crave.

Innocence is naturally eroded and corrupted as the years pass, but that alchemy of the soul by which we become adults and by which character deepens does not necessarily entail a loss of childhood. It is possible to grow up and become familiar with the ways of the world without succumbing to its cynicism. We can blend adult awareness with child-like simplicity in an attitude that is extreme in neither direction.

Paradoxically, innocence allows maturity to have depth and substance, because if our insistence on being realistic and sophisticated contains any defensiveness against childlike openness, then our maturity will not be genuine. It will simply be a way of avoiding these qualities of youthful inexperience and not have any inherent value in itself. The defense against innocence adds a neurotic weakness to maturity, while a creative tension between knowing and unknowing, between innocence and experience, makes for an interesting and complex personality.

Some people seem to think that intelligence has to be cynical, that innocence is simple unknowing. They equate wisdom with a dark, suspicious, paranoid view of life, and conversely they identify innocence with naiveté. This attitude carries over into cultural ideas about sex. It may appear wise and sophisticated to have a complicated sex life, and when a relationship ends, it may seem necessary to find a new lover quickly. It can be embarrassing to be chaste and celibate.

Lovemaking can be experienced and innocent. The polymorphous play in sex gives innocence an appropriate milieu and therefore sustains it. How valuable it is in sex to experiment, take plenty of time for foreplay, use the imagination, seize the opportunities for uncynical humor and ribaldry, and playfully transgress the rules of propriety and responsibility. Of course, we have to be responsible in relation to pregnancy and disease and to the emotions of our partners, but joined to that necessary and valuable sense of responsibility, and completing it, is the spirit of play.

I was giving a series of lectures to psychiatrists once when a man stood and summarized his experiences in the week outside the lecture hall. He spent some of his time, he said, in meditation and in collecting skeletons and bones he found on the beach. On the other hand, he and his wife for the first time made love in a rather public setting, obviously enjoying the childlike transgression of propriety and the spontaneity of it. His story, warmly accepted by his colleagues, was the tale of Freud's two principles: life and death. I suspected a paradoxical and intimate connection between his interest in the carcasses his found and his delight in his own and his wife's bodies. Innocence and experience, childhood and maturity, life and death are all encapsulated in sex.

The Possibility of a Pure Society

Celibacy can take the form of dry, defensive avoidance of sex or rabid moralistic antagonism toward it, while chastity can become fearful self-protection. Both attitudes can also be haughty and superior or part of a life-denying, oppressive philosophy or political agenda.

The trick is never to allow sensuality to be separated from purity. The spirit of chastity and celibacy has much to offer in the midst of a sensual and sexual life, while for those who choose to live as celibates, the subtle forms of sex have a place. I've known several nuns and priests, fully dedicated to their lives of celibacy, who find ways to weave into this life-style moments of sensual intimacy that to the outside may appear to contradict their vows. Literal celibates usually need to cultivate sexual sophistication, while the rest of us have to work at finding a workable innocence.

The spirit of purity may also make an appearance, perhaps unexpectedly, during lovemaking, as when a person feels the need to cover his or her body or to refrain from certain acts. One simply has to be close to one's nature to distinguish between such a visitation and anxiety. I suspect that, given the culture's lack of sophistication about chastity and its slavery to normalcy, our tendency might be to explain all sexual inhibitions as ego problems.

Purity can be a form of deep-rooted inhibition that tells us that something is wrong or that we're going too far in a certain direction. I've worked with men and women who were having affairs that reached a point where one of the partners could no longer stand the feeling of being the betrayer to their marriage. They felt a strong need for a clear conscience and confessed to their spouse as a way to get relief. Other men and women I've known have entered relationships where the sex was very aggressive and experimental, and they enjoyed it at first but then reached a point where the joy disappeared. Then they craved some purity and sometimes found it difficult to convince their partners that their sudden inhibition didn't spring from fear but from a deep need for purer sex.

Society has as much trouble finding sexual purity as individuals do. Graphic sexuality is widespread, and there doesn't seem to be a corresponding sexual purity that is not moralistic or prudish. Maybe what is wrong with pornography is that it doesn't have much innocence in it. Hollywood, too, doesn't seem free of this neurosis enough to make a movie that is innocent without being naive.

In short, we need rich and thoughtful images of sexual purity. Otherwise we will continue to think of purity as a problem or as an anxious and unnecessary inhibition. We may have to find a middle way between moralism and indulgence, a sophisticated appreciation for what in the East might be called the fruitful emptiness within sex, affirming the soul's need for erotic purity and pure eros.

CHAPTER 10

The Marriage Bed

Creating a Marriage Through Sex

O NE INSTITUTION that unwillingly and unexpectedly draws us deep into the fertile but confounding humus of the soul is marriage. Nowhere else in life is there such opportunity to envision the future, enact old memories, feel the strongest of emotions, and constantly struggle between individuality and togetherness. And in the center of this maelstrom lies sex—mysterious, alluring, demanding, comforting.

On the surface marriage appears to be a simple living arrangement: two people fall in love and decide to share a home, have a sex life, and maybe raise children. At this level a wedding is usually a small ritual followed by a big party. It marks the beginning of the marriage, and has family, personal, and legal effect. In this structure sex is the expression of mutual love and the procreation of children. At anniversaries we celebrate the tenacity of marriages and the wisdom and good luck of the couple who have been able to live their lives together over a long period of time.

This picture of marriage is familiar to most of us, but we also know that beneath the facade there is often intense and long-lasting emotional struggle. If we were to define marriage in its totality, we would have to include the tenacious conflicts that often appear in the midst of love and companionship. Could it be that there is more to any marriage than biology and psychology, more than the personal ambitions of the partners, and more even than the dynamics of their relationship? Thinking that marriage is simply a living arrangement, many couples are surprised and profoundly disturbed to discover that it is also a playing field for the soul, an arena in which the individuals, the family, and the couple go through many ordeals and near tragedies.

The wedding rites of many cultures hint at the deep mysteries that lie in wait for the enraptured couple. In many places, the couple walks in a circle, tracing out the special *temenos,* the sacred precinct of their marriage. They may wear masks or carry a mirror that shows the inner or heavenly dimension of their marriage. These masks, magic circles, and mirrors denote the realm of the soul, the virtual space where the mysteries and initiations that constitute the soul of marriage take place.

The history of religion has also brought to light ancient stories about the *hieros gamos,* a sacred marriage of a god and goddess, or a goddess and a king. While scholars have long been tempted to reduce such marriages to fertility rites, at the very least we could take the word "fertility" to refer to the soul as well as the body, to an abundance of life and not just an abundance of children. Every marriage is outwardly a legal contract and inwardly a sacred union, and only when we consider both dimensions can we find the appropriate role for sex.

Religious stories and rituals give us ways of picturing marriage that may seem mystifying in a psychological age, when the tendency is to imagine marriage only in terms of interpersonal struggle and fulfillment. They describe extraordinary unions of gods and goddesses, such as Zeus and Hera, the supreme Greek deities who enjoyed a three-hundred-year honeymoon, and Aphrodite and Hephaestus, the goddess of absolute beauty married to the dwarfish god of dirty mines and steamy forges. In India, the mysterious union of Shiva and Kali hints at the mystery of life itself, and in many cultures the divine figures are both husband and wife and brother and sister, like ancient Egypt's Isis and Osiris, yet another way of setting these marriages apart from human coupling.

These extraordinary, bigger-than-life stories invite us to examine the inner, mirror world of marriage as well as its outer form. If we could make this shift in perspective, appreciating both the outer aspects of marriage and its more mysterious inner developments, we might then understand the important role sex plays in sustaining the soul of the marriage. Marriage is not only the appropriate venue for physical pleasure, it is also an intense scene of soul-making, where sex is both the catalyst and the container.

In Greek mythology, Zeus and Hera enjoy lengthy marital bliss and give us a powerful image for tasting the sweetness of such unions. But we also read in the stories that Zeus and Hera have their difficult moments as well, so much so that Hera became an archetypal figure of insane jealousy and Zeus a complicated image of rage and infidelity. The *Iliad* tells us that, angry at Hera for stirring up bad winds against the hero Hercules, Zeus had her suspended by her wrists from a golden chain, with anvils attached to her feet. For her part, Hera was so angry at the ugly son Zeus had fathered that, according to the *Homeric Hymn to Apollo,* she tossed Hephaestus head over heels into the sea. The two were forever battling each other, and yet their union was sustained and worshiped.

These graphic scenes of love and aggression teach a lesson overlooked in our usual sentimental view of marriage: both struggle and bliss play important roles in the soul work that lies at the heart of marriage, and we should not be surprised to find an element of both in marital sex. As a marriage counselor I have witnessed bitter discussions about surrender and control in sex. I have been amazed at the intensity of anger when couples try to express their disillusionments, and at the powerful but disguised anger in partners who have turned to affairs as a way of achieving a balance of sexual power.

In the history of religions ritual sex was sometimes performed as part of liturgical drama, and it can serve a similar function in the theater of the bed in any ordinary marriage. Sex dramatizes the emotions and fantasies of the couple as they find their tortuous way toward ever deeper union. In the magic circle of passion couples enact the fantasies that currently constitute their individual soul work and that of their marriage.

The heavenly marriage of Zeus and Hera provides a pattern not only for married couples but also for marriage in the larger sense—as the achievement of union in all aspects of life. The cultures from which these passionate and complicated stories arose recognized both the harmony and the conflict that characterize any and all couplings in human life and in nature. Philosophers placed both the order of the cosmos and the union of bodies and souls in sex under the aegis of Aphrodite.

Hieros gamos portrays the mating of one aspect of reality with another, a mystery that lies just beneath the surface in all human marriages. As Mircea Eliade says in a phrase we've encountered before, the sacred lies concealed within the profane. Our marriages may appear on the surface to be plain human couplings, but deep in their core the polarities and tensions of all of life work themselves out, accounting for deep joy and absolute frustration. Married couples often confess that their pleasures and their troubles seem so deep as to be beyond understanding. No matter what they do, the tensions remain and yet, whether the marriage succeeds or fails, people have a clear sense that something absolutely meaningful is at stake.

What is at stake is peace in the world, the working out of inequalities and irreconcilable differences among nations, and peace in the neighborhood. Matrimony is a form of soul work, and marriage is the most potent alembic available to us where we can become initiated in the rudiments of community and the basics of intimacy. In this context sex is the primary ritual. It's one thing to resolve arguments and tensions in a marriage through conversation and counseling, but it's another to perform the mysterious rite that addresses the deepest mysteries of the union.

Sex doesn't have to be perfect or done in any particular way. As long as it lies at the heart of the marriage, it does the soul task of mediating between worlds, between the daily concerns of living and the eternal concerns of meaning and the heart. Even when people sense a contradiction in their marriage between good sex and bad communication, they can be certain that sexual passion is not meaningless. It points to an important attraction, a true yearning of the soul, which may or may not signify the couple's conscious goals and wishes.

In any society the many marriages play an important role in holding the society together and giving it its deep culture. Each marriage is a laboratory for the soul, and in each marriage lies the deeper laboratory of sex, the holy of holies, where passion, union, differences, pleasure, difficulties, and even work achieve their necessary balances.

If couples realized the importance of their lovemaking and its impact on the world around them, from their children and neighbors to the nation and the world, they might have a less personalistic, less psychological view of their sexuality, and in that broadening they might enter into sex with larger vision and greater joy. Everything in life suffers when our vision of it is too small and too personal.

The Soul of Marriage

Sex is the religion of a marriage. It is its contemplation, its ritual, its prayer, and its communion. As we work out our sexual difficulties and find our way to bliss, we are doing the alchemical work of the soul, transforming old and raw frustrations and emotional blocks into the golden art of erotic pleasuring. It is no small thing in a marriage to practice at sex until it is free of interference, for this is the nature of the deep alchemy by which we rough and primitive individuals become persons of refined sensibility capable of union with other humans.

Lady Chatterley wondered what Abelard meant when he said he and Heloise had passed through all the stages and refinements of passion. "Forever necessary," says D. H. Lawrence, "to burn out false shames and smelt out the heaviest ore of the body into purity. With the fire of sheer sensuality."[1] Sex purifies! In various stages of mutual generosity, showing and gazing, touching and being touched, the individuals lose their defendedness and discover what it means to be present to another, body and soul. This smelting of the ore of passion makes us people of strength and vitality.

We find the spiritual marriage not beyond the sensual but through it, by means of it. The lover explores the body of his beloved and discovers himself at his source. His partner has brought out his erotic potential and given it the opportunity for realization, but what is exposed in real love is always the deep soul, never only what mentally we intend or understand.

Over time, over many nights and days of love, marriage summons those ghosts who have been in hiding for a long time, and we gradually become more complete, but never truly complete, as we reacquaint ourselves with our selves. We do this mutually, so that, like Abelard and Heloise, we can hardly imagine living without the other—a complete interpenetration of narcissism and altruism. We find ourselves as we generously reach out toward each other. Making love we enter the true *thalamus,* the marriage chamber, a magic circle where our souls come to the foreground, where our actions, even the subtlest of them, are ritual signs, where our words speak to a separate reality, and where we can tie the bonds of marriage most effectively because we are now beneath and beyond ordinary consciousness.

This particular kind of sexuality, so deep and developing, may be found in long-term relationships outside of marriage, straight or gay, as they are equally the province of the deep work of the soul. Their rich terrain both loses and gains by the lack of the formal structure of marriage. The gains are in the creativity called for to define and refine a union without sanction and accepted bounds. The losses are the long history of models and meanings available to marriage and the untold efforts of society to diminish and destroy those couplings, as well as all the legal, social, and economic benefits of marriage. The effective ritual and the participation by family, friends, and society in a couple's marriage are a tremendous support for the deep fantasy and reality of their union. Marriage outside the legal and social forms is even more difficult to sustain than marriage within them. What a tragedy that we still refuse to allow gay men and lesbians to be married.

In our time, having lost an appreciation for ritual, some people apparently think that the ceremony and the legal papers of marriage are meaningless and optional. But ritual does, in fact, have deep repercussions, and the human soul is defined in part by the community in which it works out its necessities. Only a narcissistic psychology would understand soul work as the private activity of an individual.

Marital sex has a level of meaning that far transcends the sexuality of individuals in their search for love and experience. Marital sex is indeed a kind of ecology—a way of being in the world responsibly, helping to shape and to ground community, and sowing the seeds of love for a world in need of union. This strong communal context gives marital sex a measure of its nobility.

Married but Separate

Married people often struggle with the issue of togetherness and individuality, and this struggle appears blatantly in sex.

Even in wedding ceremonies it is common for couples to quote Kahlil Gibran saying, "Stand together yet not too near together: for the pillars of the temple stand apart,"[2] and Rainer Maria Rilke's letter on marriage where he says, "A good marriage is that in which each appoints the other guardian of his solitude."[3] It is understandable that in an age of individuality and personalism we want to preserve our solitariness even as we continue to need the embrace of love.

Religious literature often describes the human condition as a state of temporary separation, suggesting an original or primordial unity. In Plato's *Symposium,* Aristophanes' story about love describes the original humans as spheres who were later split in two, an image picked up by a number of Jewish theologians.[4] We are all trying to find our original unity. This image can be understood superficially as the proverbial two halves seeking to make a whole, but the mystery here is more complex and profound.

Deep in every human life lies a feeling of incompleteness and separation, archetypally and existentially. We may bring this anxious attitude to marriage, hoping that the other person will fill the gap or make whole what has been divided, but it doesn't take much thought to see the sentimentality and oversimplification in this hope. Plato's story suggests a deeper way in which our inherent division may be healed in marriage. It's not the other person who makes us whole, but marriage itself that addresses the issue of existential incompleteness and absolute loneliness.

Some of the trouble we meet in marriage comes from a failure to allow the change from the single life to the married state to take place. We may not like the feeling of loneliness that may inspire us to get married, but neither, sometimes, do we like the change from being a single person to living with another, with all the limitations and challenges that arrangement entails. Many married people confess to deep ambivalence about being married, and many secretly harbor strong fantasies of divorce and the single life. Sometimes it seems that those quotations from Gibran and Rilke are a way of hedging one's bets in matrimony.

While the ambivalence comes in part from the challenge to enter a fundamental change of life, it may also derive from too shallow a notion of marriage. If we understand marriage only as a literal living arrangement, then it entails a literal giving up of the solitary life. But as an initiation of the soul, marriage takes us deeper into ourselves. In our discussion of celibacy, we have already seen that it isn't necessary to give up solitude altogether to be married. But even more deeply we can imagine marriage as something we do for ourselves as well. Marriage is not a surrender to another person but to another condition of life, one that can be deeply rewarding.

When I have wishful fantasies of being single, I recall how limited and narcissistic that lifestyle has been for me. I see that marriage makes me softer, more engaged with life, and more involved with community. I sense something in those fantasies that is escapist, running away from an engaged life. At the same time, I recognize that some part of me, very central and strong, would choose the single life, probably for all its many benefits for a perpetual student and writer, but there is something else deep in my soul that wants to be married and has urged me in that direction. The deeper urge has overcome the narcissism I feel in my surface wishes.

Something in the soul evidently likes to be single and alone. Some people live pleasant lives of celibacy as they enjoy their calling to the single life. I've been around monks and nuns enough to know how much they appreciate the fact that they don't have to spend their days caring for children and making a living and never having solitude. Most parents will attest that their single friends may enjoy children and a family home for a brief visit, but they are usually anxious to return to their single life. Some people have no interest in celibacy, but they dearly want sex without commitment.

It's easy to judge a person negatively who is hesitant to make the commitment to marriage, but that person's hesitancy may represent an important and valid inhibition. From one point of view the choice of a marriage partner is indeed a momentous one, and divorce statistics make it clear that half the time people later regret the choice they have made. On the other hand major life decisions are never without the risk of failure. Such hesitancy may also represent a valid fear of losing oneself literally in another person or in a way of life. Many of us leap into marriage and then find out later that it is a tolerable initiation that doesn't necessarily take away our freedom or individuality.

Marriage is a rite of passage, not just into a role in life but into a new level of being. If we were to consider marrying primarily as an initiation, a ritual act that profoundly affects the underlying structures and dynamics of a person's life, then we might have a deeper appreciation for marriage, and sex might make more sense as an expression of marriage.

Sex is the opus of the soul, a work in which the pursuit of a partner, meeting, becoming acquainted, and going to bed work out deep, secret elements in the mythology of the heart. In sex we seek out the soul or anima, but not just my soul or the other's soul. We are always looking for the breath of life itself, the spark that will allow us to feel our vitality. When we talk about the pursuit of happiness, maybe what we're really after is that spark or *scintilla,* as the ancients called it, that is the sign of a wakened soul. We also seek the animus, that spirit that brings with it a sense of meaning— not an intellectual quantity that we can find with our minds, but a spirit of wisdom and understanding that dwells in us. We might glimpse soul and spirit in another person and desire that person sexually, hoping to find with him or her at least a moment's acquaintance with the scintilla, vibrantly feel the pulse of life, and catch a glimpse of meaning.

The modern individual likes to think that he or she is distinct and separate from the world around, and modern sexuality reflects this sense of separation. We can't seem to get our life intentions together with our sexual passions. We get into relationships that may be sexually fulfilling, at least for a time, but then fall apart because the sex has no connection to the rest of life. It is full of sensation but lacking in meaning; it satisfies the self but not the whole of life.

In sex we seek and sometimes find the scintilla that keeps life sparkling, and in marriage we keep it close, not identified with our mate but felt in our coming together and in living an abiding, lengthy sex life. Everyone claims to be on a hunt for meaning, and many seem to be hot in the pursuit of satisfying sex, but too often we look in the wrong places for the fulfillment of our desires, and we fail to see how our problems with sex and meaning might be resolved together. The best glimpse of meaning we may ever enjoy could be found in regular sex with our spouse in the holy sacramentality of the marriage bed.

The Marriage Bed

The bedroom is truly holy ground. Coming home at last, Odysseus expressed his joy at finding the special bed he had made years before for Penelope and himself. His description of it is one of the most beautiful passages in the *Odyssey*:

> I myself, no other man, made it.
> There was the bole of an olive tree with long leaves
>   growing
> strongly in the courtyard, and it was thick, like a column.
> I laid down my chamber around this, and built it, until I
> finished it, with close-set stones, and roofed it well over,
> and added the compacted doors, fitting closely together.
> Then I cut away the foliage of the long-leaved olive,
> and trimmed the trunk from the roots up, planing it with
>   a brazen
> adze, well and expertly, and trued it straight to a chalk-
>   line,
> making a bed post of it, and bored all holes with an
>   auger.
> I began with this and built my bed, until it was finished,
> and decorated it with gold and silver and ivory.[5]

The scene ends with the line: "They then gladly went to-gether to bed, and their old ritual."

The attention to beauty, craft, and ritual in this ancient scene could teach us that the bedroom is a place of holy mysteries and that sex is closely connected to what is going on in the rest of the universe. Just as Jesus died on a tree, according to old traditions, a tree that St. Augustine mysteriously described as a marriage bed, so Odysseus and Penelope, archetypal figures representing every marriage, have their special tree of love and intimacy that forms the structure of their marriage bed. Each of us who is married has such a bed, both literally and figuratively. We could become more aware of its deeper nature if we were to imitate Odysseus and bring our personal craft and sense of beauty to bear on the construction and adornment of the actual bed and also on our thoughts about the role of sex in our married life.

The marriage bed is alive with memory, fantasy, taboo, desire, jealousy, transgression, and intimacy. Few material things can be as sacred, for all the mystery, meaning, and passion that center on it. When my wife and I travel, we are sometimes given separate beds, and we have to make our *letto matrimoniale,* as they call it in Italy, by pressing two narrow beds together and making them up as one. Even a hotel bed stands in for the bed at home, for the bed is both a particular object and a sacramental construction that can be translated, more or less, from place to place.

It would be easy to dismiss fantasies about the marriage bed as sentimental or impractical, and yet this kind of concrete imagination helps sustain a marriage. In classical Rome adultery was seen as an affront to the genius, the guiding and defining local spirit, of the sacred couch or marriage bed. The marriage bed was frequently adorned with the bronze figure of the genius, who was the generative spirit of the family and marriage.[6] At Roman weddings, prayers and the preparation of the marriage bed were all focused on the genius.[7] The genius was also represented by the snake, an image of sex, and the cornucopia, an image of the abundance of life that sex generates. In these ancient Roman images we see sex, home, family, and abundant life all related to each other and honored in a spirit that transcends the personal psychologies of the married couple and yet is honored concretely as the very heart of the marriage.

This is one of those mysteries so foreign to modern ways that it is almost impossible to appreciate—the focus on the bed rather than the couple as the site of the marriage vows—

but it is a fruitful image. We all know that certain precious things can become stuffed with memory and value so that they represent the intense feelings in a marriage better than any verbal expression could. At the time of separation or divorce it can be very difficult for a couple to divide their possessions, as their things bear the most bitter and most cherished feelings about the relationship. Adultery is one thing, but adultery committed on a couple's marriage bed is something truly sacrilegious.

Jung describes the alchemical vessel, that mystical container in which transformations in the psyche take place, as a bed, and it seems reasonable to reverse that description to consider the marriage bed as an alchemical vessel.[8] The sleeping, dreaming, talking, and lovemaking that take place in the marriage bed weave the couple together. It may be more important in this respect to care for the accouterments of the marriage bed than to work at analyzing the psychologies of the married couple. A furniture maker or lace maker might do as much good for a marriage as a psychoanalyst.

The intellectual understanding sought so fervently by the modern mind is not necessarily of much value to the soul. More important might be days and nights of conversation, passionate expressions of love and devotion, words as ritual rather than communication, or even the mutual attachment to the marriage bed. All of these together weave a tapestry of fantasies and memories that becomes, over many years perhaps, the main creation of a marriage and the web that holds a couple together. Even when a married couple has become tired of their life together or caught up in painful arguments, they may find it difficult to end the marriage, because it is something other than their combined ideas and experiences. It has its own reality, and the life spark of that reality, the *genius,* has great power even though it is not strictly a personal creation.

The act of sex is not as personal in every respect as modern thinking would lead us to believe. A married person might complain that his partner is thinking of someone else during sex, and yet the soul doesn't seem to take marriage as personally as we moderns do. Turning to thoughts of perfect intercourse with an ideal mate or with a particular person who stands in for the ideal may signal the soul's interest in imagination and the transcendent aspects of sex; it may not imply any disrespect of the marriage or one's spouse. Interest in anonymous sex might also suggest not a shameful neglect of love and affection or a reduction of a person to a sexual object, but rather attention to the transpersonal and transcendent dimensions. When we are distrustful of the soul, we tend toward suspicious and negative interpretations of feelings and fantasies, but if we were less anxious about our own egos we might see that the soul is rather cool even in matters of love.

Driven compulsively at times by the personalistic thinking of our culture, we can be hard on ourselves for not being sufficiently personal and interpersonal in our attitudes toward sex. Love and personal regard are of great importance, but they aren't the only aspect of sex that serves the soul. The soul has a certain objective quality, while our sense of personality is usually made up almost entirely of ego. If we imagine marriage as a yoking of egos, and sex as the emotional fulfillment of egos, there is no room for the soul, for the soul is not at all an ego but more an objective spring from which life flows, or a vast group of characters, some of whom we feel as part of our own identity and others we find in the persons in our lives.

Even talk of my soul can be a screen for egotistic self-absorption. When a married couple give their attention to the soul, they are less focused on their own and each other's egos and more concerned with their marriage, the life they are creating together, their children, their extended families, their neighborhood, their work, and the situation of the world. All of this is intimately connected to marriage, and, perhaps oddly, to sex as well. The whole world climbs into bed with us, because the soul doesn't know the hard-and-fast, clearly marked boundaries of the ego. Ego is a boundary maker, as the familiar psychological phrase ego-boundary suggests, but the soul is forever overlapping its edges, so that the individual's soul, the family soul, and the world soul are inseparable and profoundly implicated in each other.

Traditionally the soul has been honored as the body or as a nonhuman figure of some kind. Kerényi describes the Roman view that a man has a genius resident in his forehead, while a woman has a corresponding Juno or Genia in her eyebrows.[9] Both were represented as snakes, sometimes as serpents bearing fruit and perhaps signifying fruitfulness.[10] It isn't necessary to understand ourselves, our partners, or marriage itself in order to enjoy the abundance of life that married life and sex provide, but it is necessary to have the equivalent of what the Romans honored. We need a cornucopia, a phallic and vaginal horn of plenty. We need an appreciation for the genius and the Juno that still live in our heads and our eyebrows, and we need the will to live a life of fullness in which sex has a prominent place precisely because it contributes so much to a sense of vitality.

Like the approach of the *Kama Sutra*, which places discussion of the sexual arts within the context of an ethical and abundant life, we might do more for marital sex by living

fully and meaningfully than by trying to be sexually correct
and healthy. In marriage good sex goes along with a full life,
because sex gives to the emotions and to the sense of coupling a sensation of fullness. Many people today complain
about sexual emptiness both within and outside of marriage,
and in reaction they may isolate sex from the rest of life and
make constant efforts to improve it. Another way to approach that emptiness would be to tend life in all its aspects,
making sure that it feels full rather than starved. It's difficult
to have good sex on an empty heart or in an impoverished
home. By impoverished I don't mean a home without money,
but rather a home without the spirit of abundant life, a spirit
that can be evoked in a poor home as well as in a rich house.

Eroticizing Matrimony

Sex can become routine in marriage, especially if all the accouterments remain plain and familiar, but if sex is seen as an
art rather than mere self-expression or duty, then the whole
of one's life can prepare for it and at the same time be carried
on in the afterglow of sex. My ideal would be a couple making love in a bedroom, lovingly prepared for sex, in a house
pulsing with the sexual sensations of color, aroma, and
touch, in a world rich in sensuality that appropriately holds
and sustains the couple's sexuality.

In his beautifully sensuous book *Touch,* Gabriel Josipovici discusses the importance of simple presence achieved
through touch. Touching something, he says, confirms its
presence, "its presence to you, but also your presence to it.
The doubleness is crucial."[11] He describes his first journey to
the Pacific Ocean, when he felt moved to dip his hand in the
water, confirming that he had been there. Touching gives a

vivid sense of presence, and this is one of the main purposes of sex—to be palpably present to the other.

It makes little sense to be absent from the world and then try to be present to a person in the physical intimacy of sex. I doubt that it's possible. But to be present in the world means being in touch with it, smelling it, seeing it in its presencing of itself, hearing its sounds, knowing it as a body. The senses offer a kind of knowing that is sure, reliable, confirming, and immediate, a knowing, epitomized in sex, that spreads through the whole of a person's awareness, affecting emotions, thoughts, and the sense of meaning. If we were truly present to each other in our marriages, being sexual both in bed and outside of it, we might know each other in a way that would ground our feelings for each other, keep them steady amid the ordeals of ordinary living, and interlace our hearts—a uniting of ourselves and our world that the mind simply can't make happen.

What is marriage but a mysterious, indescribably complete way of being present one to another, where sex is the epitome, ritualization, source, and celebration of that presence? We seem to see sex and marriage often as reward and prerequisite, but in fact they are two sides of a coin, inseparable. Marriage is the mythological narrative in which our lives work themselves out, while sex is the ritual presencing of that felt and sensed narrative. The sexual touch echoes the sensuality entailed in being present in everyday life, present to one's partner, present to the world, and open to the world's presence.

Marital sex is different from nonmarital sex. In some ways it is richer, more complete, steadier, growing ever deeper, unless it has fallen into an entropy caused by neglect. It gives rise to emotions and fantasies that are different from those occasioned by nonmarital sex. The latter may evoke more excitement, danger, and the important and perhaps necessary feelings of anonymity. But marital sex has its particular pleasures as well: a fuller presencing of persons, the involvement of a life, the security of faithfulness, a history of memories and fantasies, a greater contextualizing of sex that offers profound meaning, and the opportunity for the development of sex as an art.

Sometimes it seems that what marital sex lacks is simply our appreciation of its benefits and pleasures, perhaps because we are lovers of novelty, a taste that creeps into our sex lives. But not all cultures are so impressed by and preoccupied with novelty. Many peoples of this world live with the comforting security of traditions that they hold dear, and this way of life, built on attitudes that are deeply imbedded in the people's philosophy and narrative, can carry over into sex, where tradition takes the form of familiarity and custom. Rather than growing stale, a relationship can find its security, and sex its artfulness, through its history.

It is also typical of modern Western thought to compartmentalize every aspect of life, so one reads frequently about the various functions of sexuality—mutual expression of affection, dealing with biological urges, and procreation—but there is no need to separate these ways of being sexual. You don't have to produce children physically in a night of lovemaking to make the creation of a child part of your sex life. That would be to take procreation too literally and narrowly, for even after a child is born, marital sex may be in part about having children and making a family. A thousand nights of lovemaking may produce a child and keep that child cared for and educated in the full sense of the word, because sex in the marriage embraces, among other important things, the creating and tending of children.

In marriage sex is not a one-night stand, although that fantasy may creep in deliciously and effectively now and then. In marriage, one long night of sex or a morning's stolen moment are part of the eternity of the marriage that we engage on our wedding day. Eternity means both infinitely extended in time and always present. In marriage, sex is not a quantified number of encounters but the continuing development of a lifelong sexual relationship.

In a hymn to marriage, the ancient Greek poet of Lesbos, Sappho, makes the connection between sex and the holy mysteries of marriage.

Come now
          to your
bedroom to your
bed
          and play there
sweetly gently
with your bridegroom

And may Hesperus
lead you not at all
unwilling
                until
you stand wondering
before the silver

Throne of Hera
Queen of Marriage.[12]

This lovely hymn suggests that sex is the preparation for the sacred marriage by which a couple finds their way to Hera, the great patroness of marriage. Marriage is achieved through sex and is the goal of the bride and groom's bed play. Marriage is not simply an approved context for sex, and sex is not a marital obligation. Rather, sex makes the marriage at its deepest level, where the holiest spirit of marriage, honored with utmost respect by the Greeks in the sanctity of Hera, is revealed and attained. In this way, nothing could be holier than sex, nothing more profound.

CHAPTER 11

The Mystery Lover

The Sex Life of the Soul

H OW CAN WE understand people confessing that sexual desire is never completely satisfied? "Remember this," seventy-two-year-old Thomas MacGreevy said to me quietly in his office at the National Gallery in Dublin, "your sexual imagination will never grow weak or stop working, no matter how old you are and no matter what the circumstances of your life may be." This was the final advice I received from that elegant man when I was twenty-one. He died a few years later.

I have reflected on these words many times over the years since, and I've added to them the haunting reflections of my friend James Hillman, who writes about the importance to the soul of impossible love—those unrequited loves that will never find their way into life, those potential mates who are of the wrong generation, happily married, or simply unavailable.

Sexual desire still goes on when there is little or no chance of concrete satisfaction. I remember working with a man in his mid-seventies who had lived a long, celibate life in a general state of unconsciousness. In old age it suddenly occurred to him that he should give his sexuality some expression. He tried, but the obstacles were great. Further years went by as he tried to come to terms with his desire, with the feeling that he had wasted his erotic life, and with the apparent impossibility of any truly satisfying outcome. He had memories of a single affair with a young woman, but those memories were unbearably painful to him. The impossibility took the form of self-pity and depression, a deep pit of despair that eclipsed all other sources of joy he could imagine.

We are sometimes haunted by the ghosts of love. Former lovers come to mind in stray or delicate moments, and they appear in our dreams. People we are happy to be disconnected from may, in a moment of reverie, take on startling allure. Celebrities, or just people we have never known personally but only at a distance, may become the compelling object of desire.

When we actually meet someone who seems to be a potential lover or mate, we may see them surrounded by fantasy. They glow for us, though they do not for their friends. The lover becomes a double star—one radiance branches out from their real presence, while another shines from an unknown source, intensifying the total effect.

The soul's loves seem to carry on with a different tempo, with different dynamics, and with different results when compared to the ego or to the lived relationship. And so lovers talk to each other about their fathers and mothers, seeing in themselves echoes of their parents' erotic struggles. We go to movies that tell story after story about love's romantic ideals and its tragedies. A good deal of our imagination of love and sex is connected to a world of memory and fantasy, and this evidently is as it should be.

In Eric Rohmer's film *Claire's Knee (Le Genou de Clair)*, an intelligent, self-reflective man becomes infatuated with a young girl's knee. In *Shampoo*, a young man has more sex in his life than one can imagine, and yet he acts depressed and his life seems empty of pleasure. In *Belle de Jour*, Catherine Deneuve's character discovers to her amazement that men come to her as a prostitute to act out fantasies that have nothing at all to do with her. In *Last Tango in Paris*, Marlon Brando's character has a profound need to have sex with someone who is nameless. These movies all reflect fantasies that an ordinary person might have, and they show how far the life of the soul sometimes is from ordinary, rational meaning.

Claire's Knee is an essay on mysterious desire. It was filmed on a lake surrounded by mountains, and nature is palpably and sensuously present in almost every scene. The water, Aphrodite's element, carries the subject of the story, Jerome, from place to place. With the help of his friend Aurore, an alternate name for Aphrodite, whom he describes as a magician and a sorceress, Jerome tries to be open to the desires that stir in his heart. He seems to be in complete control, until one day he happens to notice the knee of the sister of the young woman he's been flirting with. Suddenly, he loses all control, and his desire gets out of hand.

"She troubles me. . . ."

"Her body?"

"Yes. The way she looks . . . She arouses in me a desire yet undefined. All the stronger because it is undefined. A pure desire. A desire of nothing. I don't want to do anything, but this desire bothers me. . . . The knee. It was the magnet of my desire."

"It's easy. Put your hand on her knee. That's the exorcism."

"You're wrong. It's the hardest thing to do."

In the end Jerome remains true to his inhibitions. There is no resolution, except that life goes on. The audience knows that Jerome will face more ordeals of desire as he lives his life with unusual openness and reflection. The film offers no conclusions, and that is its special virtue, because desire is unending and mysterious.

Jerome has an extraordinary friend, a love-magus in Aurore, with whom he can talk with remarkable candor about his mysterious attraction. There we have an ordinary but crucial factor in living through our desires—honest conversation in the context of rare and intelligent friendship. With Aurore's help Jerome acts boldly on his desire, but he also holds back strongly, and this dialectic could be the key toward living with unknown desire.

It isn't always easy to know what is going on in sexual attraction. The scenario of sex seems to have much in common with the special place of dreams, except that in dreams it often feels as though most of the action and setting are surreal or of a separate reality, with occasional intrusions from life. Sometimes in a dream we may confuse the dream for life, or we may momentarily become aware that we are dreaming. Sex is slightly different. The major sensation is that we are in life, but there is a considerable element that is separate from life, a separation that may be conscious or unconscious.

The venue of sex may have a hole in it. We slip out of the time and space of our lives and enter the theatrical milieu of the soul. Theater, in this case at least, is also alchemy, so that the space fabricated by our sexual creativity is also an alembic, an oven where the elemental stuff of the soul, its values, emotions, and memories, is transformed. Much happens to the soul in sex that is not visible to the literal eye.

I remember once in a class with David Miller, who introduced me to the work of James Hillman, someone asked him why Jung never wrote about sex. His answer: sex is on every page of Jung. This response could be simply clever, but there is a profound truth in it. For all the *scopophilia*, or love of gazing, in sex, the substance of sex is largely invisible. Much of the mating, gazing, pleasuring, touching, disrobing, and rubbing up against is the activity of ghosts.

The generosity with which lovers give themselves to each other involves the willingness to play the roles of many lovers, and some of the delight in sex comes from sighting or sensing the presence of one of the mystery lovers. A mother or father might well make an appearance, or a brother or sister. I remember several instances in therapy where the deep object of desire was a brother, who would often be the sexual partner in dreams; the lover in life was always measured in comparison to the brother. Sometimes the person would speak to her lover using her brother's name by mistake.

In our desire to possess our lover, an important fantasy in sex that need not be acted out belligerently, we may find it difficult to acknowledge the crowd that has joined us in bed. A need for Sadeian control sometimes comes over a lover who wants the full mental and emotional dedication of his partner to himself. But here is one of the ironies of the soul in sex: deeper pleasure requires an opening to the soul, not just the body, and the soul is full of quirky life. Good sex requires the ability to live from someplace other than the ego.

It may seem that sexual desire moves in the direction of our own pleasure, but in fact the pleasure may not be ours at all. The intensity of pleasure may be in direct proportion to the loss of ego, and there, perhaps, lies the focus of the irony and paradox of sex.

Could it be that the appeal of pornography lies in its capacity to present sex in a way that is not ego-centered? In pornography we may see group sex, unusual postures and actions, penetrations that one has never experienced in life, and an atmosphere of performance rather than love—a generally impersonal display of eros. The point in pornography, the reason for its large appeal, might be to see some of the personalities and scenarios that do in fact enter fantasy during lovemaking but are not related to actual life.

Epiphanies of the Mystery Lover

While writing this book, I was tempted not to include this chapter on the mystery lover. It is too difficult to describe and too elusive and fantastic for a pragmatic, literalistic world. And yet the mystery lover is the very heart of sex. In some ways, it is the most important consideration, because the sex of the soul is the key to the soul of sex.

The soul's craving for its own lover, or lovers, is so strong that sometimes we search madly for some manifestation of that figure, or we try to arrange life so that he or she becomes incarnated in an actual relationship. In Alfred Hitchcock's film *Vertigo*, the James Stewart character goes to every effort to transform an ordinary woman, Kim Novak, into the mystery woman he once loved. He insists that she wear a certain dress, put on precisely the right makeup, and color her hair perfectly to match his memory of his beloved. Because she wants his love, she agrees to everything. But then they ascend a bell tower, which, high and rickety, represents the man's obsessive idealization of the woman, the sublimation of an ordinary person into a perfect love-image, and she falls to her death. The great effort to give flesh to his haunting love fails, just as anyone's anxious attempt to literalize the mystery lover may end in failure and disillusionment.

We can all, men and women, suffer this amorous vertigo in which we try to realize the loves of the soul in actual life. It is commonly recognized that women often agree to transform themselves into the love-object for men, and this is certainly a problem for the woman who falls into the cultural assumption that women can and should disappear into male fantasies. But men have a similar problem, perhaps not as evident, as they play their role of apparent independence, while still subject to the demands of sexual fantasies of the culture, their partners, and themselves.

An alternative might be generously to help and accompany our lovers as daily they find some life for their deep cravings, and, at the same time, equally generously to stand apart as an individual unwilling to be somebody else. This pattern reflects the openhearted surrender and aggressive distancing proper to human love.

Vertigo also shows how superficial our desires may look when we bring them out of private imagination into life. James Stewart is maddeningly obsessed with every detail of external appearance, and he seems to treat Kim Novak as a mannequin. While it is bitterly true that we can reduce one another to dolls in the playhouse of our own fantasy, still, the realm of soul is theater, and surface details are important in

the theatrical realization of our fantasies. The personal col-
umn in any newspaper reveals how precise are the measure-
ments and characteristics of the fantasy lover.

As lovers we will want to know what kind of sex our partner dreams about. We may discover that some of it is questionable or repulsive to us, and we can refuse to participate in
that. This insistence on one's own individuality plays an important positive role in sex. But we also want to be that secret
lover, and so we can gradually and quietly find out what kind
of sexuality lies behind the doors of our lover's private imagination. As Jung says, a sexual relationship always involves
soul figures who are part of the psychological world of the
lovers.

As we saw toward the beginning of this book, sex is never
plain, literal behavior. Like all human experience, it is always
shaped and colored by invisible stories or fragments of story.
Sex is always myth. In some sex the transgression of propriety may be thrilling. Some form of exhibitionism may be extraordinarily liberating and delightful, as in the case of the
psychiatrist who made love with his wife on a rather public
beach. I've heard some women say how much they appreciate an insensitive, virile man, a minotaur of a lover. Some, of
course, enjoy scenarios of bondage and other kinds of theater. In recent times the public has been treated to revelations
of celebrities sucking toes and cross-dressing. Any experienced therapist knows that these are tame examples compared to the sex rituals that many couples enjoy together or
the fantasies that fill an individual's sexual imagination.

The specific rites of sex are designed to engage one's relationship with the mystery lovers we usually encounter only
in night dreams and daytime fantasies. Because the soul lover
is really not of this world, our attempts to give body to those

loves may always fall short of the mark and be somewhat dis-appointing, but we can keep trying.

There is always the possibility of confusing private fantasy with life. Some people seem to keep changing partners, look-ing for the full embodiment of the soul lover in a real person. Or, a person may feel disillusioned when actual sex doesn't measure up to the sexual experiences enjoyed in pure fantasy. We may have to learn how to live in the two worlds of dream and life, allowing each its own validity and importance, and occasionally enjoying a momentary overlap.

The arts play an important role in bridging the gap be-tween fantasy and reality. They bring us to an imaginal space where emotions and meaning are real but the sensuous de-tails are not literal. There we can meet the mystery lover on his or her own terrain, because the time and space of art are identical to the time and space of the imagination. It is an in-between world that is neither fully interior or exterior, but it does provide a place where we can catch a glimpse of the fig-ures and narrative themes that preoccupy the soul.

In practicing therapy I never went out of the way to ini-tiate art projects, but very often people played the piano, brought objects they had found or made, and painted their dreams and images. Usually the images were done without much intention and consciousness, purposely to reveal what was happening at a deeper level, and often we saw portraits of lovers.

One woman in a college course I taught did a series of paintings, accompanied by written reflections, chronicling the appearance of a fantasy figure she saw as a mysterious man who wanted something from her. In her drawings he sometimes took the form of her father and sometimes was completely unknown. She felt strongly that this new pres-

ence asked something of her, and she suspected it was something big and important. But she didn't know what it was.
Only after many months of dreams and drawings and conversations did she realize that she was coming to a major
turning point in her life. The mystery lover of her dreams
took the form of a new relationship, but it also represented
an entirely new shift in her way of life.

Her method of dealing with the change was remarkable, I
thought, and a good model for anyone. She didn't make any
quick decisions during the time of these dreams and sensations. She kept a diary of her inner life, complete with many
different kinds of drawings and poems. In these journals she
admitted her fears, her ignorance, her attractions, and her
changing attitudes. Only long after her life had settled in a
new direction was she able to gain some understanding of
the developments sketched out in her journals.

She published these journals, in a limited way, and I was
impressed more than anything with her respect for the presence of an unknown invitation to move deeper into life.
Usually one is tempted to act, even if it isn't clear just what is
to be done. It takes self-possession and courage to be the container of developments rather than the actor. In this way eros
does its traditional work without interference, creating new
life and planting the seeds of pleasure.

The Soul's Sexuality

The time of the soul is different from that of life. Events
sometimes move more slowly, sometimes faster. In life it
may seem that past affairs are settled, when in the soul they
are still active. The loves of the soul are many. Several rela-

tionships and even marriages may be developing simultane-ously. Dreams of lovers fade in and fade out.

It is not uncommon for a happily married man or woman to wake up in the morning from a powerful erotic dream in which the sex partner is someone else, known or unknown, and the couple may feel uneasy discussing the dream. It isn't clear whether the dream has any connection to life or if it is only from the soul's private theater. The dream leaves the couple on the cusp between their relationship and pure imagination.

The truth is that the dream may have a great deal to do with the relationship, but not literally. Our sexuality is not limited to what we choose or intend in life, and that deeper, less intentional eroticism will likely play a role in the mar-riage. As we enter more deeply into the soul of sex, we may be called upon to expand our ideas about what sexuality is, allowing it to stand somewhat outside the range of will and intention, allowing each other our private sexual develop-ments, all the while knowing that they are relevant to the re-lationship. I would alter Rilke's famous statement about mar-riage being a guarding of the other's solitude to marriage as solicitous care for the other's soul, particularly their eroti-cism, their struggles with desire and fear.

The mystery lover may be present at some level through-out life, as we find ourselves attracted to one person after an-other, some accessible for relationship, others distant and maybe even fictional. The deep lover may also be felt only as a yearning that never seems satisfied, and in life we are left with the longing, the waiting, and the search. This lover may also make an appearance at a certain time in life, maybe dur-ing a time of significant transition, when he or she may be an understandable presence, since change is usually powered by desire.

When I published the book *SoulMates,* several people wrote to tell me how they ache for the partner they know could come into their lives but so far has been elusive. A few even asked me if I was available—a flattering invitation to a middle-aged, settled, happily married man. I assumed they were confusing the messenger with the message. The hunger for deeply meaningful sex can sometimes get desperate, and we get confused as we try to give life to the powerful, driving fantasies of the soul.

What, then, are we to do when deep eros suddenly rises up from some reservoir of desire? Paint pictures of imagined lovers? The point of diaries, drawings, poetry, and other art forms is to meet the soul, aflame with desire, on its own terms and avoid confusion between life and fantasy. Simple, uninvolved drawing would be a pointless and ineffective exercise. It's difficult to describe, but the woman whose father was somehow involved in the appearance of her mystery lover created her diary in the midst of deep, wrenching, completely unsettling emotional struggle. The artistic expression of those struggles can be so engaging and so demanding that they effectively become the imaginal material out of which developments appear. A pen or crayon may be a crucial tool in this alchemy in which nothing less than the soul is at stake.

Honest conversation can play a similar role. It takes courage to speak openly about what is happening in the soul, especially since the soul's sexuality is so often incompatible in literal terms with the life situation. Therapy, as I understand it, is little more than dramatically heightened conversation— the telling of dreams and stories, the mutual discovery of themes and motifs, the call for courage, and the presence of relatively uncontaminated support.

Because sex is so enveloping and inclusive, because it can't be separated from the fabric of life and personality, and because it is so often essentially implicated in developments and transitions, people faced with unexpected and unintended or even unwelcome sexual longing feel profoundly confused. It helps to find ways of focusing on the soul rather than anxiously feeling the need to make immediate life decisions. But this shift in focus is not easy for modern men and women who have been conditioned to see everything, including their own psychology, in purely external terms. In these situations people often feel pressured to do something rather than sit in confusion, swamped by emotions and images that are both alluring and disturbing.

Care of the soul is a simple phrase that seems to represent an easy adjustment of life's basic elements. But at times it may take all the courage and wisdom at a person's disposal to have the patience and presence of mind to keep the soul distinct from life, to reflect deeply on developments rather than take the easier, though more dangerous path of acting out. In therapy I never believed it was my role to set the tempo or make rules about decisions and choices, but frequently I witnessed what appeared to be premature decisions and actions. People feel sexual pressure, an urgency to act, even when the meaning of their actions is far from clear.

Sexual interest is always meaningful and always has something to do with deep desire, whether that sex is directed toward a lifelong partner or a haunting lover of the imagination. Sex is not always sweet, constructive, and positive, and yet it can be profoundly meaningful.

Sexual acting out can also make visible society's erotic

struggles. A family, a community, and a nation can have their own mystery lovers and their own soul-centered sexuality. Our struggles with pornography, the great number of rapes, the high percentage of divorces, our interest in notorious sexual transgressions—this intense public sexual confusion betrays a failure to deal with the erotic life of the collective soul.

In this regard our movies, television stories, and popular fiction may be to society the equivalent of an individual's dream life. In these places we glimpse the unknown lovers who drive us mad with confusion and desire, but who also promise profound satisfaction. Our public moralism is only a temporizing, a refusal to respond to the erotic challenges that might revitalize us if we could only open our minds and hearts to the possibilities.

Sometimes people express their astonishment and out-rage at the public's focus on a politician's sexual escapades, instead of on major political developments and the real-life needs of citizens. But the outrage is empty, because no mat-ter what you say, people are going to be fascinated by sex. Evidently it is deeper and more significant to the soul than technology and politics.

Our collective fear of homosexuality, our hypocritical judgments and condemnations of public figures, our prud-ishness about sexual imagery, our continuing sexist anxieties about women's power, and our overall moralism regarding sex all hide deep, repressed loves that, released and acknowl-edged, would certainly challenge the status quo. They might also bring fresh life to a civilization quickly becoming soul dead.

In our symptoms lie the seeds of our revitalization. If we want to know how to gain new life and a fresh sensibility, all we have to do is look closely and appreciatively at our problems. We have to be careful not to leap into compensation—championing the opposite of what our symptoms embody. Rampant pornography, for instance, suggests that we might consider the value of sexual imagery. Rampant divorce suggests that our idea of marriage might need some space. Rape suggests that we have not learned to use the power of love. Excessive sex in the media suggests that we have not built an erotically rich society.

These are simplistic equations but they suggest a direction for recovering the soul of sex in a public way. Will we have the courage to come out from hiding behind moralism and hypocrisy? Probably not, if we don't learn to educate for deep values or courage of heart. We take more interest in making our children into data managers than in handing on any wisdom we may have acquired from our follies. We are attached to our moralisms because they protect us from the rich possibilities of life. Fundamentally, we don't trust our sexuality. We feel compelled by its allure, but we wish it didn't complicate life and interfere with our plans.

We could find our way in life, and maybe peace in the world, by easing up on our anxieties around eros and, even further, taking our desires seriously, if not literally. In the fifth century B.C. Greek poet Pindar offered some advice that holds true in our time: "You must harvest desires at just the right moment, heart, at just the right age."[1]

Learning how to harvest desires is perhaps the greatest skill a true education could impart. Often we get into trouble because we have harvested our desires too soon or too late. In the first case, we find life a mess. In the second, we feel empty, full of regret and remorse, and depressed.

Intercourse in the Soul

In Jung's remarkable book *Mysterium Coniunctionis,* he probes deeply into the nature of marriage, discussing the idea of sacred marriage in the Jewish kabbalah tradition. In this complex mythology the heavenly king and queen, Tifereth and Malkhut, are separated from each other in this world—Malkhut is called a widow. But with the coming of Messiah, it is believed, they will be reunited.

In human sex a similar mysterious union is always hoped for: "The *absconditus sponsus* [hidden husband] enters into the body of the woman and is joined with the *abscondita sponsa* [hidden wife]. . . . The human being is made up of the world above, which is male, and of the female world below. The same is true of woman."[2] In the sex of two people worlds unite.

The traditional rabbinical wedding rites are a celebration of the eternal condition in which we are whole, symbolized by the ideal reunion of Tifereth and Malkhut and the archetypal union of Adam and Eve, and fundamentally without loneliness. In these rites religion invites us to see marriage as the restoration of an original happiness and state of wholeness that need not be taken as a literal personal memory. It is an archetypal memory, an imaginal recalling of days so long past that they leave history altogether and work in our heart eternally.

This is a sacred union to which we could all aspire. Sex asks us to be open to the spirit that creates our lives and sustains the world, so that we may achieve in our lives a marriage of spirit and body, a realm of meaning wedded to a full sensual and active life. This fundamental task of living both spiritually and sensually reaches a high point in sex and finds ritual expression there. As we let the ego fall away the spirit enters. The resulting passion is the sign that we have attained the necessary sexual state where we are vessels for the spirits that want to join together in our expressive bodies.

The evocation of the mystery lover—or the hidden spouse—doesn't require special rituals or language. It presupposes something more difficult: the generous surrender of our control to another person. Like the mystic who is advised to surrender to the autonomous processes of divine union, the marriage partner is asked to give himself to his partner and to the marriage without reserve and without fully knowing who that sex partner really is. What is required is not a masochistic act of literal debasement, but a gesture of deepest charity, the agape love that fulfills and completes the erotic passion of marriage.

Reuniting Tifereth and Malkhut and echoing the union of Adam and Eve, the wedding rites celebrate and put us in touch with the eternal condition in which we are whole and fundamentally without loneliness. Prayers in the traditional rabbinical wedding ceremony remind the couple of the first parents and ask God to give them the happiness he gave the couple in Eden. In these rites religion invites us to see marriage as the restoration of an original happiness and state of wholeness that need not be taken as a literal personal memory. It is an archetypal memory, an imaginal recalling of days so long past that they leave history altogether and work in our heart eternally.

The horror felt in rape of all kinds and degrees elucidates this sensual spirituality. The violation is not just personal, certainly not simply physical and psychological. It reaches down to the level of our very being, where everything that holds us together and keeps us alive as a person is overturned, so that rape is a sacrilege, an offense to the spiritual realm implicated in every aspect of our sexuality. We may have spent years, perhaps a lifetime, men and women, trying to reach that place in our being where we could be truly open and ready sexually. When someone comes along and disrupts that process of sexual initiation, we may be profoundly disturbed, not emotionally alone but ontologically. We may need more than a psychological counselor; we may need someone who can address the very structure of our being, and not just feeling, but meaning and identity as well. Counseling in the case of a rape requires the most weighty spiritual considerations because psychology can't go far enough into the depths of our existence.

The mystery lover comes not just to satisfy our sexual longing, but to complete our lives. Sexual gratification always points to a greater satisfaction of absolute longing. In sex we are always under the wedding dome, our physical union always a reflection of and participation in a divine intercourse. We should take our desires seriously, even the most mundane, because they may signal the presence of the angel partner, the deeply interior lover, who alone is responsible for the creation of a life.

In classical Orphic mythology Eros is one of the primeval beings born of the cosmic egg. He fertilized the great darkness, and heaven and earth came into being. That myth speaks to our personal lives. Eros is so deep that it is among the constituents of our being. It creates our spirituality (heaven) and our lives (earth). It is represented in all forms of desire, all of which can be traced to the great source of our being and our deep unfolding.

This creative eros is difficult to distinguish from our sexuality, and maybe we should not make the distinction. We could simply see that within the most mundane sexual fantasy and longing lies the great creative eros out of which our lives come into being.

We might take care not to act on our desires prematurely, because we may not yet know where they belong in the context of our lives, but we can trust that in their depth lies the secret to our ultimate fulfillment. They are the seeds of the soul's sexuality, somehow sorted out among our earthly lovers and the mysterious partners known only to the soul.

CHAPTER 12

The Sexuality of the World

The Erotic Life of Things

T HE MYSTERY lover is a pantheistic eros, a spirit that dwells in every desire, every fantasy, and every sexual encounter. This permeating eros is present not only in our personal and interpersonal lives, but also in our relationship to the world. The world itself pulses with the presence of this electric source of creativity and pleasure. Even when we feel the strong desire to possess or to buy something, this is not just a completely human subjective act. It is an interaction, and the thing itself participates in the erotic exchange. If, as the ancient philosophers intuited, Aphrodite and Eros lie in the very constitution of the world, they are there in a dynamic way.

If things could talk I would expect them to complain about being treated impersonally as mere instruments and objects, just as people complain about being reduced to cogs in a machine. Many of our ordinary experiences make it clear that things offer themselves to us in relationship and intimacy. We enjoy being in their presence. We miss them when they are lost or taken away or when we go away from them. We keep them in the family as though somehow they were indeed members of the family. We hold them as accomplices in our childhood and treasure them as friends or departed loved ones.

Things are not only capable of true intimacy, they also bring a high degree of sensuality into our lives. We touch them, look at them, listen to them, clean them, oil them, decorate them. Imagine a room without things, like an apartment or house between owners. The emptiness is eerie, and life can't truly commence until the things have been brought in.

When we speak of things and places in this way we usually focus on the objects and romanticize and sentimentalize them. But I want to focus on the dynamic between human feeling and the presence of things. Eros is the go-between, and in our relationship to things the erotic life becomes enriched.

Given this combination of relatedness and sensuousness it isn't far-fetched to suggest that there is sexuality in our relationship with the world, and that this sexuality has something to do with our sexual lives, and therefore even with our spouses and lovers. A discussion of sexuality isn't complete unless it takes into account the extended erotic life of the objects, large and small, that fill our world and contribute immensely to our lives.

The most erotic object in my world is the modest, often ill-tempered, heavy, brown elephant of a treasure that I carry with me as I move from home to home—my piano. I touch the piano with the tips of my fingers, and it responds with a beauty I can hardly imagine, even when I'm not playing it terribly well. My fingers caress the keys while my toes play the pedals, and my eyes watch the hammers and strings making contact and exploding in small, multiple paroxysms of sound. And nothing is sweeter than to hear the piano tuner gently bring the strings into pure attunement.

My books, too, as many people say of theirs, are my friends. Each has a history, and even if I haven't read one, I am still connected to it and feel that I need its presence. One day I was visiting a friend when, passing through his library, I spotted a book that was mine on a long bookshelf. He had borrowed it from me long ago. I felt quite emotional, seeing it there on someone else's shelf, and didn't know whether to ask for it back or work through my jealousy.

The care my piano needs from me and the work entailed in keeping a small library remind me that ownership is not always the proper term for the relationship between things and persons. In many cases we are companions, and the things appear to own me as much as I own them.

This love between persons and things is of great importance for society. The buildings, roadways, bridges, parks, and public buildings that give body to our social existence are our lovers of a sort, and our relationship with them is in some way sexual. If we see the physical world as one of lifeless objects and mechanical functions, a great portion of our love lives will be lost. We are willing to spend much of our time in a loveless, sexless environment, but if the working hours of our days are not enlivened by the nymphs of sex and the spirits of eros, how can we suddenly and without context fall into lovemaking? How can we divorce sex from life and expect it to season our lives?

Losing Touch with the World

Having and enjoying a physical life is not the same as being materialistic. Materialism is the neurotic expression of our relationship with matter, in which we become compulsive about accumulating things and demean all that is not material. Quite rightly we say that we in the modern West have become a materialistic society, more interested in wealth and technological conveniences than in more humane values, but this materialism is only a sign of our neglect of matter. Only a materialistic society would be so numb to the needs of the physical world as to poison it routinely and threaten its very existence, and we can be obsessed with material objects only if we have a confused relationship with them.

If materialism is indeed a neurosis, then our symptom—excessive attention to the plain physical world—shows that we are not giving the physical world the kind of attention that it needs. We become inordinately absorbed in that which we neglect, and we display outlandishly what we do not deeply possess. This inversion of values, full of paradox, is a pattern that makes sense of our extreme interest in things and our tendency at the same time to treat things badly.

Obsessive fascination for material objects creates an equal and opposite reaction in the realm of spirit. At the very same time that we are becoming absorbed with things, we are also experimenting with the most unworldly or otherworldly forms of spirituality. Institutional religion becomes preoccupied with governance and authority, and the individual's private quest for spiritual vitality, no longer tethered to tradition and guided by rational intelligence, ventures into highly questionable and often dangerous experiments.

Currently our society seems to be destructively split between rabid materialism and runaway spirituality. People are either defensively aggressive in protecting their familiar religious institutions, or they are leaving them behind. For years many people have had their sexual lives contained by church teachings, but once they leave the institution they don't know how to make sense of sexuality. Once, the purpose of life was fairly clear and had a strong spiritual direction; now the only purpose visible to many is the ownership of things, as either the reward of success in work or as a means of feeling that life is justified. Confusion about sex and a rapacious appetite for things go together, because both arise when a solid and clear appreciation for values falls apart. Both sex and possessions fill the gap, numbing our sense of emptiness symptomatically without offering anything of substance that might satisfy our hunger.

When I was a child my family lived on a pleasant working-class street on the east side of Detroit. Many of our neighbors were employed at one of the automobile factories. My grandfather, who lived with my grandmother across the street from us, worked in the supply room at the Dodge factory. My father and several of my uncles were plumbers. We were all Catholics and attended church regularly. There were some problems among the family and our friends, but for the most part life seemed to hold together. I don't remember any signs of lust for possessions in my circle. We all seemed to be content with what we had and with small economic gains.

I remember well the day a television arrived in our house. I think I was eight years old. We were the second or third family on the block to get one, and in those first few days neighbors crowded into our living room to catch a glimpse of wrestling, the roller derby, or the evening news. I didn't realize it at the time, of course, but this new possession marked a rite of passage, not just for our family, but for our society. An appetite for technology began to grow on that day, and a certain kind of innocence departed for good. I have memories of happy times with the television set—my mother and father laughing uncontrollably as Red Skelton conducted an orchestra, tense minutes of the final game in the ice hockey playoffs, and the thoughtful silence that entered the room when Bishop Sheen ended one of his dramatic televised lectures. But my pretelevision memories of the family rolling back the rugs to dance or simply sitting around listening to the radio have a magic far beyond that of rich moments in television.

With the arrival of television, families on the block turned inward, if only to a small degree, and the commercial world of hard sell business broke into our private lives, seducing us to ever-increasing possessions. My memories are surely colored by nostalgia, and perhaps my thoughts about childhood and family are conditioned by the myth of the golden age, a deep story that can easily rumble in the basement of family memory, but there is no doubt that we have undergone a revolution in values during my lifetime.

It seems that if we hope to find our way toward sexual pleasure we have to work out our relationship to things and to the total economic dimension of our lives. Sex may follow the lead of things—if we are filling the emptiness of our lives with objects, we may do the same with sex, and then we may be satisfied with neither things nor sex. Developing a philosophy of life that regulates our acquisitiveness has a central place in getting our lives in order generally, and without that piece in place nothing else, including sex, will have a place.

Our American spirit has an element in it that keeps body and spirit divided and often we seem to live as though we

don't have bodies. We are boldly spiritual and obsessively materialistic, but these two opposites seem rarely reconciled in
a true spiritual love of the world. For all our consumerism
we don't have many things of quality in our homes and public places, and for all our spirituality we are not world leaders
in the area of spirituality and values.

Life in a body extends to the many things made by human
ingenuity and work. To care for this body means to have
beautiful, well-made things in one's environment and to keep
them in good condition. The excess of garbage, noise, graffiti, and broken roads and bridges in our society demonstrates our neglect of the body, and this neglect is not unrelated to our problems with sex. Failure in both areas hints at
our inability to love the body as much as we love the mind
and reflects our habit of investigating the invisible while paying little attention to the visible.

It is still possible to fall in love again with things, to regain
an appreciation for the beauty and satisfying sensuousness of
nature and material existence. With a different imagination,
one less abstract and distant, we might restore old ways of
fabricating and ornamenting the world in which we live and
recover the important relationship between ourselves and
the things around us.

Roads and the Phallus of Hermes

A good road can be one of the most beautiful things in the
world, and it can have rich metaphorical depth, as countless
movies attest as they begin and end with a road trailing off
the screen. It is significant that Jesus, using the Greek word
for road, *hodos,* refers to himself as the way (road), the truth,
and the life (John 14.6).

In the spirit of the times we usually build our roads for

speed, convenience, and volume of traffic. Our roads are political as well, designed sometimes to keep certain sections of
society separate from others. But once in a while, against the
odds, a beautiful road comes into being.

What does a road have to do with sexuality? A roadway is
a dramatic means of shaping our world, rising up from deep
in the imagination. We see ourselves in our roads, because
they are an external manifestation of our values and sensibilities. If they are noisy and speedy, they reflect our insensitiv-
ity to noise and our impatience. If they are beautiful and
calming, they reveal our own appreciation for beauty and
peace. In turn, the roads we build determine in large measure how we feel as we go to work, do our shopping, visit
friends, and take vacations. They often filter our view and
therefore our imagination of nature.

A road is an emotional and imaginal entity, and it is also a
body. A road that takes away from nature or intrudes on a
neighborhood is brutal. Truly, our cities are raped by over-
sized highways and overpasses. Some people find sexual excitement in brutality, but most of us don't. On the other hand
a road that enhances nature and serves a neighborhood well,
has its own beauty, and invites us to enjoy driving on it obviously contributes to the sexuality of our world.

While writing this book I had occasion to discuss roads
and sex on a radio program. The host informed me that in
her East Coast community some people wanted to rebuild a
beautiful parkway that twists and turns through their area.
They say, "It's too slow, out of date. We need to straighten it
out. Make it more efficient. Get more of us to work a little
earlier." Others appreciate the beauty and indeed the slow
tempo of the road. The radio host had no trouble seeing the
political issue as a sexual one.

Writing about the lovely Merritt Parkway in Connecticut,

art historian Bruce Radde points out that you can't even see the amazing details on its underpasses and overpasses at speeds over thirty to forty-five miles per hour, the speeds for which the road was designed in the 1930s.[1] It is a road that curves constantly and with its subtle landscape design fits beautifully into its bucolic yet highly populated surroundings. I drove the Merritt not long ago from Hartford to New York City, and my family was delighted with the variety of appealing bridges, its rich overgrown trees and plants, and the leisurely pace it demands of a careful driver.

The Merritt Parkway, as beautiful as it is, was a compromise among pragmatic, budget-conscious politicians, citizens concerned about their own seclusion and perquisites, and a team of enthusiastic, inspired, and cooperative designers. It isn't easy to get sex into public life. We're more interested in work than in pleasure, and sexual values fall to the bottom of our list of priorities, where they become little devils causing all kinds of trouble for the very people who don't appreciate their public value.

It seems clear to me that the plague of sexual images that fill the Internet and line our city streets, and the so-called gratuitous sex that spices most grown-up movies are exaggerated, autonomous, and noisome because we don't understand the importance of a sexy road or an appealing building or a sensuous workplace. The principle at play is simple: whatever we don't have the imagination to weave into our human lives beautifully and intimately will haunt us in the form of autonomous temptations and shadow values. There seems to be no middle ground. Either we build a beautiful road or the ugly version will soon begin to destroy the culture we are striving so hard to make. As always, our choices are basic: Eros or Thanatos, sex or death.

The ancient Greeks lined their roads with herms, piles of stones dedicated to the god Hermes, which later became pillars fixed with a highly visible phallus. Roads in many parts of the world are still lined with shrines, and they still give way to nature's beauty rather than bulldozing through it. The most beautiful roads are the slow ones and those that allow nature to take us unexpectedly into her dark interiors and tumescent promontories. When people travel, the adventurous ones say they always take the back roads, knowing that it is there that pleasure is to be found. The Greeks had their road pillars, but the closest to a road herm we have is a telephone pole.

If a town or region decided that it needed more soul and sought a way to find it, they could do worse than build sexy roads or adjust the existing ones so that their sexuality might be uncovered. At all costs they would have to resist the antierotic forces that want to make a culture of metallic efficiency, forcing sex into undesirable places and increasing the pressure on our own personal sexuality.

Bridges

There are few things as romantic as a bridge, and a good bridge naturally and mysteriously attracts lovers. People walk the Golden Gate Bridge in San Francisco not just to get a view of the bay and the city but because of the bridge itself, which adds to rather than detracts from the beauty of the place.

A bridge is a liminal place, a place *between* two locations. Being neither here nor there, it echoes the mediating function of the soul, which seems to show itself particularly between waking and dreaming and in other liminal points.

From a bridge, one can usually see life on both ends without being part of either. In this way a bridge is a place of intensified imagination and vision, where fantasies are strong and emotions unusually poignant. Lovers may also enjoy the lower liminality of a bridge—the private space of the bridge's own underworld.

In a short essay, Sándor Ferenczi offers his psychoanalytic meanings of bridges: (1) the penis in sex, of course; (2) the connection between the beyond of the womb and this life; (3) the connection to the beyond after death; and (4) transitions in general.[2] He discusses a patient of his who suffered both a fear of crossing bridges and a sexual dysfunction. Ferenczi believed that this man's fear of surrendering to a woman in the deep waters of sex matched his fear of the deep water beneath the bridge and the unknown life on the other side.

No longer do we adorn our bridges with images, graceful arches, and ornament. We're interested in efficiency rather than romance, and so, what was for centuries part of the sexual landscape has lost its body, becoming a mere functional skeleton that allows our lives to be speedy at the cost of eros.

In therapy I have sometimes heard the complaint from both men and women that the sex in their marriage had become perfunctory, a word that means getting through with. But I was also getting the idea that life in general for these people was perfunctory. In daily life they didn't take time to look, touch, contemplate, wonder, or listen. It wasn't surprising that their sex reflected the same concern to go on to the next thing and keep life moving at a pace. When life is perfunctory, sex is perfunctory.

A romantic road, full of memory and nature, and a romantic bridge, full of mystery and beauty, can respond to our daily need for beauty and reflection. Both roads and bridges may give more to the soul than to the body, as they transport us to places in imagination and memory, as well as to places on the map. They are both profoundly sexual, and the sexuality of our world and ourselves suffers when they are made purely for the transport of objects.

Erotic Buildings

My family's old homestead in Upstate New York was a modest house with three entrances. The front porch, which was never used, had a door into a parlor, and that parlor led to a small back bedroom deep in the interior of the house. I would love to go into that musty parlor, which was another century away, and then into the isolated back bedroom, far from the life of the house, where the air always felt still and timeless. This house would fail all flow-charts, but it was full of delightful mysteries and haunting memories.

The old New England mills that grace most towns in my part of the country are worth taking the time to contemplate. Their bricks have the color of earth, their windows have curve and shape, their doors and doorways seduce you into entering them, and their interiors flirt with you and make you want to tarry. The old houses in these mill towns are dressed up for a good time. You don't get the sense that they are mere boxes with good flow patterns. Clearly they have pleasure in mind and want to appeal to your senses. For all the influences of puritanism and pragmatism and the industrial revolution, Venus found her way into these homes and factories.

In *The Old Way of Seeing*, Jonathan Hale says that eighteenth-century homes were built in such a way that the outside was to be enjoyed during the day and the inside at night: "The furniture faces into the dark. The shadows belong there, by candlelight they become deep rather than dreary. Little objects off in the corners sparkle. The ceilings and the windows are no longer too low, because we are sitting down."[3] Or lying down. Darkness, the deepening of shadow, sitting, candlelight—these are all soul images of intimacy and seduction. Maybe if we planned our buildings for nights as well as days they would have more soul and sexuality.

Upon entering a sexual building you have an erotic response, a physical reaction. I felt this on my first visit to the Pantheon in Rome, where you are in the bowels of religion, or better, in the vagina of ancient mysteries. You feel a certain transgression, a clear and potent leaving behind of the world of light, even though the building is open to the sky. That opening increases the illusion of sexuality, for in sex we are usually on the threshold between temporal life and time-stopping bodily contemplation.

The sexuality of a building may be borrowed from the human form. A building can be phallic, but not simply because it is long and tall: a glass skyscraper isn't necessarily phallic. A phallic building will have some allure and will manifest its sensuality.

The acres of mirror and plain glass we lay upon our skyscrapers suggest not only the narcissism of the age, but also our emphasis on looking rather than touching. The good old brick, wood, or stone building has an exterior and an interior. You want to look at it but also touch it and enter it. Glass buildings are ambivalent, keeping the world out by offering the world its own reflection from the outside.

Church spires are not predominantly, if at all, phallic. In New England we have such spires all around us, but you never get the sense that the landscape is saturated with sexuality. On the contrary, these spires look like rockets waiting to blast off from the earth—not in orgasm, but in lovely, towering spiritual escape from earth and body. They represent New England's spirituality more than its sensuality.

We can find the curves of the erotic human body in public architecture, for example in the domes that top churches, temples, concert halls, and civic buildings. Domes suggest many different levels of meaning, such as the canopy of the sky brought down to earth to give our activities a cosmic context. At the same time, the sexuality in these architectural forms is clear, and they help give a city whatever mysterious associations and spirit that are connected to the body, and in the case of domes, to the female breast.

About the dome and the canopy, architectural theorist Donlyn Lyndon writes: it becomes "an enveloping presence, lending a protective aura to everything underneath. . . . Bringing the elements of a structure palpably close increases the sense of a building's embrace."[4] St. Peter's Basilica at the Vatican has a dome that is the visual center of the city of Rome, and it complicates the image many have of the pope and St. Peter's as the center of religious patriarchy. Catholics refer to this basilica and all that it represents as mother church, reflecting the protective, caring, and embracing aspect of the Church.

Especially in its doorways a building may borrow from a woman's body. A good door or gateway is an invitation to enter, and we may identify either with the one who penetrates the door or with the building being entered. The study of doors around the world is the study of human interactions and worldviews. The best doors are thrilling to see, to open, and to walk through.

A purely functional door, like the glass and stainless-steel portals built into hospitals and schools, can be redeemed erotically by an articulated entryway or portico, or even by drawings and messages taped to the glass. Joseph Campbell once described the initiatory power of the caves at Lascaux in France, where the visitor has to crawl through a narrow channel to reach the interior, as a concrete enactment of the return to the womb. I feel the same about all good doors and doorways. When you pass through them you have gone somewhere, not just physically, but in imagination and feeling.

When you walk through a door and don't have at least a slight sexual experience, perhaps the door should be changed. I have an old, simple, wood batten door on the room where I write, and it is clearly the most important detail of the room. When I touch it, press its iron latch, squeak it open, and shut it with a metallic certainty, I have truly entered my room, and I can start writing. I've never wanted to live in a house that has few doors and only suggestions of rooms—the open-plan style. But then I'm someone who prefers a highly sexual environment that is full of privacy and hiddenness.

Some buildings are sexy because they inspire fantasy. I remember doing business at an old bank in Brookline, Massachusetts, that had a beautiful highly polished wood balcony high above the tellers' windows, and stained glass windows. These elements softened the emphasis on money and the abstraction typical of finance, added beauty, and brought pleasure to customers, and I assume, workers in the bank. I would sometimes walk in, sit down, and just look around. I wondered what kind of imagination built this bank and why other banks have to be so cold, their architecture demanding business and efficient use of time?

The whole of a city lies in each citizen's imagination, even though no citizen knows every inch of the place. What is in the city is important, whether or not the citizen actually uses or frequents it. Citizens are often infatuated with their cities, and when traveling, they may speak of their home towns with the enthusiasm of a lover. They jealously defend them against criticism and find it difficult to part from them.

Sex in the Garden

Recently I was told of an old New England town that must have been glorious in the last century. Its old buildings are still captivating. In the center of the city flows a beautiful river spanned by a bridge that reflects a perfect wide arc in the river. Mysterious columns rise along its span. There is only one park of any size left within the city limits now, a wilderness park full of special plant varieties and trees. Some residents have initiated a move to cut down the trees and change the park into a golf course. Other residents complain that they need the park, and the golf course would be available only to a few who like the game and can afford the fees. In such a scenario, the woods are all too likely to lose.

This conflict demonstrates a typical contest between pleasure and entertainment. In one sense, it makes no difference how many citizens use the woods and how many play golf. The city needs the woods—every civilized area is incomplete without its nature preserve keeping raw nature and civilized city life in dialogue. Maybe golf wins out so often because we can see the obvious entertainment value in golf, while we don't perceive clearly the important and more subtle pleasures of the woods. Furthermore, we seem not able to distinguish the nature of our pleasures. Maybe we think that golf can substitute for a walk in the woods. Ancient cultures knew that different spirits inhabit raw nature and the manicured playing field, but apparently we have lost that discernment.

Certain things in a city give it life, while others merely make it work well. Among the life-bestowing sites are gardens, parks, lanes and cemeteries. Each offers a suitable place where the soul can do what it needs to do—play, converse, reflect, flirt, and court. Each of these also accounts in great measure for a city's sensuality and erotic appeal. Take the parks out of New York City, and the frenzy of business and sophisticated living there would become unbearable. The city would be a body equipped only with a brain, hands, and legs.

We may not realize that a city has a body, and that the sexual centers of that body are precious—a flowing river, a wilderness park, a beautiful facade, some breastlike domes, a phallic rise here and there, some private parts. Gardens have special importance as they provide the soul with the beauty it requires.

It is not surprising that Adam and Eve discovered their sexuality in the garden of Eden, that Jesus prayed before his death in the Garden of Gethsemane, that Epicureanism was created in the Garden School in Athens, that the Buddha gave his great sermons in Deer Park in Varanasi, a place once known as Anandavana, the forest of bliss. Any garden or park can be a forest of bliss, if the city perceives and honors the special spirit that resides there. It is usually a spirit of pleasure, play, tranquillity, and love—ultimately more important for a city's soul than its transportation system or its civic headquarters.

Renaissance gardens were places where the earth and plant

artist could spell out the archetypes from which human life takes definition and meaning. There might be section devoted to Saturn, a remote, shady place for withdrawal and reflection. Another area might be dedicated to Diana or Artemis, where the feeling of nature's purity was strong and a person could enjoy pristine beauty. Venus always had her part as well, and, in fact, the garden as a whole might be dedicated to her. The garden of Venus was a common image in Renaissance art and literature; Botticelli's *La Primavera* is one extraordinary example among many.

We could easily emulate this excellent form of natural magic—bringing the spirit of Venus, a sexual spirit, into our homes and cities through a special kind of gardening where the emphasis is on sensual delight, on abundance, color and texture. This is different from the healthy garden or the intellectual one where the classification of flowers and plants is paramount. These other fantasies of gardening are valuable, but the Venusian approach is distinct and has a special place in our effort to eroticize all of life.

Eros and the Workplace

We've already had occasion to consider the film *Shampoo*. Wonderfully scripted and acted, it contains many subtle insights into modern life and love, among them a comparison between love in work and love in sex. George, the confused and depressed antihero hairdresser, has sex many times in the long day of the film's time-frame, but he seems to get no pleasure and certainly no lasting satisfaction from it. The women in his life desire him, but they, too, are frustrated in their sexual relationships with him. But every so often, in the middle of an argument or a crisis, George will notice the condition of their hair and make a comment. They stop and earnestly ask him his opinion about their hair and beg him to fix it for them. The really creative eros in these lives is not at all in sex but in work, a work that significantly is centered around beauty, sensuality, and pleasure.

The fact that modern work is often devoted to mechanical and technical values may obscure the potential sexuality in work itself. We see the erotic elements more clearly, perhaps, in avocations, where people work with unusual devotion, attention, and tenacity. I know from woodworking how much sensuous pleasure can be drawn from hard work, and how hours go by like minutes from sheer absorption in the work.

One woodworker describes his introduction to his avocation using an erotic term: "I needed furniture. Then I started looking at woodworking magazines. I began *lusting* after tools and hanging out in shady hardware stores."[5] Another emphasizes the intimate connection between teacher and apprentice:

> A personality alchemizes into interesting forms when one has spent a lifetime doing anything that matters. But something particularly interesting occurs when someone has spent years up to his elbows in the physical world.[6]

The something that happens from immersion in the physical world is certainly in part a discovery of body—your body and the body of the world.

Most work, of course, doesn't have the obvious sensuousness of woodworking, or the freedom and art. Still, our avocations teach us that work has many potential pleasures, depending in large part on our basic fantasy of what we are about. With a little imagination we could bring more erotic values to our work. We could take care to choose the precise work and the working conditions that give something to our need for pleasure. We could give some attention to the physical environment. A painting, a vase of flowers, some incense, good music, a single piece of furniture or craft, a child's drawing—anything that contains the spirit of Venus can magically infuse the workplace with at least a modicum of pleasure and sense. We could also give serious attention to friendship, food, clothing, conversation, and, of course, the style with which we work, all with the idea of infusing some sexual values into this area of life that is often imagined from a completely different archetypal fantasy.

There is a great deal of interest today in new forms of management and even in the soul of business. One way to get soul into business might be to examine carefully the erotic aspects of the workplace. Usually we are only too painfully aware of sexual problems, from sexual harassment to affairs, but we could also become more sophisticated about the human need for sexual values even at work. The list, familiar by now, includes desire, pleasure, sensuousness, imagination, intimacy, joy, physicality, bodily comfort, friendship, attention to food, beauty, leisure, nature, and privacy. At a subtle level a company could also work in a sophisticated way with sexual problems, discovering in the symptoms exactly where the erotic life of the business is faltering.

Eros in Food

I know a family in which the father works an hour away from home, and so he leaves home early in the morning and returns after dinner. He usually brings home a take-out Chinese dinner, the same dinner almost every night. The mother also works during the day and eats her own breakfast, lunch, and dinner alone, often take-out or a quick sandwich. Their son is in the care of a nanny who prepares his food. Every day she thaws and heats prepared dinners for him. The little boy is in therapy, and the parents wonder what could have gone wrong to make him neurotic—they are giving everything of themselves on his behalf.

This is an efficient family, a caricature perhaps of contemporary American culture, or maybe its epitome. The parents are doing everything right in relation to the work ethic, but in connection with sex, eros, and the life principle, they are doing everything wrong. Because of their hard work, they have in their home the machinery that most American parents consider essential—televisions, microwaves, stereo systems—but it seems their home doesn't have a soul, and one of the clearest indications of soullessness is the sexless nature of the food they eat.

Sex and food are closely related, in obvious generic ways— they're both bodily, sensual, physical, and pleasurable—and in subtle ways, as in the sexual shape of many foods like bananas, peppers, carrots, apples, figs, and melons. Sexual slang gives us a large vocabulary, demonstrating the connection between sex and food. Oral sex is called eating, of course, but there is also eating at the Y, where the legs fork; eating out, and even eating poundcake, where the buttocks are seen as cakes. A woman is sometimes a tart, and testicles are eggs in a basket. Juice is a word for semen or vaginal fluid, and chickpeas are breasts. A sailor is seafood.[7]

In his brilliant book *American Mythologies,* the philosopher of popular culture Marshall Blonsky describes an interview with a French food critic who tells him how to eat salmon without chewing it, by squeezing it against the palate and sucking it. "There was too much intimacy," he writes, "in her description of food, too much erotic saliva for one trained mainly in visual sensuality, from luscious food to shining bodies. . . . The American I was had forgotten that food is the Great Metaphor, able to transport us to the sexual." [8]

But food does indeed transport us to the sexual, and without a joyous, attentive, and imaginative life with food one wonders if we can find any other transportation to a soulful sex life. A good cook, like a good lover, works with all senses in play. An eye for color, a nose for scent, fingers for touch, and ears for subtle sonorities prepare the body for the sensations of both sex and cooking. The many facets of food preparation and presentation keep the senses well-tuned and alert, trained to catch nuances, and eager for new experiences.

A good cook keeps an eye on the color of food in a pot and knows exactly what to do when aromas shift ever so slightly. Even the cook at home deals with ice, fire, water, mold, rot, burning, browning, settling, and liquefying—primal conditions of nature's body. The nonvegetarian cook handles raw fish and meat, knows well the signs on their flesh of freshness and spoiling, and has a feel for organs, veins, sinews, and skin. The ordinary cook is an expert about the body, and it isn't such a long way from animal and vegetable bodies in the kitchen to the human body in the bedroom.

In his book *Tomato Blessings and Radish Teachings,* one of the most thoughtful books on food I have read, Zen priest Edward Espe Brown has a section called "Tomato Ecstasy," in which he writes: "When we fail to notice the essential juicy, lush, and meaty vibrancy of tomato, somewhere inside us our 'heart' shrivels up, our succulent fecundity is unrecognized and uncalled-for. We too are dry and mealy, and longing for something to break us open and make us feel alive and flowing."[9] Here the parallel between food and sex be-comes identity—they seem to be different aspects of the same experience. It makes sense to give food as much atten-tion as possible as a way to care for sexuality, and maybe we could add a course on cooking in our sex education classes.

The Sexuality of Everyday Life

More detailed study of the sexuality of everyday life could be, and maybe should be, done to the advantage of individu-als, couples, and the society as a whole. From this point of view we could address problems such as absenteeism and dissatisfaction at the workplace, which translates into poor quality of work and financial loss. We might temper the ten-dency in political life toward aggressive conflict and failure to respond to community needs. We might build towns, cities, buildings, roads, and houses for human beings who have bodies and desires, who need basic pleasure to feel good about themselves and their lives. We might take care of lovers by tending the liminal places they enjoy. Responding to erotic symptoms in the culture, we might find our way to-ward more satisfying sex and happier marriages and families.

If we stick to the work ethic and exaggerated devotion to the mind, we will wind up with a well-functioning world that no one will enjoy living in. How could we have neglected eros as the extension of our sexuality in so many ways? For-tunately, there are still individuals and communities, even a few cultures, where sexuality has not been compressed into the plain physical categories of medicine or the psychology of human coupling, where the world is granted its body.

It would be a simple thing to allow the world's inherent sexuality to blossom and be seen and enjoyed in the world around us. It would only take some leisure, less exploitation and more honoring of nature, some openings of time and space at work, some relief from the purely health and convenience aspects of food, some imaginative building in public and private life, and public gardens, the keeping of old buildings. This is all sex, and all of it is directly connected to what happens in the bedroom.

CHAPTER 13

Sublime Sex

Erotic Intelligence and Vision

S EX TAKES US deep into the body, deep into the emotions of love and desire, and deep into the entanglements of relationship. Because of this inward and downward movement, sex has been regarded as a temptation against the higher human aspirations and has been relegated to a dark trinity of values known as the world, the flesh, and the devil. From that place in us where we imagine a life of virtue, orderliness, and social responsibility, sex may appear as a threat or an obstacle. In imagination it is often placed low, as though it were a weight holding us down from our more exalted concerns.

From an archetypal point of view, where we try to find a place for all human inclinations and fantasies, it is valuable and necessary to be pulled down by our sexuality. We need depth as much as we need higher vision. We need the shadow side of all life, and sex offers plenty of opportunity to experience the shadow. We also become persons of character by dealing courageously with the many challenges sex offers during the course of a life.

But there is another aspect to sexuality that can easily be lost in the dark and downward emphasis on the sensuous life. Sex also has a role in the upper regions, where the spirit is dominant. Sex can lift our attention upward and offer a visionary experience of life based in love and passion that is the equal of any abstract philosophy or highly spiritual form of contemplation. Sex is not only earthy, it is also sublime.

The Role of the Sublime in Ordinary Life

Writers have been exploring the role of the sublime in human life for two thousand years. They point to the grandeur and beauty of nature as the source of awe at life's immensity, and they honor the human imagination for its capacity to transcend our small personal lives to arrive at a grand vision of humanity with all its promise.

The European Renaissance, an era of amazing achievements in the development of culture, celebrated the sublime potentiality of the human imagination. The young, passionate scholar Pico della Mirandola wrote in his celebrated *Oration on the Dignity of Man,* "Mankind is, with complete justice, considered and called a great miracle and a being worthy of all admiration." During our own American renaissance, Ralph Waldo Emerson based his idea of self-reliance not in an antisocial individualism but in an expansive view of the human person. "We lie in the lap of immense intelligence, which makes us receivers of its truth and organs of its activity," he wrote.

At the end of the twentieth century we may be experiencing the beginnings of a renaissance of our own culture. There seems to be a new upsurge of interest in what people are carefully calling "spirituality," to distinguish it from institutional religion. They seem interested in personal transcendence, and it remains to be seen if this new spirit will mature into a full-blown social renewal.

It isn't surprising that a new fascination for the spiritual life would spring up at the end of a century of material and technical progress. We have been studying nature technically and exploiting it for its material resources, losing a sense of its mystery and immensity. As we watch our little machines on the moon and on Mars and see the dust and rocks of those far off landscapes, our image of the universe grows small. In some ways the sublime is fed by those voyages, as when we look at the whole lovely blue earth from many thousands of miles out, but at the same time our appreciation for the beauty and greatness of the universe is diminished by the narrow vision of the technologist.

Another reason why we may be returning to a sense of the sublime is the frustration and hopelessness many feel in modern life. Violence still plagues our city streets and is still used as the instrument of political change. It is difficult for many people to create satisfying intimate relationships at home, and to raise children in this increasingly materialistic culture. It is as though we have lost our sense of the sublime and now crave it, seeking it out in ancient mythologies, spiritual practices, and new psychologies that give a place to the spirit as well as to the emotions. The current interest in personal fitness and health may also be part of a deeper longing for transcendence, expressed in the wish for a long, fruitful, and healthy life.

Scientific understanding of human life and behavior, with its emphasis on chemicals, genes, and environmental influences, affects our very image of the human being today. Daily the media give us increments of information and explanation about the body and about human behavior in materialistic terms. Experts often discuss human emotions in terms of the brain, and it's easy to be convinced that we are nothing but chemicals and genes.

In this context sex, already imagined as part of the lower aspects of human life, becomes further distanced from the sublime. Our talk about sex takes on more and more of the medical patois of the laboratory or the vulgar slang once used only in special contexts for bite and passion. This vulgarization of sexual language both further reduces our appreciation for the sublimity of sex and expresses the low level to which our sexuality has fallen.

While the soul embraces the shadowy and unrefined aspects of all of life, including sex, it also needs the vision and clarity of its upper, spiritual dimension. Judging from books and articles on spiritual themes, there seems to be renewed interest in finding a place for sex in spirituality, but often that concern leads only to borrowing language and techniques from Tantric practices in India or from some other esoteric tradition. When general interest in spirituality first began, we saw this kind of borrowing from old traditions, which later turned into a more sophisticated and integrated pursuit of the spiritual life. Perhaps it is time to refine our approach to the sublimity of sex and to see how sex might be part of a new sublime vision of human potentiality.

Sublimation: The Ladder and the Circle

One way to connect the abstract idea of the sublime to everyday life, and especially to sexuality, is to shift from the idea of the sublime to the process of sublimation. Our notion of psychological sublimation is strongly influenced by the work of Freud, whose ideas still permeate our culture, where to sublimate is to defend oneself against erotic passion by translating bodily desire into lofty artistic and intellectual expression. If we take away the judgment of defensiveness in that definition, we are left with a positive view of sublimation. In our arts and writing we may simply be extending our desires and pleasures into realms not literally physical but full of imagination.

Jung sees sublimation as part of the overall process of transforming the literal details of our daily lives into the stuff of the soul. Sublimation is that part of the work of soul-making where our dense emotions and unreflected thoughts rise to a more refined level. At that higher place we can articulate our experiences with more precision, using language and imagery in subtle ways to express the depth of our feeling. A heartfelt letter, an honest poem, or even a poignant song might sublimate a painful or joyful experience to a level where it can be appreciated and understood and even have wider appeal.

Jung uses the traditional image of a ladder to describe this valuable process. He refers to ancient stories about the ascent of the soul on a ladder that winds through the planets and ends at the sun. He also mentions that the Egyptians used to place a small ritual ladder in the tomb when they buried their dead, an image of the ascent of the soul. Shamans sometimes carry ladders as emblems of their office, since they serve as go-betweens connecting the deep soul, ordinary life, and the high regions of spirit.

In every area of life the soul needs grounding in the depths and inspiration in the heights. For thousands of years the soul has been described as a mediator, that element in us that can span the highest and lowest reaches of human experience. Marsilio Ficino said that the greatest tragedy in human life is for the spirit to become disconnected from the body, and he advised that the way to keep these two valuable dimensions connected is through the activities of the soul. The soul itself is the ladder that allows us to keep our humanity intact as we move freely between our bodily and spiritual experiences.

In sex the soul has an unusually powerful opportunity to join body and spirit. Sex focuses our attention, as perhaps nothing else can, on our sensuous presence in this world and on another person, while at the same time it fulfills our desire for emotional and spiritual union with another, for transcendence of our self-consciousness, and for meaningful experience. If our sexuality has soul, the whole range of human experience is contained there.

Sex can put us in touch with the sublime. While making love, or afterward, we may feel utterly fulfilled, and the whole of life may be renewed by the experience. British composer Philip Heseltine, known as Peter Warlock, wrote his lover after first making love with her: "I am so transcendentally happy, I can find no words to tell you: but I feel as though new life and an infinite source of new power and ability has been bestowed upon me." Rainer Maria Rilke wrote to Lou Andreas-Salomé: "Only through you am I linked with the human, in you it is turned toward me, senses me, breathes on me." Their cherished moments of love obviously meant the world to these lovers, and gave them a feeling of transcendence.

In addition to the ladder, Jung offers another alchemical image for the process of sublimation—*rotatio*. In alchemy various materials, understood as images for the stuff of the soul, were subjected to heating, mixing, and distilling in a long and complicated series of treatments. One key process involved rotating the material—introducing it again and again into processes of refinement until it became extraordinarily subtle and pure. Alchemists believed that this highly refined material could be used as an elixir to transform all of life.

We could imagine sex in this way, as a highly refined part of life capable of transforming everything with its elegance and power. In this sense sex is indeed the most important element in a person's life because it has the power to transmute everything. If our sexuality is free of anxiety, everything in life may be comfortably creative, but if our sexuality is crude, then the whole of life suffers a parallel lack of refinement.

In alchemy the rotation of the material was crucial for several reasons. It showed that the work of the soul is dynamic, not static. You can never stop and say that you have arrived at the final point. There is always room for further refinement. Rotation also asks us to be faithful to the soul in its various phases, to notice its changes, and to keep it moving between the realms of body and spirit.

We could apply the same ideas to sex. Our sexual lives are not static. We tend to think of all movement as linear and developmental, but we could just as easily imagine our sexuality as rotating. At one time in life sex may feel pressing and dominant, while at another time it may recede into the background. The focus of our sexual interests may keep changing—the kind of person we're drawn to, our fantasies about lovemaking, our tendency to be more active or receptive. Sex has cycles that are not only physical but emotional and full of meaning.

Rotation demanded that the alchemist be engaged with the process faithfully. We may be tempted to give up on sex or feel that we're failures because of ever new developments in our sexuality or because of the return of old issues. But, appreciating our own sexual cycles, we might be faithful to our own eccentric sexuality. Sometimes it is easier to be judgmental about sexuality than to allow it its many turns and returns.

Being faithful to our sexuality, over time we may notice that it does become more refined. Our compulsions may lessen and our discomfort in some areas ease. As we make love with our partner many times we are rotating the sexual mysteries that we share, and this process is a form of sublimation. Repeated sex, carried out with devotion and constancy, can lead to a sense of the sublime in life in general.

When people complain that sex is confusing and unsatisfying, maybe it is simply raw. It may need the kind of attention the alchemist gave to his vessel full of coarse material. It may need months and years of gentle, patient tending. Over time it may gel into an exquisite aspect of personality, relationship, and general living where eros is extremely subtle and weaves neatly among other values and other areas of life.

Erotic Intelligence

When I first read the *Kama Sutra*, the ancient sex manual from India, I was surprised to discover that it doesn't immediately launch into styles of lovemaking but begins with a discussion of how to live. It recommends that lovers first give attention to two critically important areas of life: discovering their own destiny and proper route in life (*dharma*), and finding their own way to make a living and a home (*artha*). This advice points us in a fruitful direction where we might reflect on the roles of desire and pleasure, and sexuality in general, in the way we live and think.

In order to discover the sublime joys of sex, we may have to develop a special kind of intelligence about the erotic life. As a therapist I found that one word characterizes most people's attitude toward their own sexuality—confusion. They don't understand their attractions and desires. They feel generally that their sexual lives are and have always been a mess. They believe that they are blind and powerless in the face of passion. They sustain the hope that one day they will find sexual bliss, but so far that hope has not been realized.

A central area of confusion concerns the difference between soul pleasure and ego need. The soul embraces the deepest and highest levels of our being. It is not as tied to rapidly developing life as is the ego, and its longing seems to be focused on deep-seated and lasting pleasures. The ego, on the other hand, is that aspect of the self that gets us through this fast-paced and relatively brief life. It can easily get snagged on passing satisfactions. It is also the part of us that falls victim to complexes. If we are out of touch with our own soul, we may experience it, as many psychological theories suggest, as the unconscious. The ego may chase after people and things that will satisfy its narcissism, its long repressed desires, and its wishes for salvation and happiness, and all this activity may feel at least slightly compulsive because of its disconnection from the deeper soul.

The objects of desire that the ego settles on so quickly often are hollow and short-lived. They reveal that they are not the true objects of desire but only substitutes. It becomes apparent that the ego was temporarily stunned by an attractive person or object, but its craving persists and perhaps has worsened. Sexual experiences long fantasized and hoped for may fail to give the promised satisfaction.

The ego is an effective instrument in making one's way through life, but it must be connected at all times to the deeper soul. Desire emerges from the soul and usually needs to be satisfied at a deep level and with precisely the right object. Just getting a job that pays well, for example, may not satisfy the soul's need for creative and personally satisfying work. Just having sex may gratify the ego momentarily, but it may also leave the soul feeling empty, because it is in search of a particular partner and sexual experience that is full of emotion, friendship, and life.

Erotic intelligence begins with familiarity with one's own soul—with its strong desires and inclinations, its cycles and phases. Rilke recommends that we live from a deep place in order to have creative experiences, and this principle applies to sex. It is possible to be close enough to the soul's fundamental desires that we have the presence of mind to forego temporary gratifications in favor of its deeper needs.

Living from a deep place may require periods of quiet and silence, when we can hear the soul speaking. Long, honest, and open-minded conversations with good friends can often reveal what the soul wants. Dreams give many good hints about developments in the soul and about the ego's defenses. Diaries, walks, retreats, hikes, and certain kinds of travel are traditional ways for keeping in touch with the soul, and they are as relevant today as they ever were. These simple practices can be the foundation for erotic intelligence and can help us bring our sexuality to a point of refinement.

The ego trusts the mind, and so we often look to a book or an expert for guidance through sexual confusion. The soul, on the other hand, operates primarily on the principle of eros. Desire and pleasure are signals of its current condition and need. Erotic intelligence requires that we appreciate these usually neglected feelings and use them as guides.

Among my colleagues in archetypal psychology, I often heard this idea condensed into the simple question: What does the soul want? We might take time to consider just what the real object of our desire is and which kinds of pleasure offer lasting and deep satisfaction.

Desire has its own intelligence. If we think that the mind is the best guide through life, we will make choices by gathering opinions and weighing the options. But if we follow the soul, we will understand that desire is also an indicator of what is needed and what is best. We may be confused, especially at the outset of desire, about the exact nature of our soul's longing, but over time we will become clearer about what the soul is seeking. This is a dynamic way of life rooted in deep longings that call for a response, rather than a static way based on fixed ideas about what is prudent. Some people, for example, assume that making a good living financially is the one and only proper goal in life. Everything else fits under its umbrella. But they may later realize, after much torturous experiment and self-examination, that they need to live more simply, on less money, and with less prestige in order to feel fulfilled. They may wake up to the awareness that their heart has needs that are primary and are not being met by living according to widely accepted standards. The laws of desire and pleasure sometimes contradict those of prudence.

Being close to the soul's desires we might better know whom to marry, whom to befriend, and where to live. These are all choices involving desire and pleasure and require erotic intelligence, and they all have a direct connection to our sexuality, which, after all, is nothing less than the erotic life.

The soul is like a spring from which life-giving water bubbles up. We find our vitality there, but also our identity, which is infinitely larger and more supple than the personality offered by the ego. Because the soul is so deep and so high, when we are connected to it—mainly by being responsive to its desire—our very sense of self has a sublime quality. Today some would call it personal excellence. Renaissance people spoke of it as virtue, by which they meant not moral integrity so much as personal power and capacity.

Many studies on sexuality and aggression make it clear that eros requires a solid sense of power. In mythology Mars is a special lover of Venus. She smoothes his harshness, and he gives her sensuality an attractive measure of strength and forcefulness. Powerful and creative people are often sexually attractive because of the mysterious connection between sex and strength. People often get into trouble in their sexual relationships because of an imbalance in personal forcefulness or the acting-out of power issues. Developed and refined exercise of personal power is an aspect of erotic intelligence.

Sexual confusion sometimes arises out of our timidity in the presence of desire and sexual fantasy. We can respond to these attractions intelligently: Would they exploit or harm others? Are they suspiciously extreme or exaggerated? Do they make sense in relation to other values, commitments, and ideals we hold? This kind of thoughtful reflection is an alternative to heavy-handed dismissal of new and challenging desires or to thoughtless acting-out. The refinement of desire is an effective alternative to both repression and sexual license.

Sublime Sex and Society

Society tends to be preoccupied with the tawdry side of sex. It has to deal with disease, unwanted pregnancies, prostitution, and pornography. It stands for the moral containment of sex and is usually inundated with many kinds of unwholesome sexual behaviors. Magazines and newspapers are full of stories about sexual misbehavior, with little positive insight beyond medical interpretations and advice-giving. Overall, the public image of sex falls far short of the sublime.

Historical and cultural studies, on the other hand, give us many examples of public sexuality that is highly spiritual and visionary. In India the lingam and yoni are everywhere to be seen, even today, and they inspire religious awe and devotion rather than prurience. In ancient Greece and Rome powerful sexual images were to be found in public architecture, in sculpture and in painting, again representing the highest aspirations. On many churches in England the image of a woman displaying her genitals is intended not only to protect against evil spirits, as is often observed, but also to give social recognition to the most profound mysteries of human life, including birth, sex, and death. In many places such images were believed to be healing, and it is not far-fetched to consider that a more positive, indeed sublime presence of sexual imagery in our own culture might have healing effect.

Modern society's combined moralism against and obsession with sex indicates that we have not yet discovered the deeper meaning of sexuality. We think of it in purely personal terms, in contrast with many cultures that treat sex as a sacred cosmic force. We try to keep sex hidden, apparently thinking that what we can't see won't hurt us. But like all powerful elements in the soul, sex needs to be manifested. Otherwise we suffer not only from the sudden return of the repressed—sex breaking through our repression in negative and uncontrollable ways—but also from a diminishment of life and vitality. Sex gives life color and vivacity. When we hide it out of fear, our personal lives and our social life become flat.

Because we are so far from an appreciation of the sublimity of sex, it may be difficult to imagine how it could be different, but there are simple things we could do as a society to move in the direction of sexual maturity. We could understand our prudishness about sexual imagery as an unnecessary, self-protective fear of vitality, and allow our artists to present images that honor the mysteries of the human body with delight and dignity. We could foster films and television dramas that move beyond the typical timid formula and explore the higher implications of human sexuality. Small and private presses are publishing excellent erotic poetry written by men and women of vision, who capture the sublime in appropriately earthy language. But this work is almost repressed, as it remains accessible to only a small number of readers.

In another direction we could bring sexual qualities and values to the making of culture and public life. Pleasure and sensuousness often disappear from public institutions and architecture because we allow function and efficiency to dominate city planning and building codes. It isn't unusual to sit through a town meeting or a city council discussion concerned with business development without hearing a word about beauty, sensuousness, and imagery. Yet beauty is one of the main sources of the sublime.

An expanded sexuality might allow us to consider our social problems and the development of culture from a visionary point of view, one that is neither mired in pragmatic issues nor too extravagant and unrealistic in its literal flights into futurism. When our notion of sexuality expands, we turn to serious consideration of such things as deep pleasures, beauty, and individuality. In turn public and private worlds constructed from such erotic, visionary fantasies offer the kinds of pleasure and security that help us lead tranquil and satisfying lives.

Old, mystifying illustrations of the alchemical process can give us insight today into ways society might become visionary through sexuality. Many pictures of the late stage, when the raw elements have been purified, show a bird rising out of the material—a peacock may stand majestically at the mouth of the vessel or a dove may be flying up out of the morass, each signifying the sublimation that has been accomplished.

Our sexuality could contribute positively to social concord and creativity if it could reach this stage where it has wings. At the moment our imagination of sex is largely stuck in the thick and muddy details of its problems and inadequacies. But we could refine it to the point where it would make a significant contribution to the social recovery of sublime values. This development of the higher end of the spectrum of human sexuality would also help at the lower end, where we try to make sense of our desires and failures in everyday life. As individuals and as a society we need vision and inspiration, and nowhere more so than in our sexual lives, where we can find the passion and meaning necessary to transform the raw material of our personalities and our world into the subtle stuff of a soulful life.

CHAPTER 14

Earthly Pleasures

The Epicurean Life

IN THE FIFTEENTH century Marsilio Ficino met with his fellow artists, architects, and philosophers in the enchanted villa of Careggi, just outside Florence, in an upper room where the walls were decorated with inspiring words. "Laetus in praesens" was one of the favored sayings, "Happiness now." These honored words expressed one piece in the humanist philosophy shared by those present, a Renaissance version of Epicureanism, which is the belief that pleasure is not only valid, but a necessary and inspiring goal in everyday life.

Today the very word "pleasure" can have hedonistic, and therefore negative, associations, and for many it is hardly a worthy motive in daily living. We use the word "epicurean" to refer to the glutton, the gourmet, and the dandy, the person who makes good food and pleasant living their primary values, and we usually infer that this person goes to extremes and lives a superficial life.

The philosophy of Epicurus, the Greek philosopher who taught his students, men and women, in his garden school in Athens, bears almost no relation to this modern notion of Epicureanism. Epicurus described pleasure as *ataraxia*, sometimes translated as tranquillity or peace of mind. You accomplish this state by living simply and avoiding pain when possible. According to an Epicurean epigram: "It is better for you to lie on a bed of straw and be free of fear, than to have a golden couch and an opulent table, yet be troubled in mind." Epicurus recommended a simple diet of bread and vegetables and advocated the cultivation of friendship as being among the most important activities in life.

It is with this ancient notion of Epicureanism in mind that I set out to explore the role of earthly pleasures for the soul and try to give sexual pleasure a place of esteem in a philosophy of life. In our efforts to make our lives spiritually vibrant, responsive to the needs of people who are close to us, and personally rich and full, we can take pleasure, if it is grounded and genuine, as a measure of the soul's presence. Epicurean pleasures include deep satisfactions like friendship, family, and community, and also the sensuous delights that may not appear at first glance to be so meaningful.

With Epicurus we could distinguish between the pleasures that make us feel driven and those that make us feel deeply satisfied. The former are not real pleasures but may instead be gratifications that are not deep enough to stir the soul. They may be symptomatic pleasures—not the real thing but only a sign that we are lacking real pleasure in life. Sexual pleasure can either move the soul or offer gratifications that in the end feel empty. Its pleasures are not necessarily the passing kind disparaged by Epicurus, for they can be deep and lasting and have a profound effect on the whole of life.

Ficino was a vegetarian, but he also loved and kept fine wines. Edgar Wind, an insightful Renaissance scholar, says of Ficino that "he tried to infuse into Christian morals a kind of neo-pagan joy" and believed that "pleasure *(voluptas)* should be reclassified as a noble passion."[1] Following a long-standing custom among the ancients, Ficino kept a painting of two philosophers in his study—the laughing Democritus and the weeping Heraclitus. He wrote a great deal about depression and confessed to being a melancholy man, but he also advocated joyful living and dedicated a major essay to the theme of pleasure.

If we keep in one frame these two images that represent such different yet compatible emotional states, we need not lose sight of the one as we become absorbed in the other. Both melancholy and pleasure play important roles in the emotional complexity of the heart. When we divide them we end up with stern puritanism on one side and thoughtless hedonism on the other. The true Epicurean brings these two positions close to each other, so that pleasure has a degree of restraint and depth, while virtue doesn't aim at destroying the joy of life.

There is a difference between sexual hedonism and sexual pleasure. Most of us are familiar with the compulsion for sex and perhaps as well the fantasy that an unlimited sex life would be bliss. But we have probably also tasted the pleasure to be found in making love with a person we know well, for whom we feel deep affection, and for whom we wish equal pleasure and happiness. With this kind of partner sexual pleasure is not separate from the joys and challenges of daily life or diminished by the struggles involved in living together or the restriction of having only one lover.

Epicurean sex consists of sheer sensual delight in the touches, smells, sights, and sounds of bodies pleasuring each other, accompanied by feelings of love, emotional peace, and deep friendship. One rarely hears about the connection between friendship and sex, but for Epicurus friendship is a central need of the soul, and it gives sex a comfortable base. If sex is narcissistically self-absorbed or if it represents an anxious escape from loneliness, its pleasures will be diminished. They won't reflect the central Epicurean doctrine of ataraxia, "without disturbance."

Sex and Friendship

It may seem axiomatic that marriage and friendship go together and that lovers are always friends, but, of course, that is not always the case. When sexual troubles appear, we might think of Epicurus and examine the role of friendship in our relationship. Friendship is a special kind of connection that serves the soul's need for lengthy and deep intimacy. Other kinds of love are important, but they serve other purposes. Romantic love takes us to a different, more volatile place in the imagination and the emotions, and community, though essential to the soul, is not as intimate as friendship.

Friendship usually endures the changes that inevitably appear in life and is not destroyed by the ups and downs of emotions. Friends often come together to talk about both the exciting and the devastating events of life from the distance of longtime mutual observers, and the abiding nature of their connection gives constant nourishment to the soul.

Lovers who are also friends will have something to say to

each other before, after, and during sex. They will be aware of their deeper ties as they make love, and their lovemaking will be tightly woven into other dimensions of their intimacy. Their friendship will give sex a loving context that is more stable than romantic love or physical attraction. Friendship may also inspire the kind of kissing and caressing that extend lovemaking, give foreplay reason and purpose, and keep a glow in the slow decay of orgasm. Friendship also helps channel the pleasures of sex into ordinary life: friends want to be together after making love, and they have a life outside the bedroom that is intimate and loving.

This blending of friendship and sex is simple but not necessarily easy to do. The key is to cultivate a guiding philosophy of life in which friendship and sex are important and have a connection with each other. We may dismiss the importance of such ordinary pleasures simply because we have been brought up to doubt the value of pleasure and to exclude it from the company of virtue and responsibility.

A spirited people, we recognize the value in exciting and exhilarating elements in daily life and often neglect the need of the soul for deeper, more ordinary delights. This esteem for the enduring comforts of the heart is the essence of an Epicurean lifestyle, and it gives sex the rooting, the context, and the tranquillity that are difficult to find in a driven society.

Pleasure and Affection

Epicurean pleasure is a particular kind of joy and comfort. In our culture it's difficult to imagine pleasure without extreme longing, anxious questing, and disturbing neediness, but these qualities make our pleasures neurotic. For us pleasure is often accompanied by guilt, and it's almost facetious to confess to anyone that whatever you're doing, you're doing for the pleasure of it. We have not yet caught up to fifteenth-century Florence, where, in the remarkable hands of a dwarfish, hunchbacked, untraveled priest and magus, pleasure was "reclassified as a dignified passion."

Occasionally when I lecture on Epicurean themes and accent the importance of a rich sensual life, and especially when I recommend it for married people who are having trouble staying together, someone will complain that I'm not speaking about love, when love is the most important factor in sex. When I hear this objection, at first I'm brought up short. "Of course love is central. Why am I not talking about love?" I ask myself. But then I notice a sentimental tone in the talk of love and affection—an indication that our ideas are suspiciously shallow and maybe defensive. Often popular psychology leans toward the sentimental in human relationships, while professional and academic psychology tends to be dry. The soul, as usual, is somewhere in the middle.

When we try to give sex more substance, in effect to justify its pleasures with something more meaningful than sensuality, we often appeal to affection. We assume that sex is valid only when it expresses a loving *feeling* toward the partner. Just as some moralists might justify sex as the means to procreation, the psychologically minded person validates sex as the expression of affection. In some circles sex is appropriate only when it is understood to be an expression of tender regard, and to discuss the sensual dimension without love is to rip out the ethical core of sex. Such people tend to hear the suggestion of sensuality as essentially inimical to love.

In many cases insistence on affectionate love is motivated by anxiety, a worry not so much about sex as about pleasure. Because the defense of affection comes from anxiety, it tends toward sentimentality, and so this kind of affection may not have much substance. A married couple may not feel terribly affectionate at times when they make love, but as they make love they may bring to each other loyalty to their marriage, to their home, and to their children. After a few years or months of marriage the quality of their loving emotions may change—but they may come together as friends who want a real marriage and a meaningful sex life.

On some occasions lovers may find in sex an effective way to celebrate their passion, their desire to give something to each other, and the joy of exploring their sexuality with a partner with whom they feel safe, comforted, and honest. They may indeed want to express their affection sexually, but the other motives are also worthy. The mutual exploration of sensuality may do more for the relationship than any anxious attempt to keep the affection constant, and their focus on their physical pleasuring doesn't have to take away from their love. In fact the need to place a veneer of love on the sensuality of sex may indicate a resistance against vulnerability and openness to the partner. What seems to be a virtue—insisting on affection—may be only a way of protecting oneself from the challenge in sex to be utterly and completely present.

Affection is an important part of sex, but so is lust. Lust can refer to two different emotions—wanton and extreme interest in sex or simple desire for the sensual delights of sex. If lust appears as wanton desire this may be a sign that sex has not been woven into the fabric of life. On the other hand sensual desire can be welcomed into the community of emotions and values that make up a rich life, and in the topsy-turvy world of Aphrodite lust can be a virtue. In an Epicurean life, especially, lust may have a place and yet at the same time be influenced by the fundamental values of friendship and deep tranquillity.

In sex we are also called upon to be generous, to be extraordinarily giving of our bodies and emotions. It's a simple thing, this virtue of generosity, and yet we might easily overlook its importance when we become entangled in the complexities of interpersonal communication and the subtle dynamics of relationship. In matters of the heart and the sexual body generosity is one of the central virtues, because sex usually requires the sensation of abundance—full presence, overflowing love, extraordinary attention, and volumes of pleasure. Two people give themselves to each other, and each hopes that the other has something to give and is free to give it abundantly.

Along with the modern tendency to overanalyze a relationship goes the more traditional attempt to hold people together with principles, rules, and obligations. Yet if we were to trust pleasure and sensuality, we might discover that they, too, can keep people together, and perhaps in the long run do the job more effectively. Why do people go outside the marriage for sex other than to seek pleasures they believe can't be enjoyed within the marriage? Many married people stay in their marriages out of obligation and not joy. They may hold their lives together by sheer effort and self-denial for years, and then either they break out inexplicably in rash behavior or they fall apart emotionally and physically.

In my practice as a therapist I worked with many men and women who lived their lives out of obligation and remained in painful marriages for reasons of propriety or responsibility. These marriages were sustained by discipline and not by love or pleasure. Many felt that their old and tormenting longings for pleasure with a real partner were selfish and had to be overcome. They believed that their lives would be more virtuous, and therefore more meaningful, if they denied themselves the pleasure they craved and remained attached to a partner with whom they felt no joy, and this lack of joy ranged from a vague feeling of unsettledness to the torments of physical abuse.

None of them made a connection between the sense of dry discipline that kept them in their marriage and the exciting sexual desire that lured them away from their obligations. It never occurred to them that sex is a meaningful and telling aspect of marriage, and in one case that I remember a woman who "forgot" to inform me, as over months she wrestled with her fears and hopes, that she hadn't had sex with her spouse for several years. For weeks before this confession she had been asking me if I had any clue why her marriage felt dry and dead.

Imagine placing sex at the top of our priorities in marriage or other intimate relationships—prior to love, affection, duty, communication, parenthood, and mutual support. If it sounds irresponsible or superficial to give sex such prominence, then maybe we have indeed lost sight of the soul of sex. By short shrifting sex we give it a power and autonomy that ultimately comes back to haunt us and to tempt us into extreme mistreatment of our partners. When we allow sex its potency, its allure, and its pleasure, we may find that it can be the most effective glue to keep all the pieces and parts together. This, of course, is the dynamic role of eros—to hold together the pieces of our universe, the world of the person and the cosmos.

One advantage in this reclassifying of sex and pleasure is to shift the focus of our lives away from a purely mental place where we feel we must understand everything we do and everything that happens, and where we believe we must have full control of it all. Sex eases us away from the intellectualized life and places us in a different position where intuition, emotion, and physical sensation take on special importance. This is not a dumb position where we are at the complete mercy of instinct—that's the typical moralistic and intellectualistic criticism of sex—but rather a different set of intelligences, each of them equal in effectiveness to the intellect.

Here we are not moved by obligation but by pleasure. The right place, timing, setting, clothing, lighting, and touching give the greatest delights. Pleasure is the gauge and the single criterion—the pleasure we give and the pleasure we receive. We don't ask the mind to tell us what is correct and smart, and we don't consult the voices of the superego to make sure we are approved and justified in what we are doing. We don't try to figure out how it all works as we are doing it. We don't measure our actions and responses according to a code that has been given to us and to everyone for all times and all places. We are individuals in a particular time and place in search of deep pleasure. For the moment, we are in the garden of Epicurus learning how to live from the soul.

We might place a plaque above the bed quoting an ancient Epicurean suggestion: "Stranger, here you will do well to spend some time. Here our highest good is pleasure." For the Epicurean, pleasure is good, the highest good. The ancient theologian Orpheus supposedly said that Cupid is blindfolded because love has no eyes—not that it is ignorant in its blindness but that it is above the intellect.

Today, we are strangers to the garden school where a courtesan was a star pupil and discussions were focused on friendship and the convivial life. We seek pleasure every day and pursue it with vigor and blind energy, but this is the search of those who profess not to believe in it and believe it to be the enemy of the moral life. For the most part our pleasure-seeking is a compulsion that contradicts our stated values and spiritual ambitions, and as such it is a stranger to us, dissociated from the rest of our purposes and the essential fabric of our lives.

Pleasure and Pollution

Jung's famous dictum, inscribed above his doorway, has sexual implications: *Vocatus atque non vocatus deus aderit,* Called or not, the god will be present. We may make all the preparations for sexual pleasure, but it will appear in its own good time. It isn't possible to force pleasure into life, although it seems we often do try hard to have a good time. Pleasure will not be coerced, but we can request that it make its presence felt, and sometimes it will appear unexpectedly. The true Epicurean is a person alert to the opportunities for deep and abiding pleasure, who weaves these pleasures into a life where labor and pleasure intertwine in a beautiful knot where one may be profoundly implicated in the other.

The secret of pleasure is that it is infinitely more religious, sacred, and virtuous than any of its contraries. It may seem virtuous to resist pleasure, but the satisfaction that results may well come from an inflation of the ego, the pride of one who has wrestled with the angel of desire and won. When we design life according to deep desire and honest pleasure, we sink deep into our humanity and find collegiality with our fellow humans. We are not above the ordinary pleasures of life in our superior intelligence and virtuous self-control, but rather deep in the thick of human existence where the soul is to be found and enjoyed.

When I consider the people I have known who manifest

strongly in their lives what I consider to be soul, I think of men and women who enjoy life, who eat well, who have a good sense of humor, and who avoid many of the moralisms of the day. They are not without blemishes. They are not necessarily easy to get along with. They are not always appropriate in their speech and conduct. They are strong individuals, not terribly balanced in their views. They seek out pleasure, deep pleasure, and they don't make excuses for it.

On the other hand it makes sense that culturally we would place strong taboos on a force as potent, passionate, and creative as sex and suffer the guilt that accompanies transgression. But taking the taboos literally results in a worrisome distancing from sex in some people and a rebellious disregard of inhibition in others. We could realize instead that sex is indeed holy and should be approached with the kind of reserve we give to sacred places and activities. Not to take the taboos literally means to observe them as necessary means of inhibition and caution, but not to place a moral shield around sex or to disregard its enormous potency by engaging in it without reserve.

Taboo is an aspect of the soul's morality, a deep sensation of inhibition, surrounded by a halo of holiness, inexplicable and yet unarguable. There is the sense in taboo that the inhibition lies at the very core of the issue subject to taboo. The taboo against incest is difficult to explain, but its presence is certain and can be grasped without explanation. The taboo against abusing children sexually is strong as well, and its violation is more than a mere transgression of a law or principle. One feels the resulting pollution as a physical and emotional trauma—miasma, the Greeks called it. They believed that the pollution of adultery might incite an attack by bees, who abhor adulterers and are disgusted by their smell.[2] Bees might well indeed smell out an adulterer and sting him in punishment, for they are the animal representations of the pure virgin goddess Artemis, whose priestess was known as Melissa—honey, or bee.

A strong, well-founded sensitivity to pollution protects our purity and at the same time reflects the profundity of sexual passion. Pleasure is not the product of genes or instinct; it transcends human life, for animals, plants, and even the stars, as the ancients said, are governed by the erotic dynamic of the cosmos. When we violate the inhibitions of sex and conscience we are polluted, and our community becomes polluted by a felt moral participation in the violation.

Sexual pollution is contagious and communal. When we read about atrocious sexual abuse and rape happening every day in our society, we are reading about ourselves, and we may feel the pollution. We may worry about the society we live in and wonder where it is heading, feeling soiled ourselves by what is happening. This is not the same as individual responsibility and culpability but another kind of participation in the sexual confusion of our times.

Pollution calls for an absolute cleansing. A halfhearted expression of remorse will not do, although remorse plays an important role in the psyche.[3] In ancient times people restored their purity through fire, water cleansings, chasing scapegoats from the community, impressive ceremonies, and symbolic expulsion of the polluting element.[4] The sense of invasion and the profound need for renewal that accompany pollution hint at its depth. With taboo, pollution, pleasure, and sex, we are in the realm of religion, and no psychological or sociological interpretations will suffice to describe their intensity and meaningfulness. Mental excuses, rationalizations, and resolutions don't even come close to the source of pollution, and in fact they merely keep us protectively distant from moral responsibility and the care of our souls.

The point in ancient rituals of purification after pollution was to make a fresh start and to establish a spirit of renewal. Part of our work of restoring soul to sex involves positive efforts to weave eros and the arts of Aphrodite into our daily lives and into the culture at large, but another piece of that work includes purification and a sense of erotic renewal. All signs indicate that our society needs a profound change of mind and heart, especially in the area of sex, and a purification as well that is not moralistic. We need a substantial reorientation in relation to sex, eros, pleasure, the human body, and the body of the world. Medicine and the sciences, physical and social, have secularized the human body, and in the process sex has lost its sacred character. We could recover the mystery in sex that many cultures of the past honored in ritual, story, and daily living, but that rediscovery of the sexual mysteries would entail a fundamental shift in perspective.

To appreciate how the idea of pollution might help elucidate the sacredness of sex, it might help to consider other forms of pollution. When we hear of a person who has gone berserk and has killed a number of people, we are horrified and then immediately wonder about that person's childhood, family, and personal psychology, anxiously looking for an explanation. If we do consider that the community or nation, indeed the culture as a whole might be implicated, we still look for reasonable causes and cures—we talk extensively about poverty and family breakdown. We feel an overwhelming need to understand how such a terrible thing could happen. We could learn from older cultures that such a deed is a social pollution requiring some kind of deep ritual cleansing.

Our intellectual inquiries shed some light, but they don't reach the deep roots of our behavior in the soul.

The same is true of sex. We may feel polluted if we engage in adultery, but we defend ourselves, offer explanations, and hope for a cleaner future. The Greeks, like many other cultures aware that Eros is divine, believed that sexual misconduct has much deeper consequences. Transgressions in the erotic realm are not mere mistakes calling for resolutions and explanations; they are a form of sacrilege requiring a deep cleansing that goes beyond reason and psychology.

To talk about adultery and other sexual transgressions as pollution helps us avoid becoming moralistic. The sense of pollution is a stronger incentive to avoid sexual misbehavior precisely because it is not accusatory. The best of people hurt their partners grievously, and we all may have to find our way toward an effective, genuine sexual morality free of anxiety. Sensing pollution, we also keep our community in mind. When violation is serious, we all get involved, and even before violation happens, we are all connected as we provide whatever rituals and inspiration we need to live moral lives.

When newspapers sensationalize a celebrity or politician losing his moral compass in the sexual area, it's easy to become judgmental and defend ourselves against the pollution that heads our way as part of the national community. At such times columnists take the moral high ground and freely dispense their judgments, and even the Congress looks for ways to condemn and punish. Such accusations and condemnations do not serve the common soul, and they don't offer any means of limiting such behavior in the future. They are a moralistic indulgence trying to keep the challenging spirits of sex at bay.

The Ordinary Erotic Life

What, then, does it mean to live our ordinary, daily lives erotically? It doesn't mean to exaggerate the importance of sex; that's what happens when we repress eros. It doesn't mean to abandon our spiritual and moral sensibilities. If they are based on the repression of eros, which is another name for the life principle, then they are fundamentally inimical to a vital and vibrant way of life. It doesn't mean to create a sentimental philosophy that denies the dark and difficult aspects of everyday living. Eros is involved in our pain and struggle as much as it is in happy moments, and ultimately it makes a tougher and more demanding life than one based on intellect.

An erotic life begins in a fundamental affirmation of life in the face of opportunities, challenges, and defeats that crop up in daily experience. It doesn't give in to despair. This is a key idea in Epicurean teaching: no matter how much pain there is in life, don't give yourself entirely to it.

In everything we do we can take the path of desire and this special kind of Epicurean pleasure. We can become educated erotically, following the turns of the heart. We can read erotically, selecting books and passages that attract us and that we come to love. We can teach for the pleasure of it and train others for the pleasure they receive in our pleasuring. We can notice the faintest of desires stirring in us and consider ways to give them flesh. We can allow ourselves to be caught up in a theme or a subject until it exhausts us with its desire for our attention. The mind need not be distanced from the heart, for it is as erotic as any other body or soul part.

By saying yes to the offerings and challenges of ordinary life we can find the gift of vitality, the lack of which might account for widespread depression people of all ages experience today. But to make that affirmation wholeheartedly requires that we agree to the moments of loss, failure, disillusionment, and ending that come with a full-bodied life. We may discover that eros is not so much concerned with our loving the people, the events, and the objects we find in the world as much as allowing ourselves to be loved and pursued by destiny, fate, and life itself. It's an illusion to think that we are always the subjects in the sentences of daily living. We are mainly the objects, the ones who are done to, not only the ones doing.

In this context sex takes on immense meaning. The expression of love, desire, passion, and attraction to one's partner are ritual ways of saying yes to life's grander offerings. With our partner, we dance the aesthetics of sex, expressing the deepest nature of things, and that realization goes so deep that it makes relationship meaningful and makes sex the spring from which a full life flows. As we embody our love with another, we make a significant contribution to the erotic dynamic that keeps all things fully alive and connected. Sex mirrors the contours, movements, qualities, and sensations of everyday life recapitulated, celebrated, and made into art.

It is too literal and reductive, for example, to explain as superstition the ancient ritual of the farmer and his wife making love in the field as a way to make the field fertile. There is indeed sympathy between their action and the fructification of the earth, but their act transcends simple procreation. The man and woman having sex are doing the same thing the earth is doing when it lives out its life—they are deepening their bond and increasing the quality of their life together. As a holy ritual sex gives body to the life principle among people and in nature. Nature and human life are intimately connected. In sex especially, we relax our tight grip on reason and allow nature to course through our bloodstream and quicken the imagination.

The rush of vitality we find in sex can make us feel in our bodies that life is meaningful—one reason why sex has such powerful attraction and why, when sex is lacking or unsatisfying, life seems dull and empty. The vitality in sex also accounts for its humor, because comedy breaks the barriers that keep life contained and restricted. It's important that sex be fun and that we joke about it and discuss it with good humor. Sexual vitality also helps keep couples together, because sex can give their daily lives the optimism they need to carry on. We might remember that the Roman god of abundance, Ops, lies hidden in our word optimism.

The Radical Epicurean

The Epicurean life, rooted in a profound appreciation of the roles of desire and pleasure, offers a rich and fertile ground for soul-filled sexuality. By definition it is a philosophy of life in which sexual longing and pleasure have a home. It may appear that our culture is dedicated to pleasure, because we seem so preoccupied with entertainment and convenience, but these are shallow substitutes for the abiding rewards Epicurus described over two thousand years ago. The pleasures he recommended are those deep-seated satisfactions that arise from friendship, family, and creative work and that lead to tranquillity—not passivity, but to a calming of anxiety and craving.

The suggestion to resurrect Epicureanism is radical because our culture places a high value on immediate gratifications rather than on pleasures that slowly take form as though they were growing from the earth. Modern life is fundamentally impatient. It sets aside those soul-soothing delights like thoughtful gardening and traditional cooking because they take time away from the job and from the many activities that cram a calendar. The Epicurean life can be slow and uninventive, when we may want to keep to a fast tempo and be forever creative.

For these very reasons the Epicurean style can affect our sexuality for the good. It gives us time to be sensual, and it fosters the nurtured intimacy that gives sex its personal substance and depth. It fosters deep pleasure rather than passing gratification. It prefers delight to thrill, and it is not demanding. The whole point of it is to reach a point of abundant tranquillity.

The Epicurean life has a certain simplicity and immediacy. People obviously enjoy sex on television and in the movies—vicariously and at a distance. But Epicurean sex is set in an Epicurean life: it is direct, relatively simple, and bodily and emotionally satisfying. It doesn't have the quality of desperation and anxiety that sometimes surrounds sex in the media. Epicurus often discussed the relation between pain and pleasure and he insisted that life can have deep pleasure in the presence of pain, although he also said that it's possible, if your idea of pleasure has limits, to find a way toward a life that is always more pleasurable than painful. "The person who appreciates the limits in living knows that one can always find whatever will ease the pain caused by desire and whatever perfects the whole life."

Epicurean sex is deeply pleasurable because it has a place in a relatively tranquil life and because it doesn't have unrealistic ambitions; it enjoys rather than suffers limitations. If you can't have great simultaneous orgasms every time, that's fine. If you have sex with the same person all your life, all the better. It's exciting to allow the imagination to roam about picturing heavenly bodies and uncomplicated lovers, but at the same time real pleasure may come along only when we inhabit our own chunky, blemished bodies and make love with a body that is changing, aging, and perhaps falling apart. If you are not the world's greatest lover, but you live by the principles of love and pleasure in your own modest way, then you will enjoy the soul pleasures of Epicurean sex.

People sometimes bring to sex impossible expectations that they have picked up in popular magazines, books, or movies, and these demands on themselves and their partners add a high level of anxiety to their sex life. Readers sometimes tell me that the gist of my writing is self-acceptance. When pressed to reduce hundreds of thousands of words to a phrase, I'd rather speak of soul-acceptance, an acknowledgment of your own and life's limitations, an acceptance of fate and destiny, in particular an acceptance of the friends, lovers, and family members that fate has chosen for you. This kind of acceptance seems to me truly Epicurean, modestly but deeply pleasurable and therefore completely livable and satisfying.

The history of Epicurean philosophy shows that over the ages individuals have chosen the elements in Epicurus's thought that please them and have ignored the rest. I confess to my part in this tradition: I admit that I am emphasizing certain themes that seem especially relevant to a reimagination of sex and pleasure. But, as we continue to make physical and mental life faster and have less time for simple pleasures, we could do worse than imitate Epicurus in our own way. One subtitle I might have chosen for this book is: *A*

Guide to Ordinary Sex. And that title, I believe, would be thoroughly Epicurean.

As I interpret it, the Epicurean approach is an active way of life where we do things that give pleasure. We cultivate friendships, we write letters, we invite friends and family into our homes, we play music and paint, we make good food, and we contribute to society. In Epicurean sex we cultivate a sensuous life, we go to the trouble of making sex an art, we give pleasure to our partner, we live from love and affection, and most of all, in great tranquillity and in the absence of ambition, we enjoy ordinary nights, mornings, and days of lovemaking.

Epicurean Sex

As I imagine it, the Epicurean life is rooted in moderate attention to the deepening of pleasure and to the honoring of desire. This kind of life takes more courage, I believe, than a life of repression. Its morality lies deeper than the moralism that surrounds us because it is based in an affirmation of life and, being less controlled, is less contaminated by egotism, defensiveness, and narcissism. Admittedly, it may be a challenge to those brought up to believe in discipline and self-denial as primary principles, but it is not at odds with an orderly and moderate life. In fact, as I have tried to show, affirming life rather than repressing it doesn't set us up for exaggerated compensations like denying ourselves and then bingeing on gratifications and entertainments.

When sex is Epicurean, the accidentals are important: timing, setting, atmosphere, sounds, tastes, and sensations. Foreplay becomes all-play, and afterglow an invitation to the sexualization of daily life. The perimeters of lovemaking blur:

it's difficult to tell where sex leaves off and an erotic life begins. The qualities of sex become the standards of life, and we can dare to live from love, pleasure, and desire.

Epicurean sex is precious in itself; it doesn't require any justification. It doesn't have to make a baby or avoid a baby. It doesn't have to be emotionally perfect or politically correct. It doesn't have to help a relationship or hurt one. It can have some jealousy in it, some anger, some humor. It can be filled with passion, and even more with friendliness. It is based on pleasuring and has nothing to do with hurting another person emotionally or physically. It is not self-serving, abusive, or manipulative.

I don't mean that this kind of sex has no shadow. Sex is a great place to give shadow its due. But the absolute focus on moderated pleasure as a way of life precludes some of the suppressed aggression often brought to sex. By not giving serious value to pleasure, we use sex for other purposes, and it can turn cold and aggressive.

The beauty of the Epicurean life is that there is nothing to figure out, nothing to understand, nothing to subject to painful analysis. The work, rather, is one of educating the senses, giving them their due in abundance, finding the soul in them, and loving with such consistency as to appear foolish and imprudent. The ultimate Epicurean is the holy fool, whose wisdom is judged by a standard made in heaven.

CHAPTER ONE: THE NYMPH OF SEX

1. Charles Boer, trans., *The Homeric Hymns,* 2nd edition, rev. (Dallas: Spring Publications, 1970), p. 79.

2. *Hesiod,* "Theogony," trans. Richmond Lattimore (Ann Arbor: University of Michigan Press, 1959), p. 130.

3. Paul Friedländer, *Plato: An Introduction,* trans. Hans Meyerhoff, Bollingen Series LIX (Princeton: Princeton University Press, 1969), p. 50.

4. C. G. Jung, *Dream Analysis: Notes of the Seminar Given in 1928-1930,* ed. William McGuire, Bollingen Series XCIX (Princeton: Princeton University Press, 1984), p. 172.

5. Anne Carson, *Eros the Bittersweet* (Princeton: Princeton University Press, 1986), p. 172.

6. Georges Bataille, *Eroticism: Death and Sensuality,* trans. Mary Dalwood (San Francisco: City Lights Books, 1986), p. 107.

CHAPTER TWO: THE EROTIC BODY

1. Neil Grant, *Marilyn in Her Own Words* (New York: Crescent Books, 1991), p. 25.

2.   Graham McCann, *Cary Grant, A Class Apart* (New York: Columbia University Press, 1996), p. III.

3.   C. G. Jung, *Alchemical Studies,* trans. R. F. C. Hull, *Collected Works of C. G. Jung,* vol. 13, Bollingen Series XX (Princeton: Princeton University Press, 1967), § 107.

4.   Marsilio Ficino, *Commentary on Plato's Symposium on Love,* trans. Sears Jayne (Dallas: Spring Publications, 1985), Speech V, p. 90.

5.   James Joyce, *Portrait of the Artist as a Young Man* in *The Portable James Joyce,* ed. Harry Levin (New York: Viking Press, 1968), p. 481.

6.   Graham McCann, *Marilyn Monroe, The Body in the Library* (Polity Press, 1988), p. 81.

7.   Apuleius, *The Golden Ass,* trans. P. G. Walsh (Oxford: Oxford University Press, 1994), pp. 92–93.

CHAPTER THREE: PHALLIC AND VAGINAL MYSTERIES

1.   George R. Elder, "Phallus," in *Encyclopedia of Religion,* ed. Mircea Eliade, vol. 11, (Macmillian Publishing Co., 1987), p. 268.

2.   J. N. Adams, *The Latin Sexual Vocabulary* (Baltimore: The Johns Hopkins University Press, 1982), p. 63.

3.   Helene P. Foley, ed., *The Homeric Hymn to Demeter* (Princeton: Princeton University Press, 1994), p. 46.

CHAPTER FOUR: ARCHETYPAL PATTERNS IN SEX

1.   David L. Miller, *Christs: Meditations on Archetypal Images in Christian Theology* (New York: The Seabury Press, 1981), p. 131.

2.   Peter Lamborn Wilson and Nasrollah Pourjavady, ed., *The Drunken Universe* (Grand Rapids: Phanes Press, 1987), p. 4.

3.   Walter M. Spink, *The Axis of Eros* (New York: Penguin Books, 1975), p. 147.

4.   Miller, *Christs,* p. 134.

5.   Rosemary Ruether, "The Sexuality of Jesus," in *Christianity and Crisis,* vol. 38/8(May 29, 1978), p. 134, 137.

6.   For a sketch of this history, see: Robin Lane Fox, "Living Like Angels," chap. 7 in *Pagans and Christians* (New York: Alfred A. Knopf, 1987).

7. Neil Grand, ed., *Marilyn in Her Own Words* (New York: Crescent Books, 1991), p. 38.

8. Roger G. Taylor, ed., *Marilyn in Art* (London: Elm Tree Books, 1984). n.p.

9. Margot Fonteyn, *Autobiography* (London: Star Books, 1976), p. 184, quoted in Graham McCann, *Marilyn Monroe,* pp. 96–97.

CHAPTER FIVE: SEXUAL FANTASY AND DREAM

1. Laura Kipnis, *Bound and Gagged: Pornography and the Politics of Fantasy in America* (New York: Grove Press, 1997).

2. Erica Jong, *The Devil at Large* (New York: Grove Press, 1993), p. 40.

3. Meister Eckhart, *The Essential Sermons, Commentaries, Treatises, and Defense,* trans. Edmund Colledge and Bernard McGinn, *The Classics of Western Spirituality* (New York: Paulist Press, 1981), p. 206.

4. Charis Wilson, *Edward Weston Nudes* (Millerton, NY: Aperture, Inc., 1977), journal entry, May, 1930, n.p.

5. Kenneth Clark, *The Nude,* Bollingen Series xxxv.2 (Princeton: Princeton University Press, 1972), p. 83.

6. Charis Wilson, *Weston,* journal entry, April 24, 1930, n.p.

7. W. T. H. Jackson, *The Anatomy of Love: The Tristan of Gottfried von Strassburg* (New York: Columbia University Press, 1071). For an excellent commentary see pp. 122–134.

8. Louis Frédéric and Raghu Rai, *Khajuraho* (London: Lawrence King, 1992), p. 13.

9. C. G. Jung, *Memories,* pp. 277–78; *Aion,* trans. R. F. C. Hull, Bollingen Series xx (Princeton: Princeton University Press, 2nd ed., 1968), par. 339, n. 131.

10. In Frédéric, *Khajuraho,* p. 9.

11. Alan Watts and Eliot Elisofon, *Erotic Spirituality* (New York: Collier Books, 1974), p. 64.

12. K. Kerényi, *The Gods of the Greeks,* trans. Norman Cameron (London: Thames and Hudson, 1974), p. 81.

13. Anne Hollander, *Seeing Through Clothes* (New York: Penguin Books, 1978), p. 145.

CHAPTER SIX: PRIAPUS THE SCARECROW

1.   "The Priapeia, An Anthology of Poems on Priapus," 1937.

2.   Rafael Lopez-Pedraza, *Hermes and His Children* (Switzerland: Spring Publications, 1977), p. 119.

3.   Richmond Lattimore, trans., *The Odyssey of Homer* (New York: Harper & Row, 1965).

4.   Samuel Beckett, *Dream of Fair to Middling Women,* ed. Eoin O'Brien and Edith Fournier (New York: Arcade Publishing, 1992), p. 97.

5.   Carl C. Schlam, *The Metamorphoses of Apuleius: On Making an Ass of Oneself* (Chapel Hill: The University of North Carolina Press, 1992), pp. 110–111.

6.   William Bright, *A Coyote Reader* (Berkeley: University of California Press, 1993), p. 3.

7.   Walter F. Otto, *Dionysus: Myth and Cult,* trans. Robert B. Palmer (Bloomington: Indiana University Press, 1965), p. 158.

8.   Thomas Moore, "Six Characters, Ivy Crowns, No Authors," *Sphinx 2, Journal for Archetypal Psychology and the Arts* (London: London Convivium for Archetypal Studies, 1989), p. 42.

9.   Ralph Waldo Emerson, "The Poet," in *The Portable Emerson,* ed. Carl Bode and Malcolm Cowley (New York: Penguin Books, 1981), p. 255.

10. Kerényi, Gods of the Greeks, p. 76.

CHAPTER SEVEN: THE MYSTIC'S ORGASM

1.   George L. Hersey, *The Evolution of Allure* (Cambridge, MA: The MIT Press, 1996), p. 36.

2.   *The Harper/Collins Study Bible: Revised Standard Version,* ed Wayne A. Meeks (New York: HarperCollins, 1993).

3.   "Rabi'a," Jane Hirshfield, trans., in *Women in Praise of the Sacred* (New York: HarperCollins, 1994), p. 45.

4.   Miranda Shaw, *Passionate Enlightenment: Women in Tantric Buddhism* (Princeton: Princeton University Press, 1994), p. 37.

5.   William McGuire, ed., *The Freud/Jung Letters,* trans. by Ralph Manheim and R. F. C. Hull. Bollingen Series XCIV (Princeton: Princeton University Press, 1974), p. 294.

6.   Alan Richter, *Sexual Slang* (New York: HarperPerennial, 1995),

p. 49. Richter records the following anonymous advice: "A little coitus never hoitus."

7. Henry George Liddell and Robert Scott, *A Greek-English Lexicon*, 9th ed. (Oxford: Oxford University Press, ninth ed., 1940), pp. 1245–46.

8. Thomas Moore, *The Planets Within* (Hudson, NY: Lindisfarne Press, 1990), p. 143.

9. J. N. Adams, *The Latin Sexual Vocabulary* (Baltimore: The Johns Hopkins University Press, 1982), p. 189.

10. James Hillman, *Re-Visioning Psychology* (New York: Harper-Collins, 1975), p. 184.

11. Edgar Wind, *Pagan Mysteries in the Renaissance* (New York: W. W. Norton & Co., 1958), p. 62.

12. *Ibid.*, p. 263.

13. Victor Turner, *The Ritual Process* (Chicago: Aldine, 1969), p. 94.

14. *Ibid.*, p. 95.

15. Paul Friedrich, *The Meaning of Aphrodite* (Chicago: The University of Chicago Press, 1978), pp. 134–148.

16. Thomas Merton, *Conjectures of a Guilty Bystander* (New York: Doubleday, 1989), p. 122.

CHAPTER EIGHT: EROS AND MORALITY

1. Andrew Carroll, ed., *Letters of a Nation* (New York: Kodansha International, 1997), pp. 111, 173.

CHAPTER NINE: THE JOY OF CELIBACY

1. James Hillman, *Re-Visioning Psychology*, p. 107; *A Blue Fire*, ed. Thomas Moore (New York: HarperCollins, 1989), pp. 149–52; "On the Necessity of Abnormal Psychology" in *Eranos Jahrbuch* 43 (19.4) (Leiden: E. J. Brill, 1977), pp. 91–135.

2. Robert M. Stein, "Coupling/Uncoupling: Reflections on the Evolution of the Marriage Archetype," *Spring 1981* (Dallas: Spring Publications, 1981), pp. 205–14. This essay by a Jungian analyst is a seminal one for me in the whole area of marriage and sexuality. Stein proposes a way out of the many divisions we find in marriage and sex. He recommends a deliteralization of our ideas about sex and couples. "By maintaining the

connection to both the desire to be coupled and the desire to be uncoupled, both poles of the instinct (archetype) can be experienced and lived as complementary rather than as divisive opposites." (p. 210).

CHAPTER TEN: THE MARRIAGE BED

1. D. H. Lawrence, *Lady Chatterley's Lover* (New York: Signet Modern Classics, 1959), p. 231.

2. Kahlil Gibran, *The Prophet* (New York: Alfred A. Knopf, 1951), p. 17.

3. Rainer Maria Rilke, *Letters of Rainer Maria Rilke, 1892–1910*, trans. Jane Bannard Greene and M. D. Herter Norton (New York: W. W. Norton & Company, 1972), p. 57.

4. David Biale, *Eros and the Jews* (New York: Basic Books, 1992), p. 41; Daniel Boyarin, Carnal Israel (Berkeley: University of California Press, 1993), pp. 44–45.

5. *The Odyssey of Homer,* trans. Richmond Lattimore (New York: Harper & Row, 1967), p. 340.

6. Jane Chance Nitzsche, *The Genius Figure in Antiquity and the Middle Ages* (New York: Columbia University Press, 1975), p. 9.

7. K. Kerényi, *The Religion of the Greeks and Romans,* trans. Christopher Holme (New York: E. P. Dutton & Co., 1962), pp. 232–33.

8. C. G. Jung, *Mysterium Coniunctionis,* trans. R. F. C. Hull, *Collected Works of C. G. Jung,* vol. 14, Bollingen Series xx (Princeton: Princeton University Press, 1963), § 438.

9. On "genia" see Nitzsche, *The Genius Figure,* p. 146, n. 23.

10. *Ibid.*, p. 138, n. 8.

11. Gabriel Josipovici, *Touch* (New Haven: Yale University Press, 1996), p. 59.

12. Mary Barnard, *Sappho: A New Translation* (Berkeley: University of California Press, 1958), p. 31.

CHAPTER ELEVEN: THE MYSTERY LOVER

1. Peter Bing and Rip Cohen, trans., *Games of Venus, An Anthology of Greek and Roman Erotic Verse from Sappho to Ovid* (New York and London: Routledge, 1991), p. 116.

2. Jung, CW, vol. 14, §18.

CHAPTER TWELVE: THE SEXUALITY OF THE WORLD

1. Bruce Radde, *The Merritt Parkway* (New Haven: Yale University Press, 1993).

2. Sándor Ferenczi, *Further Contributions to the Theory and Technique of Psycho-Analysis*, trans. Jane Isabel Suttie, et. al., ed. John Richman (New York: Brunner/Mazel Publishers, 1926), pp. 356–67.

3. Jonathan Hale, *The Old Way of Seeing* (Boston: Houghton Mifflin Company, 1994), pp. 90–91.

4. Donlyn Lyndon and Charles W. Moore, *Chambers for a Memory Palace* (Cambridge, MA: The MIT Press, 1994), pp. 139, 143.

5. Mike Sheffield, "Building a Guitar," *Fine Woodworking*, no. 123 (April 1997), p. 122.

6. Andrew Davis, "Learning Cabinetmaking by Alchemy," *Fine Woodworking*, no. 124 (June 1997), p. 114.

7. Alan Richter, *Sexual Slang*, passim.

8. Marshall Blonsky, *American Mythologies* (New York: Oxford University Press, 1992), pp. 72–73.

9. Edward Espe Brown, *Tomato Blessings and Radish Teachings: Recipes and Reflections* (New York: Riverside Books, 1997), p. 235.

CHAPTER FOURTEEN: EARTHLY PLEASURES

1. Edgar Wind, *Pagan Mysteries*, p. 68.

2. Robert Parker, *Miasma: Pollution and Purification in Early Greek Religion* (Oxford: Clarendon Press, 1983), p. 95.

3. Thomas Moore, "Remorse," in *The Psychotherapy Patient*, ed. Mark Stern, vol. 5, no. 11 (New York: Haworth Press, 1988), p. 83.

4. Parker, *Miasma*, chap. 1.

(continued from copyright page)

"The Works and Days: Theogony," "The Shield of Herakles" by Hesiod from *Hesiod,* trans. Richmond Lattimore, Copyright © 1959, Ann Arbor: University of Michigan Press. *The Odyssey of Homer,* trans. Richmond Lattimore, Copyright © 1965, 1967 by Richmond Lattimore, Copyright renewed, reprinted by permission of HarperCollins Publishers, Inc., New York. *The Art of the Kama Sutra* by Douglas Mannering, a compilation of works from the Brigeman Art Library, published by Shooting Star Press, New York. "Some Say a Squadron" by Sappho from *Games of Venus: An Anthology of Greek and Roman Erotic Verse from Sappho to Ovid,* trans. Peter Bing and Rip Cohen, Copyright © 1991 by Routledge, New York.

Female idol, marble, from Amorgos, National Archeol. Museum, Athens, Eric Lessing/Art Resource, New York. *Nuptials of God,* Eric Gill, The Victoria & Albert Museum, London, v.392 E.1048–1952. *The Birth of Venus,* Botticelli, Uffizi, Florence, Scala/Art Resource, New York. *Eros & Psyche,* from the author's collection. Phallic miniature figure, reproduced by permission of the Fitzwilliam Museum, Cambridge, England, Acc. No.: E.89–1914. *Venus,* Musei Capitolini, Rome, Alainari/Art Resource, New York. Statue of Venus Lifting Skirt, reproduced by permission of the Fitzwilliam Museum, Cambridge, England, E.P. 223. Marilyn Monroe in Korea, Kobal Collection, New York. Marilyn Monroe, The girl standing on a subway grating in *The Seven Year Itch,* Kobal Collection, New York. *Venus,* Lucas Cranach (the Elder), Musée des beaux-arts du Canada, Ottawa, #6087. *David,* Donatello, Museo Nazionale del Bargello, Florence, Alainari/Art Resource, New York. *St. Theresa in Ecstasy,* Bernini, S. Maria della Vittoria, Rome, Alainari/Art Resource, New York.

![HarperPerennial logo] HarperPerennial

The Wisdom of Thomas Moore

CARE OF THE SOUL
ISBN 0-06-092224-9
Drawing on ancient wisdom and modern depth psychology, this national
bestseller examines how we can find deep satisfaction and pleasure in life.

SOUL MATES
ISBN 0-06-092575-2
Examining the rich idea of a soul mate, Moore offers guidance through
the beginnings, the ups and downs, and the sometimes devastating ends of
romances, friendships, and marriages.

THE RE-ENCHANTMENT OF EVERYDAY LIFE
ISBN 0-06-092824-7
A guide to finding wonder in common events and surroundings often taken
for granted—food, home, business, politics, business, rituals, and more.

THE EDUCATION OF THE HEART
ISBN 0-06-792860-3
A selection of readings designed to animate and educate the heart and mind,
and expand the soul.

THE SOUL OF SEX
ISBN 0-06-093095-0
Thomas Moore turns to religion, mythology, literature, and visual imagery
to explore the spirituality and profound mysteries of life inherent in sex.

CARE OF THE SOUL *(The Illustrated Edition)*
ISBN 0-06-757511-0
This special edition of the spiritual bestseller, beautifully illustrated with more
than 150 full-color classic and modern works of art, creates an extraordinary
guide to finding the sacredness in ordinary, everyday life.

Available at bookstores everywhere, or call 1-800-331-3761 to order.